Phil Ballard

D0557141

Sams **Teach Yourself**

JavaScript®

Sixth Edition

in **24 Hours**

SAMS 800 East 96th Street, Indianapolis, Indiana, 46240 USA

Sams Teach Yourself JavaScript in 24 Hours, Sixth Edition

Copyright © 2015 by Pearson Education, Inc.

ISBN-13: 978-0-672-33738-3

ISBN-10: 0-672-33738-X

Library of Congress Control Number: 2015905614

Printed in the United States of America

First Printing June 2015

Trademarks

Warning and Disclaimer

Special Sales

For information about buying this title in bulk quantities, or for special sales opportunities (which may include electronic versions; custom cover designs; and content particular to your business, training goals, marketing focus, or branding interests), please contact our corporate sales department at corpsales@pearsoned.com or (800) 382-3419.

For government sales inquiries, please contact governmentsales@pearsoned.com.

For questions about sales outside the U.S., please contact international@pearsoned.com.

Executive Editor
Mark Taber

Managing Editor
Sandra Schroeder

Senior Development Editor
Chris Zahn

Senior Project Editor
Tonya Simpson

Copy Editor
Bart Reed

Indexer
Tim Wright

Proofreader
Debbie Williams

Publishing Coordinator
Vanessa Evans

Technical Editor
Siddhartha Singh

Cover Designer
Mark Shirar

Compositor
Bronkella Publishing

Contents at a Glance

Table of Contents

Part IV: HTML and CSS

About the Author

Phil Ballard, the author of various *Sams Teach Yourself* titles, graduated in 1980 with an honors degree in electronics from the University of Leeds, England. Following an early career as a research scientist with a major multinational, he spent a few years in commercial and managerial roles within the high technology sector, later working full time as a software engineering consultant.

Operating as "The Mouse Whisperer" (www.mousewhisperer.co.uk), Ballard has spent recent years involved solely in website and intranet design and development for an international portfolio of clients, as well as writing numerous technical books and articles.

We Want to Hear from You!

As the reader of this book, *you* are our most important critic and commentator. We value your opinion and want to know what we're doing right, what we could do better, what areas you'd like to see us publish in, and any other words of wisdom you're willing to pass our way.

We welcome your comments. You can email or write to let us know what you did or didn't like about this book—as well as what we can do to make our books better.

Please note that we cannot help you with technical problems related to the topic of this book.

When you write, please be sure to include this book's title and author as well as your name and email address. We will carefully review your comments and share them with the author and editors who worked on the book.

Email: feedback@samspublishing.com
Mail: Sams Publishing
         ATTN: Reader Feedback
         800 East 96th Street
         Indianapolis, IN 46240 USA

Reader Services

Visit our website and register this book at www.informit.com/register for convenient access to any updates, downloads, or errata that might be available for this book.

Introduction

This introduction walks you through a few basic things before you begin reading, including who this book was written for, why it was written, the conventions employed in this book and in the Sams Teach Yourself series, how the content is organized, and the tools you need to create JavaScript.

Who This Book Is For

If you're interested in learning JavaScript, chances are that you've already gained at least a basic understanding of HTML and web page design in general, and want to move on to adding some extra interactivity to your pages. Or maybe you currently code in another programming language, and want to see what additional capabilities JavaScript can add to your armory.

If you've never tinkered with HTML at all, nor done any computer programming, it would be helpful to browse through an HTML primer before getting into the book. Don't worry—HTML is very accessible, and you don't need to be an expert in it to start experimenting with the JavaScript examples in this book.

JavaScript is an ideal language to use for your first steps in programming, and in case you get bitten by the bug, pretty much all of the fundamental concepts that you learn in JavaScript will later be applicable in a wide variety of other languages such as C, Java, and PHP.

The Aims of This Book

When JavaScript was first introduced, it was somewhat limited in what it could do. With basic features and rather haphazard browser support, it gained a reputation in some quarters as being something of a toy or gimmick. Now, due to much better browser support for W3C standards and improvement in the JavaScript implementations used in recent browsers, JavaScript is finally being treated as a serious programming language.

Many advanced programming disciplines used in other programming languages can readily be applied to JavaScript; for example, object-oriented programming promotes the writing of solid, readable, maintainable, and reusable code.

So-called "unobtrusive" scripting techniques and the use of DOM scripting focus on adding interaction to web pages while keeping the HTML simple to read and well separated from the program code.

This book aims to teach the fundamental skills relevant to all of the important aspects of JavaScript as it's used today. In the course of the book, you start from basic concepts and gradually learn the best practices for writing JavaScript programs in accordance with current web standards.

Conventions Used

All of the code examples in the book are written as HTML5. For the most part, though, the code avoids using HTML5-specific syntax, since at the time of writing its support in web browsers is still not universal. The code examples should work correctly in virtually any recent web browser, regardless of the type of computer or operating system.

In addition to the main text of each lesson, you will find a number of boxes labeled as Notes, Tips, and Cautions.

NOTE
These sections provide additional comments that might help you to understand the text and examples.

TIP
These blocks give additional hints, shortcuts, or workarounds to make coding easier.

CAUTION
Avoid common pitfalls by using the information in these blocks.

▼ TRY IT YOURSELF

Each hour contains at least one section that walks you through the process of implementing your own script. This will help you to gain confidence in writing your own JavaScript code based on the techniques you've learned.

Q&A, Workshop, and Exercises

After each hour's lesson, you'll find three final sections.

► The "Q&A" section tries to answer a few of the more common questions about the hour's topic.

► The "Workshop" section includes a quiz that tests your knowledge of what you learned in that lesson. Answers to the quiz items are conveniently provided immediately following the quiz.

► The "Exercises" section offers suggestions for further experimentation, based on the lesson, that you might like to try on your own.

How the Book Is Organized

The book is divided into seven parts, gradually increasing in the complexity of the techniques taught.

► **Part I—First Steps with JavaScript**

An introduction to the JavaScript language and how to write simple scripts using the language's common functions. This part of the book is aimed mainly at readers with little or no prior programming knowledge, and no knowledge of the JavaScript language.

► **Part II—Cooking with Code**

Here JavaScript's data types are introduced, such as numbers, strings, and arrays. More sophisticated programming paradigms such as program control loops and timers are also covered.

► **Part III—Objects**

This part of the book concentrates on creating and handling objects, including navigating and editing the objects belonging to the DOM (Document Object Model).

► **Part IV—HTML and CSS**

Here you learn in greater depth how JavaScript can interact with HTML (including HTML5) and CSS (Cascading Style Sheets), including the latest CSS3 specification.

► **Part V—Using JavaScript Libraries**

In this part of the book you learn how to simplify cross-browser development using third-party libraries such as jQuery.

▶ **Part VI—Advanced Topics**

This part of the book covers reading and writing cookies, looks at what's new in JavaScript via the ECMAScript 6 specification, introduces the use of frameworks such as AngularJS, and shows examples of using JavaScript beyond its use in web pages.

▶ **Part VII—Learning the Trade**

In the final part you explore aspects of professional JavaScript development such as good coding practices, JavaScript debugging, and unit testing.

Tools You'll Need

Writing JavaScript does not require any expensive and complicated tools such as Integrated Development Environments (IDEs), compilers, or debuggers.

The examples in this book can all be created in a text-editing program, such as the Windows Notepad program. At least one such application ships with just about every operating system, and countless more are available for no or low cost via download from the Internet.

NOTE

Appendix A, "Tools for JavaScript Development," lists some additional, easily obtainable tools and resources for use in JavaScript development.

To see your program code working, you'll need a web browser such as Internet Explorer, Mozilla Firefox, Opera, Safari, or Google Chrome. It is recommended that you upgrade your browser to the latest current stable version.

The vast majority of the book's examples do not need an Internet connection to function. Simply storing the source code file in a convenient location on your computer and opening it with your chosen browser is generally sufficient. The exceptions to this are the hour on cookies and the examples in the book that demonstrate Ajax; to explore all of the sample code will require a web connection (or a connection to a web server on your local area network) and a little web space in which to post the sample code. If you've done some HTML coding, you may already have that covered; if not, a hobby-grade web hosting account costs very little and will be more than adequate for trying out the examples in this book. (Check that your web host allows you to run scripts written in the PHP language if you want to try out the Ajax examples in Part V. Nearly all hosts do.)

HOUR 1
Introducing JavaScript

What You'll Learn in This Hour:

▶ About server-side and client-side programming
▶ How JavaScript can improve your web pages
▶ The history of JavaScript
▶ The basics of the Document Object Model (DOM)
▶ What the `window` and `document` objects are
▶ How to add content to your web pages using JavaScript
▶ How to alert the user with a dialog box

The modern Web has little to do with its original, text-only ancestor. Modern web pages can involve audio, video, animated graphics, interactive navigation, and much more—and more often than not, JavaScript plays a big part in making it all possible.

In this first hour we describe what JavaScript is, briefly review the language's origins, and consider the kinds of things it can do to improve your web pages. You also dive right in and write some working JavaScript code.

Web Scripting Fundamentals

Since you've picked up this book, there's a pretty good chance that you're already familiar with using the World Wide Web and have at least a basic understanding of writing web pages in some variant of HTML.

HTML (Hypertext Markup Language) is not a *programming* language but (as the name indicates) a *markup* language; we can use it to mark parts of our page to indicate to the browser that these parts should be shown in a particular way—bold or italic text, for instance, or as a heading, a list of bullet points, arranged as a table of data, or using many other markup options.

Once written, these pages by their nature are *static*. They can't respond to user actions, make decisions, or modify the display of their page elements. The markup they contain will always be interpreted and displayed in the same way whenever the page is visited by a user.

As you know from using the World Wide Web, modern websites can do much more; the pages we routinely visit are often far from static. They can contain "live" data, such as share prices or flight arrival times, animated displays with changing colors and fonts, or interactive capabilities such as the ability to click through a gallery of photographs or sort a column of data.

These clever capabilities are provided to the user by programs—often known as *scripts*—operating behind the scenes to manipulate what's displayed in the browser.

NOTE

The term *script* has no doubt been borrowed from the world of theater and TV, where the *script* defines the actions of the presenters or performers. In the case of a web page, the protagonists are the elements on the page, with a *script* provided by a scripting language such as, in this case, JavaScript. *Program* and *script* are, for our purposes, pretty much interchangeable terms, as are *programming* and *scripting*. You'll find all of these used in the course of the book.

Server- Versus Client-Side Programming

There are two fundamental ways of adding scripts to otherwise static web content:

▶ You can have the web server execute a script before delivering your page to the user. Such scripts can define what information is sent to the browser for display to the user—for example, by retrieving product prices from the database of an online store, checking a user's identity credentials before logging her into a private area of the website, or retrieving the contents of an email mailbox. These scripts are generally run at the web server *before* generating the requested web page and serving it to the user. You won't be surprised to learn that we refer to this as *server-side scripting*.

▶ Alternatively, the scripts themselves, rather than being run on the server, can be delivered to the user's browser along with the code of the page. Such scripts are then executed by the browser and operate on the page's already-delivered content. The many functions such scripts can perform include animating page sections, reformatting page layouts, allowing the user to drag-and-drop items within a page, validating user input on forms, redirecting users to other pages, and much more. You have probably already guessed that this is referred to as *client-side scripting*, and you're correct.

This book is all about JavaScript, the most-used language for client-side scripting on the Internet.

NOTE

There is, in fact, an elegant way to incorporate output from server-side scripts into your client-side JavaScript programs. We look at this in Part V, "Using JavaScript Libraries," when we study a technique called *Ajax*.

JavaScript in a Nutshell

NOTE

Although the names are similar, JavaScript doesn't have much, if anything, to do with the Java language developed by Sun Microsystems. The two languages share some aspects of syntax, but no more so than either of them do with a whole host of other programming languages.

A program written in JavaScript can access the elements of a web page, and the browser window in which it is running, and perform actions on those elements, as well as create new page elements. A few examples of JavaScript's capabilities include

▶ Opening new windows with a specified size, position, and style (for example, whether the window has borders, menus, toolbars, and so on)

▶ Providing user-friendly navigation aids such as drop-down menus

▶ Validation of data entered into a web form to make sure that it is of an acceptable format before the form is submitted to the web server

▶ Changing how page elements look and behave when particular events occur, such as the mouse cursor moving over them

▶ Detecting and exploiting advanced features supported by the particular browser being used, such as third-party plug-ins, or native support for new technologies

Because JavaScript code runs locally inside the user's browser, the page tends to respond quickly to JavaScript instructions, enhancing the user's experience and making the application seem more like one of the computer's native applications rather than simply a web page. Also, JavaScript can detect and utilize certain user actions that HTML can't, such as individual mouse clicks and keyboard actions.

Virtually every web browser in common use has support for JavaScript.

Where JavaScript Came From

The ancestry of JavaScript dates back to the mid 1990s, when version 1.0 was introduced for Netscape Navigator 2.

The European Computer Manufacturers Association (ECMA) became involved, defining ECMAScript, the great-granddaddy of the current language. At the same time, Microsoft introduced jScript, its own version of the language, for use in its Internet Explorer range of browsers.

TIP

ECMA continues to issue updated versions of the ECMAScript language standard. At the time of writing, ECMAScript 6 is nearing its final version, and in Part VI, "Advanced Topics," you can read about some of the new language features soon to become available.

NOTE

JavaScript is not the only client-side scripting language. Microsoft browsers have supported (in addition to jScript, Microsoft's version of JavaScript) a scripting-oriented version of the company's own Visual Basic language, called VBScript.

JavaScript, however, has much better browser support; a version of JavaScript is supported by nearly every modern browser.

The Browser Wars

In the late 1990s, Netscape Navigator 4 and Internet Explorer 4 both claimed to offer major improvements over earlier browser versions in terms of what could be achieved with JavaScript.

Unfortunately, the two sets of developers had gone in separate directions, each defining its own additions to the JavaScript language, and how it interacted with your web page.

This ludicrous situation forced developers to essentially write two versions of each of their scripts, and use some clumsy and often error-prone routines to try to determine which browser was being used to view the page, and subsequently switch to the most appropriate version of their JavaScript code.

NOTE

The World Wide Web Consortium (W3C) is an international community that exists to develop open standards to support the long-term growth of the World Wide Web. Its website at http://www.w3.org/ is a vast resource of information and tools relating to web standards.

Thankfully, the World Wide Web Consortium (the W3C) worked hard with the individual browser manufacturers to standardize the way web pages were constructed and manipulated, by means of the Document Object Model (DOM). Level 1 of the new standardized DOM was completed in late 1998, and Level 2 in late 2000.

Don't worry if you're not sure what the DOM is or what it does—you learn a lot about it later this hour and through the course of this book.

The `<script>` Tag

Whenever the page is requested by a user, any JavaScript programs it contains are passed to the browser along with page content.

> **NOTE**
>
> JavaScript is an *interpreted* language, rather than a *compiled* language such as C++ or Java. The JavaScript instructions are passed to the browser as plain text and are interpreted sequentially; they do not need to first be "compiled" into condensed machine code only readable by the computer's processor. This offers big advantages in that JavaScript programs are easy to read, can be edited swiftly, and their operation can be retested simply by reloading the web page in the browser.

You can include JavaScript statements directly into your HTML code by placing them between `<script>` and `</script>` tags within the HTML:

```
<script>
    ... JavaScript statements ...
</script>
```

The examples in this book are all written to validate correctly as HTML5, in which no obligatory attributes are specified for the `<script>` element (the `type` attribute is optional in HTML5, and has been excluded from the examples in this book to aid clarity). However, if you write JavaScript for inclusion in HTML 4.x or XHTML pages, you should add the `type` attribute to your `<script>` elements:

```
<script type="text/javascript">
    ... JavaScript statements ...
</script>
```

You'll also occasionally see `<script>` elements having the attribute `language="JavaScript"`. This has long been deprecated, so unless you think you need to support ancient browsers such as Navigator and Mosaic, there's no need to continue writing code like this.

NOTE

The term *deprecated* is applied to software features or practices to indicate that they are best avoided, usually because they have been superseded.

Although still supported to provide backward compatibility, their *deprecated* status often implies that such features will be removed in the near future.

The examples in this hour place their JavaScript code within the body section of the document, but JavaScript code can appear elsewhere in the document too; you can also use the `<script>` element to load JavaScript code saved in an external file. We discuss how to include JavaScript in your pages in much more detail in Hour 2, "Writing Simple Scripts."

Introducing the DOM

A Document Object Model (DOM) is a conceptual way of visualizing a document and its contents.

Each time your browser is asked to load and display a page, it needs to interpret (we usually use the word "parse") the source code contained in the HTML file comprising the page. As part of this parsing process, the browser creates a type of internal model known as a DOM representation based on the content of the loaded document. It is this model that the browser then refers to when rendering the visible page. You can use JavaScript to access and edit the various parts of the DOM representation, at the same time changing the way the user sees and interacts with the page in view.

In the early days, JavaScript provided rather primitive access to certain parts of a web page. JavaScript programs could gain access, for example, to the images and forms contained in a web page; a JavaScript program could contain statements to select "the second form on the page" or "the form called 'registration'."

Web developers sometimes refer to this as DOM Level 0, in backward-compatible homage to the W3C's subsequent Level 1 DOM definition. As well as DOM Level 0, you might also see reference to the BOM, or Browser Object Model. Since then, the W3C has gradually extended and improved the DOM specification. The W3C's much more ambitious definition has produced a DOM that is valid not just for web pages and JavaScript, but for any programming language and for XML, in addition to HTML, documents.

NOTE

In this book, we concentrate on the W3C's DOM Levels 1 and 2 DOM definitions. If you're interested in the details of the various DOM levels, you can find a good overview at https://developer.mozilla.org/en/DOM_Levels.

The W3C and Standards Compliance

The browser vendors have incorporated much-improved support for DOM in their most recent versions. At the time of writing, Internet Explorer is shipping in version 11, Netscape Navigator has been reborn as Mozilla Firefox (currently in version 35.0), and other competitors in the market include Opera, Konqueror, Apple's Safari, and Google's Chrome and Chromium. All of these offer excellent support for the DOM.

The situation has improved markedly for web developers. Apart from a few irritating quirks, we can now largely forget about writing special code for individual browsers provided that we follow the DOM standards.

NOTE

The use of early browsers such as Netscape Navigator (any version) and Internet Explorer up to version 5.5 has now virtually disappeared. This book concentrates on more modern browsers that are compatible with DOM Level 1 or better, such as Internet Explorer 9+, Firefox, Google Chrome, Apple Safari, Opera, and Konqueror. You are recommended to upgrade your browser to the latest stable version.

The `window` and `document` Objects

Each time your browser loads and displays a page, it creates in memory an internal representation of the page and all its elements, the DOM. In the DOM, elements of your web page have a logical, hierarchical structure, like a tree of interconnected parent and child *objects*. These objects, and their interconnections, form a conceptual model of the web page and the browser that contains and displays it. Each object also has a list of *properties* that describe it, and a number of *methods* we can use to manipulate those properties using JavaScript.

Right at the top of the hierarchical tree is the browser `window` object. This object is a parent or ancestor to everything else in the DOM representation of your page.

The `window` object has various child objects, some of which are visualized in Figure 1.1. The first child object shown in Figure 1.1, and the one we'll use most in this book, is the `document` object. Any HTML page loaded into the browser creates a `document` object containing all of the HTML and other resources that go into making up the displayed page. All of this information is accessible via JavaScript as a parent-child hierarchy of objects, each with its own properties and methods.

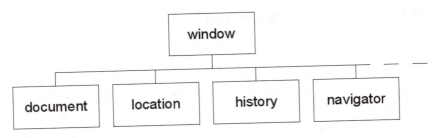

FIGURE 1.1
The `window` object and some of its children

The other children of the `window` object visible in Figure 1.1 are the `location` object (containing details of the URL of the currently loaded page), the `history` object (containing details of the browser's previously visited pages), and the `navigator` object (which stores details of the browser type, version, and capabilities). We look in detail at these objects in Hour 4, "DOM Objects and Built-In Objects," and use them again at intervals throughout the book, but for now let's concentrate on the `document` object.

Object Notation

The notation we use to represent objects within the tree uses the dot or period:

`parent.child`

As an example, referring to Figure 1.1, the `location` object is a child of the `window` object, so in the DOM it is referred to like this:

`window.location`

TIP

This notation can be extended as many times as necessary to represent any object in the tree. For example

`object1.object2.object3`

represents `object3`, whose parent is `object2`, which is itself a child of `object1`.

The `<body>` section of your HTML page is represented in the DOM as a child element of the `document` object; we would access it like this:

`window.document.body`

The last item in the sequence can also be, instead of another object, a *property* or *method* of the parent object:

```
object1.object2.property
object1.object2.method
```

For example, let's suppose that we want to access the `title` property of the current document, as specified by the HTML `<title>...</title>` tags. We can simply use

```
window.document.title
```

NOTE

Don't worry if object hierarchy and dot notation don't seem too clear right now. You'll be seeing many examples in the course of the book!

TIP

The `window` object always contains the current browser window, so you can refer to `window.docu-ment` to access the current document. As a shortcut, you can also simply use `document` instead of `window.document`—this also refers to the current document.

If you have several windows open, or if you are using a frameset, there will be a separate `window` and `document` object for each window or frame. To refer to one of these documents, you need to use the relevant window name and document name belonging to the window or frame in question.

Talking to the User

Let's take a look at some of the methods associated with the `window` and `document` objects. We begin with two methods, each of which provides a means to talk to the user.

window.alert()

Even if you don't realize it, you've seen the results of the `window` object's `alert` method on many occasions. The `window` object, you'll recall, is at the top of the DOM hierarchy, and represents the browser window that's displaying your page. When you call the `alert()` method, the browser pops open a dialog displaying your message, along with an OK button. Here's an example:

```
<script>window.alert("Here is my message");</script>
```

This is our first working example of the dot notation. Here we are calling the `alert()` method of the `window` object, so our `object.method` notation becomes `window.alert`.

Notice that the line of text inside the parentheses is contained within quotation marks. These can be single or double quotes, but they must be there, or an error will be produced.

This line of code, when executed in the browser, pops up a dialog like the one in Figure 1.2.

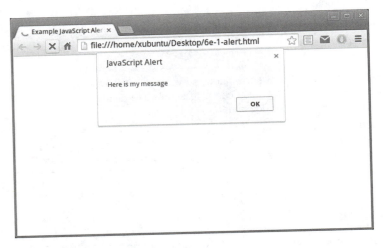

FIGURE 1.2
A `window.alert()` dialog

document.write()

You can probably guess what the write method of the document object does, simply from its name. This method, instead of popping up a dialog, writes characters directly into the DOM of the document, as shown in Figure 1.3.

```
<script>document.write("Here is another message");</script>
```

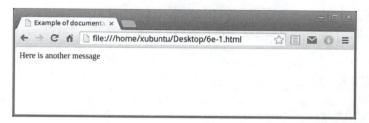

FIGURE 1.3
Using document.write()

NOTE

In fact, document.write is a pretty dumb way to write content to the page—it has a lot of limitations, both in terms of its function and in terms of coding style and maintainability. It has largely fallen into disuse for "serious" JavaScript programming. By the time you come to write more advanced JavaScript programs, you'll have learned much better ways to put content into your pages using JavaScript and the DOM. However, we use document.write quite a lot during Part I of the book, while you come to grips with some of the basic principles of the language.

TRY IT YOURSELF ▼

"Hello World!" in JavaScript

It seems almost rude to introduce a programming language without presenting the traditional "Hello World" example. Have a look at the simple HTML document of Listing 1.1.

LISTING 1.1   "Hello World!" in an alert() Dialog

```
<!DOCTYPE html>
<html>
<head>
    <title>Hello from JavaScript!</title>
</head>
```

```
<body>
    <script>
        alert("Hello World!");
    </script>
</body>
</html>
```

Create a document called hello.html in your text editor, and enter the preceding code. Save it to a convenient place on your computer, and then open it with your web browser.

CAUTION

Some text editor programs might try to add a .txt extension to the filename you specify. Be sure your saved file has the extension .html or the browser will probably not open it correctly.

Many popular operating systems allow you to right-click on the icon of the HTML file and choose Open With..., or similar wording. Alternatively, fire up your chosen browser, and use the **File > Open** options from the menu bar to navigate to your file and load it into the browser.

You should see a display similar to Figure 1.2, but with the message "Hello World!" in the dialog. If you have more than one browser installed on your computer, try them all, and compare the display—the dialogs will probably look a little different, but the message, and the operation of the OK button, should be just the same.

CAUTION

The default security settings in some browsers cause them to show a security warning when they are asked to open local content, such as a file on your own computer. If your browser does this, just choose the option that allows the content to be shown.

Reading a Property of the `document` Object

You may recall from earlier in the hour that objects in the DOM tree have properties and methods. You saw how to use the `write` method of the `document` object to output text to the page—now let's try *reading* one of the properties of the `document` object. We're going to use the `document.title` property, which contains the title as defined in the HTML `<title>` element of the page.

Edit hello.html in your text editor, and change the call to the `window.alert()` method:

```
alert(document.title);
```

Notice that `document.title` is NOT now enclosed in quotation marks—if it were, JavaScript would infer that we wanted to output the string "document.title" as literal text. Without the quote marks, JavaScript sends to the `alert()` method the *value* contained in the `document.title` property. The result is shown in Figure 1.4.

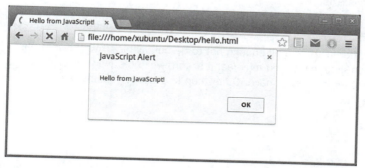

FIGURE 1.4
Displaying a property of the `document` object

Summary

In this hour, you were introduced to the concepts of server-side and client-side scripting and had a brief history lesson about JavaScript and the Document Object Model. You had an overview of the sorts of things JavaScript can do to enhance your web pages and improve the experience for your users.

Additionally, you learned about the basic structure of the Document Object Model, and how JavaScript can access particular objects and their properties, and use the methods belonging to those objects.

In the lessons that follow, we'll build on these fundamental concepts to get into more advanced scripting projects.

Q&A

Q. If I use server-side scripting (in a language such as PHP or ASP), can I still use JavaScript on the client side?

A. Most definitely. In fact, the combination of server-side and client-side scripting provides a potent platform, capable of producing powerful applications. Google's Gmail is a good example.

Q. How many different browsers should I test in?

A. As many as you practically can. Writing standards-compliant code that avoids browser-specific features will go a long way toward making your code run smoothly in different browsers. However, one or two minor differences between browser implementations of certain features are likely to always exist.

Q. Won't the inclusion of JavaScript code slow down the load time of my pages?

A. Yes, though usually the difference is small enough not to be noticeable. If you have a particularly large piece of JavaScript code, you may feel it's worthwhile testing your page on the slowest connection a user is likely to have. Other than in extreme circumstances, it's unlikely to be a serious issue.

Workshop

Try to answer all the questions before reading the subsequent "Answers" section.

Quiz

1. Is JavaScript a compiled or an interpreted language?

    a. A compiled language

    b. An interpreted language

    c. Neither

    d. Both

2. What extra tags must be added to an HTML page to include JavaScript statements?

    a. `<script>` and `</script>`

    b. `<type="text/javascript">`

    c. `<!--` and `-->`

3. The top level of the DOM hierarchy is occupied by:

    a. The `document` property

    b. The `document` method

    c. The `document` object

    d. The `window` object

Answers

1. b. JavaScript is an interpreted language. The program code is written in plain text, and the statements are read and executed one at a time.

2. a. JavaScript statements are added between `<script>` and `</script>` tags.

3. d. The `window` object is at the top of the DOM tree, and the `document` object is one of its child objects.

Exercises

▶ In the "Try It Yourself" section of this hour, we used the line

```
alert(document.title);
```

to output the `title` property of the `document` object. Try rewriting that script to instead output the `document.lastModified` property, which contains the date and time that the web page was last changed. (Be careful—property names are case sensitive. Note the capital M.) See whether you can then modify the code to use `document.write()` in place of `alert()` to write the property directly into the page, as in Figure 1.3.

▶ Try the example code from this hour in as many different browsers as you have access to. What differences do you note in how the example pages are displayed?

Writing Simple Scripts

What You'll Learn in This Hour:

- ▶ Various ways to include JavaScript in your web pages
- ▶ The basic syntax of JavaScript statements
- ▶ How to declare and use variables
- ▶ Using mathematical operators
- ▶ How to comment your code
- ▶ Capturing mouse events

You learned in Hour 1, "Introducing JavaScript," that JavaScript is a scripting language capable of making web pages more interactive.

In this hour you learn more about how JavaScript can be added to your web page, and then about some of the fundamental syntax of your JavaScript programs such as statements, variables, operators, and comments. You'll also get your hands dirty with more code examples.

Including JavaScript in Your Web Page

In the previous hour I said that JavaScript programs are passed to the browser along with page content—but how do we achieve that? Actually there are two basic methods for associating JavaScript code with your HTML page, both of which use the `<script></script>` element introduced in Hour 1.

One method is to include the JavaScript statements directly into the HTML file, just like we did in the previous hour:

```
<script>
    ... Javascript statements are written here ...
</script>
```

A second, and usually preferable way to include your code is to save your JavaScript into a separate file, and use the `<script>` element to include that file by name using the `src` (source) attribute:

```
<script src='mycode.js'></script>
```

The preceding example includes the file `mycode.js`, which contains our JavaScript statements. If your JavaScript file is not in the same folder as the calling script, you can also add a (relative or absolute) path to it:

```
<script src='/path/to/mycode.js'></script>
```

or

```
<script src='http://www.example.com/path/to/mycode.js'></script>
```

Placing your JavaScript code in a separate file offers some important advantages:

▶ When the JavaScript code is updated, the updates are immediately available to any page using that same JavaScript file. This is particularly important in the context of JavaScript libraries, which we look at later in the book.

▶ The code for the HTML page is kept cleaner, and therefore easier to read and maintain.

▶ Performance is slightly improved because your browser caches the included file; therefore, having a local copy in memory next time it is needed by this or another page.

NOTE

It is customary to give files of JavaScript code the file extension .js, as in this example. However, your included code files can have any extension, and the browser will try to interpret the contents as JavaScript.

CAUTION

The JavaScript statements in the external file must NOT be surrounded by `<script>` ... `</script>` tags, nor can you place any HTML markup within the external file. Just include the raw JavaScript code.

Listing 2.1 shows the simple web page we used in Hour 1, but now with a file of JavaScript code included in the `<body>` section. JavaScript can be placed in either the head or body of the HTML page. In fact, it is more common—and generally recommended—for JavaScript code to be placed in the head of the page, where it provides a number of *functions* that can be called from elsewhere in the document. You learn about functions in Hour 3, "Using Functions"; until then, we limit ourselves to adding our example code into the body of the document.

LISTING 2.1   An HTML Document with a JavaScript File Included

```
<!DOCTYPE html>
<html>
<head>
    <title>A Simple Page</title>
</head>
<body>
    <p>Some content ...</p>
    <script src='mycode.js'></script>
</body>
</html>
```

When JavaScript code is added into the body of the document, the code statements are interpreted and executed as they are encountered while the page is being rendered. After the code has been read and executed, page rendering continues until the page is complete.

TIP

You're not limited to using a single `script` element—you can have as many of them on your page as you need.

NOTE

You sometimes see HTML-style comment notation `<!--` and `-->` inside `script` elements, surrounding the JavaScript statements, like this:

```
<script>
    <!--
    ... Javascript statements are written here ...
    -->
</script>
```

This was for the benefit of ancient browsers that didn't recognize the `<script>` tag. This HTML "comment" syntax prevented such browsers from displaying the JavaScript source code on the screen along with the page content. Unless you have a reason to support very old browsers, this technique is no longer required.

JavaScript Statements

JavaScript programs are lists of individual instructions that we refer to as *statements*. To interpret statements correctly, the browser expects to find each statement written on a separate line:

```
this is statement 1
this is statement 2
```

Alternatively, they can be combined in the same line by terminating each with a semicolon:

```
this is statement 1; this is statement 2;
```

To ease the readability of your code, and to help prevent hard-to-find syntax errors, it's good practice to combine both methods by giving each statement its own line and terminating the statement with a semicolon:

```
this is statement 1;
this is statement 2;
```

Commenting Your Code

Some statements are not intended to be executed by the browser's JavaScript interpreter, but are there for the benefit of anybody who may be reading the code. We refer to such lines as *comments*, and there are specific rules for adding comments to your code.

A comment that occupies just a single line of code can be written by placing a double forward slash before the content of the line:

```
// This is a comment
```

NOTE

JavaScript can also use the HTML comment syntax for single-line comments:

```
<!-- this is a comment -->
```

However, this is not commonly used in JavaScript programs.

To add a multiline comment in this way, we need to prefix every line of the comment:

```
// This is a comment
// spanning multiple lines
```

A more convenient way of entering multiline comments to your code is to prefix your comment with /* and terminate it with */. A comment written using this syntax can span multiple lines:

```
/*  This comment can span
    multiple lines
```

```
without needing
to mark up every line  */
```

Adding comments to your code is really a good thing to do, especially when you're writing larger or more complex JavaScript applications. Comments can act as reminders to you, and also as instructions and explanations to anybody else reading your code at a later date.

NOTE

It's true that comments add a little to the size of your JavaScript source file, and this can have an adverse effect on page-loading times. Generally the difference is so small as to be barely noticeable, but if it really matters you can always strip out all the comments from a "production" version of your JavaScript file—that is, a version to use with live, rather than development, websites.

Variables

A variable can be thought of as a named "pigeon-hole" where we keep a particular piece of data. Such data can take many different forms—an integer or decimal number, a string of characters, or various other data types discussed later in this hour or in those that follow. Our variables can be called pretty much anything we want, so long as we only use alphanumeric characters, the dollar sign $, or underscores in the name.

NOTE

JavaScript is case sensitive—a variable called `mypetcat` is a different variable from `Mypetcat` or `MYPETCAT`.

Many coders of JavaScript, and other programming languages, like to use the so-called *CamelCase* convention (also called mixedCase, BumpyCaps, and various other names) for variable names. In CamelCase, compound words or phrases have the elements joined without spaces, with each element's initial letter capitalized except the first letter, which can be either upper- or lowercase. In this example, the variable would be named `MyPetCat` or `myPetCat`.

Let's suppose we have a variable called `netPrice`. We can set the value stored in `netPrice` with a simple statement:

```
netPrice = 8.99;
```

We call this *assigning a value* to the variable. Note that we don't have to declare the existence of this variable before assigning a value, as we would have to in some other programming languages. However, doing so is possible in JavaScript by using the `var` keyword, and in most cases is good programming practice:

```
var netPrice;
netPrice = 8.99;
```

Alternatively we can combine these two statements conveniently and readably into one:

```
var netPrice = 8.99;
```

To assign a *character string* as the value of a variable, we need to include the string in single or double quotes:

```
var productName = "Leather wallet";
```

We could then, for example, write a line of code sending the value contained in that variable to the `window.alert` method:

```
alert(productName);
```

The generated dialog would evaluate the variable and display it (this time, in Mozilla Firefox) as in Figure 2.1.

FIGURE 2.1
Displaying the value of variable `productName`

TIP

Choose readable variable names. Having variable names such as `productName` and `netPrice` makes code much easier to read and maintain than if the same variables were called `var123` and `myothervar49`, even though the latter names are entirely valid.

Operators

The values we have stored in our variables aren't going to be much use to us unless we can manipulate them in calculations.

Arithmetic Operations

First, JavaScript allows us to carry out operations using the standard arithmetic operators of addition, subtraction, multiplication, and division.

```
var theSum = 4 + 3;
```

As you'll have guessed, after this statement has been executed the variable `theSum` will contain a value of 7. We can use variable names in our operations too:

```
var productCount = 2;
var subtotal = 14.98;
var shipping = 2.75;
var total = subtotal + shipping;
```

We can use JavaScript to subtract (-), multiply (*), and divide (/) in a similar manner:

```
subtotal = total - shipping;
var salesTax = total * 0.15;
var productPrice = subtotal / productCount;
```

To calculate the remainder from a division, we can use JavaScript's *modulus division* operator. This is denoted by the % character:

```
var itemsPerBox = 12;
var itemsToBeBoxed = 40;
var itemsInLastBox = itemsToBeBoxed % itemsPerBox;
```

In this example, the variable `itemsInLastBox` would contain the number *4* after the last statement completes.

JavaScript also has convenient operators to increment (++) or decrement (--) the value of a variable:

```
productCount++;
```

is equivalent to the statement

```
productCount = productCount + 1;
```

Similarly,

```
items--;
```

is just the same as

```
items = items - 1;
```

TIP

If you need to increment or decrement a variable by a value other than one, JavaScript also allows you to combine other arithmetic operators with the = operator; for example, += and -=.

The following two lines of code are equivalent:

```
total = total + 5;
total += 5;
```

So are these two:

```
counter = counter - step;
counter -= step;
```

We can use this notation for other arithmetic operators, such as multiplication and division:

```
price = price * uplift;
price *= uplift;
```

A more comprehensive list of JavaScript's arithmetic operators appears in Appendix B, "JavaScript Quick Reference."

Operator Precedence

When you use several operators in the same calculation, JavaScript uses *precedence rules* to determine in what order the calculation should be done. For example, consider the statement

```
var average = a + b + c / 3;
```

If, as the variable's name implies, you're trying to calculate an average, this would not give the desired result; the division operation would be carried out on c before adding the values of a and b to the result. To calculate the average correctly, we would have to add parentheses to our statement, like this:

```
var average = (a + b + c) / 3;
```

If you have doubts about the precedence rules, I would recommend that you always use parentheses liberally. There is no cost to doing so, it makes your code easier to read (both for you and for anyone else who later has to edit or decipher it), and it ensures that precedence issues don't spoil your calculations.

NOTE

If you have programming experience in another language such as PHP or Java, you'll find that the precedence rules in JavaScript are pretty much identical to the ones you're used to. You can find detailed information on JavaScript precedence at http://msdn.microsoft.com/en-us/library/z3ks45k7(v=vs.94).aspx.

Using the + Operator with Strings

Arithmetic operators don't make much sense if the variables they operate on contain strings rather than numeric values. The exception is the + operator, which JavaScript interprets as an instruction to concatenate (join together sequentially) two or more strings:

```
var firstname = "John";
var surname = "Doe";
var fullname = firstname + " " + surname;
// the variable fullname now contains the value "John Doe"
```

If you try to use the + operator on two variables, one of which is a string and the other numeric, JavaScript converts the numeric value to a string and concatenates the two:

```
var name = "David";
var age = 45;
alert(name + age);
```

Figure 2.2 shows the result of using the + operator on a string and a numeric value.

We talk about JavaScript data types, and string operations in general, much more in Hour 5, "Numbers and Strings."

FIGURE 2.2
Concatenating a string and a numeric value

Convert Celsius to Fahrenheit

To convert a temperature in degrees Celsius to one measured in degrees Fahrenheit, we need to multiply by 9, divide by 5, and then add 32. Let's do that in JavaScript:

```
var cTemp = 100;  // temperature in Celsius
// Let's be generous with parentheses
var hTemp = ((cTemp * 9) /5 ) + 32;
```

In fact, we could have omitted all of the parentheses from this calculation and it would still have worked fine:

```
var hTemp = cTemp*9/5 + 32;
```

However, the parentheses make the code easier to understand, and help prevent errors caused by operator precedence.

Let's test the code in a web page, as shown in Listing 2.2.

LISTING 2.2   **Calculating Fahrenheit from Celsius**

```
<!DOCTYPE html>
<html>
<head>
    <title>Fahrenheit From Celsius</title>
</head>
<body>
    <script>
        var cTemp = 100;  // temperature in Celsius
        // Let's be generous with parentheses
        var hTemp = ((cTemp * 9) /5 ) + 32;
        document.write("Temperature in Celsius: " + cTemp + " degrees<br/>");
        document.write("Temperature in Fahrenheit: " + hTemp + " degrees");
    </script>
</body>
</html>
```

Save this code as a file `temperature.html` and load it into your browser. You should get the result shown in Figure 2.3.

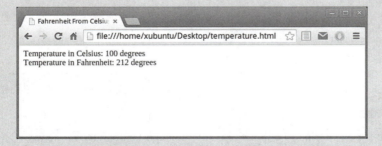

FIGURE 2.3
The output of Listing 2.2

Edit the file a few times to use different values for `cTemp`, and check that everything works OK.

Capturing Mouse Events

One of the fundamental purposes of JavaScript is to help make your web pages more interactive for the user. To achieve this, we need to have some mechanisms to detect what the user and the program are doing at any given moment—where the mouse is in the browser window, whether the user has clicked a mouse button or pressed a keyboard key, whether a page has fully loaded in the browser, and so on.

All of these occurrences we refer to as *events*, and JavaScript has a variety of tools to help us work with them. Let's take a look at some of the ways we can detect a user's mouse actions using JavaScript.

JavaScript deals with events by using so-called *event handlers*. We are going to investigate three of these: `onClick`, `onMouseOver`, and `onMouseOut`.

The `onClick` Event Handler

The `onClick` event handler can be applied to nearly all HTML elements visible on a page. One way we can implement it is to add one more attribute to the HTML element:

```
onclick=" ...some JavaScript code... "
```

NOTE
_____

While adding event handlers directly into HTML elements is perfectly valid, it's not regarded these days as good programming practice. It serves us well for the examples in Part I of this book, but later in the book you learn more powerful and elegant ways to use event handlers.
_____

Let's see an example; have a look at Listing 2.3.

LISTING 2.3   Using the `onClick` Event Handler

```
<!DOCTYPE html>
<html>
<head>
    <title>onClick Demo</title>
</head>
<body>
    <input type="button" onclick="alert('You clicked the button!')" value="Click
    ➥Me" />
</body>
</html>
```

The HTML code adds a button to the `<body>` element of the page, and supplies that button with an `onclick` attribute. The value given to the `onclick` attribute is the JavaScript code we want to run when the HTML element (in this case a button) is clicked. When the user clicks on the button, the `onclick` *event* is activated (we normally say the event has been "fired") and the JavaScript statement(s) listed in the value of the attribute are executed.

In this case, there's just one statement:

```
alert('You clicked the button!')
```

Figure 2.4 shows the result of clicking the button.

FIGURE 2.4
Using the `onClick` event handler

NOTE

You may have noticed that we call the handler `onClick`, but that we write this in lowercase as `onclick` when adding it to an HTML element. This convention has arisen because, although HTML is case insensitive, XHTML is case *sensitive* and requires all HTML elements and attribute names to be written in lowercase.

`onMouseOver` **and** `onMouseOut` **Event Handlers**

When we simply want to detect where the mouse pointer is on the screen with reference to a particular page element, `onMouseOver` and `onMouseOut` can help us to do that.

The `onMouseOver` event is fired when the user's mouse cursor enters the region of the screen occupied by the element in question. The `onMouseOut` event, as I'm sure you've already guessed, is fired when the cursor leaves that same region.

Listing 2.4 provides a simple example of the `onMouseOver` event in action.

LISTING 2.4 Using `onMouseOver`

```
<!DOCTYPE html>
<html>
<head>
    <title>onMouseOver Demo</title>
</head>
<body>
    <img src="image1.png" alt="image 1" onmouseover="alert('You entered the
    ➥image!')" />
</body>
</html>
```

The result of running the script is shown in Figure 2.5. Replacing `onmouseover` with `onmouse-out` in the code will, of course, simply fire the event handler—and therefore pop up the alert dialog—as the mouse *leaves* the image, rather than doing so as it enters.

FIGURE 2.5
Using the `onMouseOver` event handler

▼ TRY IT YOURSELF

Creating an Image Rollover

We can use the onMouseOver and onMouseOut events to change how an image appears while the mouse pointer is above it. To achieve this, we use onMouseOver to change the src attribute of the HTML <img> element as the mouse cursor enters, and onMouseOut to change it back as the mouse cursor leaves. The code is shown in Listing 2.5.

LISTING 2.5 An Image Rollover Using onMouseOver and onMouseOut

```
<!DOCTYPE html>
<html>
<head>
    <title>OnMouseOver Demo</title>
</head>
<body>
    <img src="tick.gif" alt="tick" onmouseover="this.src='tick2.gif';"
onmouseout="this.src='tick.gif';" />
</body>
</html>
```

You may notice something new in the syntax we used here. Within the JavaScript statements for onMouseOver and onMouseOut we use the keyword this.

When using this within an event handler added via an attribute of an HTML element, this refers to the HTML element itself; in this case, you can read it as "this image," and this.src refers (using the "dot" notation that we've already met) to the src (source) property of this image object.

In this example we used two images, tick.gif and tick2.gif—you can use any images you have on hand, but the demonstration works best if they are the same size, and not too large.

Use your editor to create an HTML file containing the code of Listing 2.5. You can change the image names tick.gif and tick2.gif to the names of your two images, if different; just make sure the images are saved in the same folder as your HTML file. Save the HTML file and open it in your browser.

You should see that the image changes as the mouse pointer enters, and changes back as it leaves, as depicted in Figure 2.6.

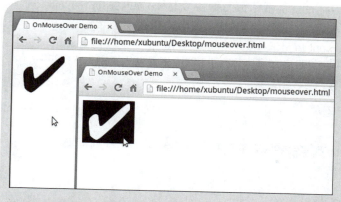

FIGURE 2.6
An image rollover using `onMouseOver` and `onMouseOut`

NOTE

There was a time when image rollovers were regularly done this way, but these days they can be achieved much more efficiently using Cascading Style Sheets (CSS). Still, it's a convenient way to demonstrate the use of the `onMouseOver` and `onMouseOut` event handlers.

Summary

You covered quite a lot of ground this hour.

First of all you learned various ways to include JavaScript code in your HTML pages.

You studied how to declare variables in JavaScript, assign values to those variables, and manipulate them using arithmetic operators.

Finally, you were introduced to some of JavaScript's event handlers, and you learned how to detect certain actions of the user's mouse.

Q&A

Q. Some of the listings and code snippets list opening and closing `<script>` tags on the same line; other times they are on separate lines. Does it matter?

A. Empty spaces, such as the space character, tabs, and blank lines, are completely ignored by JavaScript. You can use such blank space, which programmers usually call **whitespace**, to lay out your code in such a way that it's more legible and easy to follow.

Q. Can I use the same `<script>` element both to include an external JavaScript file and to contain JavaScript statements?

A. No. If you use the `script` element to include an external JavaScript file by using the `src` attribute, you cannot also include JavaScript statements between `<script>` and `</script>`—this region must be left empty.

Workshop

Try to answer the following questions before looking at the "Answers" section that follows.

Quiz

1. What is an `onClick` event handler?

   a. An object that detects the mouse's location in the browser

   b. A script that executes in response to the user clicking the mouse

   c. An HTML element that the user can click

2. How many `<script>` elements are permitted on a page?

   a. None

   b. Exactly one

   c. Any number

3. Which of these is NOT a true statement about variables?

   a. Their names are case sensitive.

   b. They can contain numeric or non-numeric information.

   c. Their names may contain spaces.

Answers

1. b. An `onClick` event handler is a script that executes when the user clicks the mouse.

2. c. You can use as many `<script>` elements as you need.

3. c. Variable names in JavaScript must not contain spaces.

Exercises

▶ Starting with Listing 2.4, remove the `onMouseOver` and `onMouseOut` handlers from the `<img>` element. Instead, add an `onClick` handler to set the `title` property of the image to `My New Title`. (Hint: You can access the image title using `this.title`.)

▶ Can you think of an easy way to test whether your script has correctly set the new image title?

HOUR 3
Using Functions

What You'll Learn in This Hour:

▶ How to define functions
▶ How to call (execute) functions
▶ How functions receive data
▶ Returning values from functions
▶ About the scope of variables

Commonly, programs carry out the same or similar tasks repeatedly during the course of their execution. For you to avoid rewriting the same piece of code over and over again, JavaScript has the means to parcel up parts of your code into reusable modules, called *functions*. Once you've written a function, it is available for the rest of your program to use, as if it were itself a part of the JavaScript language.

Using functions also makes your code easier to debug and maintain. Suppose you've written an application to calculate shipping costs; when the tax rates or haulage prices change, you'll need to make changes to your script. There may be 50 places in your code where such calculations are carried out. When you attempt to change every calculation, you're likely to miss some instances or introduce errors. However, if all such calculations are wrapped up in a few functions used throughout the application, then you just need to make changes to those functions. Your changes will automatically be applied all through the application.

Functions are one of the basic building blocks of JavaScript and will appear in virtually every script you write. In this hour you see how to create and use functions.

General Syntax

Creating a function is similar to creating a new JavaScript command that you can use in your script.

Here's the basic syntax for creating a function:

```
function sayHello() {
    alert("Hello");
    // ... more statements can go here ...
}
```

You begin with the keyword `function`, followed by your chosen function name with parentheses appended, then a pair of curly braces, {}. Inside the braces go the JavaScript statements that make up the function. In the case of the preceding example, we simply have one line of code to pop up an `alert` dialog, but you can add as many lines of code as are necessary to make the function...well, function!

CAUTION
_____

The keyword `function` must always be used in lowercase, or an error will be generated.
_____

To keep things tidy, you can collect together as many functions as you like into one `<script>` element:

```
<script>
    function doThis() {
        alert("Doing This");
    }
    function doThat() {
        alert("Doing That");
    }
</script>
```

Calling Functions

Code wrapped up in a function definition will not be executed when the page loads. Instead, it waits quietly until the function is *called*.

To call a function, you simply use the function name (with the parentheses) wherever you want to execute the statements contained in the function:

```
sayHello();
```

For example, you may want to add a call to your new function `sayHello()` to the `onClick` event of a button:

```
<input type="button" value="Say Hello" onclick="sayHello()" />
```

TIP

Function names, like variable names, are case-sensitive. A function called `MyFunc()` is different from another called `myFunc()`. Also, as with variable names, it's really helpful to the readability of your code to choose meaningful function names.

TIP

You've already seen numerous examples of using the **methods** associated with JavaScript objects, such as `document.write()` and `window.alert()`.

Methods are simply functions that "belong" to a specific object. You learn much more about objects in Hour 4, "DOM Objects and Built-in Objects."

Putting JavaScript Code in the Page `<head>`

Up to now, our examples have all placed the JavaScript code into the `<body>` part of the HTML page. Using functions lets you employ the much more common, and usually preferable, practice of storing your JavaScript code in the `<head>` of the page. Functions contained within a `<script>` element in the page head, or in an external file included via the `src` attribute of a `<script>` element in the page head, are available to be called from anywhere on the page. Putting functions in the document's head section ensures that they have been defined prior to any attempt being made to execute them.

Listing 3.1 shows an example.

LISTING 3.1 Functions in the Page Head

```
<!DOCTYPE html>
<html>
<head>
    <title>Calling Functions</title>
    <script>
        function sayHello() {
            alert("Hello");
        }
    </script>
</head>
<body>
    <input type="button" value="Say Hello" onclick="sayHello()" />
</body>
</html>
```

In this listing, you can see that the function definition itself has been placed inside a `<script>` element in the page head, but the call to the function has been made from a different place entirely—on this occasion, from the `onClick` event handler of a button in the body section of the page.

The result of clicking the button is shown in Figure 3.1.

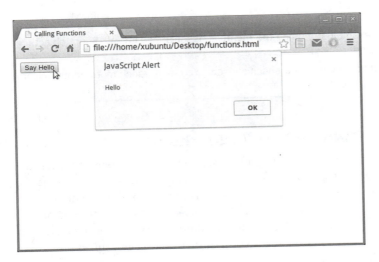

FIGURE 3.1
Calling a JavaScript function

Passing Arguments to Functions

It would be rather limiting if your functions could only behave in an identical fashion each and every time they were called, as would be the case in the preceding example.

Fortunately, you can extend the capabilities of functions a great deal by passing data to them. You do this when the function is called, by passing to it one or more *arguments*:

```
functionName(arguments)
```

Let's write a simple function to calculate the cube of a number and display the result:

```
function cube(x) {
    alert(x * x * x);
}
```

Now we can call our function, replacing the variable *x* with a number. Calling the function like the following results in a dialog box being displayed that contains the result of the calculation, in this case 27:

```
cube(3);
```

Of course, you could equally pass a variable name as an argument. The following code would also generate a dialog containing the number 27:

```
var length = 3;
cube(length);
```

NOTE

You'll sometimes see or hear the word *parameters* used in place of **arguments**, but it means exactly the same thing.

Multiple Arguments

Functions are not limited to a single argument. When you want to send multiple arguments to a function, all you need to do is separate them with commas:

```
function times(a, b) {
    alert(a * b);
}
times(3, 4); // alerts '12'
```

You can use as many arguments as you want.

CAUTION

Make sure that your function calls contain enough argument values to match the arguments specified in the function definition. If any of the arguments in the definition are left without a value, JavaScript may issue an error, or the function may perform incorrectly. If your function call is issued with too many arguments, the extra ones will be ignored by JavaScript.

It's important to note that the names given to arguments in the definition of your function have nothing to do with the names of any variables whose values are passed to the function. The variable names in the argument list act like placeholders for the actual values that will be passed when the function is called. The names that you give to arguments are only used inside the function definition to specify how it works.

We talk about this in more detail later in the hour when we discuss variable *scope*.

▼ TRY IT YOURSELF

A Function to Output User Messages

Let's use what we've learned so far in this hour by creating a function that can send the user a message about a button he or she has just clicked. We place the function definition in the `<head>` section of the page and call it with multiple arguments.

Here's our function:

```
function buttonReport(buttonId, buttonName, buttonValue) {
    // information about the id of the button
    var userMessage1 = "Button id: " + buttonId + "\n";
    // then about the button name
    var userMessage2 = "Button name: " + buttonName + "\n";
    // and the button value
    var userMessage3 = "Button value: " + buttonValue;
    // alert the user
    alert(userMessage1 + userMessage2 + userMessage3);
}
```

The function `buttonReport` takes three arguments, those being the `id`, `name`, and `value` of the button element that has been clicked. With each of these three pieces of information, a short message is constructed. These three messages are then concatenated into a single string, which is passed to the `alert()` method to pop open a dialog containing the information.

TIP

You may have noticed that the first two message strings have the element `"\n"` appended to the string; this is a "new line" character, forcing the message within the alert dialog to return to the left and begin a new line. Certain special characters like this one must be prefixed with \ if they are to be correctly interpreted when they appear in a string. Such a prefixed character is known as an *escape sequence*. You learn more about escape sequences in Hour 5, "Numbers and Strings."

To call our function, we put a button element on our HTML page, with its `id`, `name`, and `value` defined:

```
<input type="button" id="id1" name="Button 1" value="Something" />
```

We need to add an `onClick` event handler to this button from which to call our function. We're going to use the `this` keyword, as discussed in Hour 2, "Writing Simple Scripts":

```
onclick = "buttonReport(this.id, this.name, this.value)"
```

The complete listing is shown in Listing 3.2.

LISTING 3.2   Calling a Function with Multiple Arguments

```html
<!DOCTYPE html>
<html>
<head>
    <title>Calling Functions</title>
    <script>
        function buttonReport(buttonId, buttonName, buttonValue) {
            // information about the id of the button
            var userMessage1 = "Button id: " + buttonId + "\n";
            // then about the button name
            var userMessage2 = "Button name: " + buttonName + "\n";
            // and the button value
            var userMessage3 = "Button value: " + buttonValue;
            // alert the user
            alert(userMessage1 + userMessage2 + userMessage3);
        }
    </script>
</head>
<body>
    <input type="button" id="id1" name="Left Hand Button" value="Left" onclick
    ➥="buttonReport(this.id, this.name, this.value)"/>
    <input type="button" id="id2" name="Center Button" value="Center" onclick
    ➥="buttonReport(this.id, this.name, this.value)"/>
    <input type="button" id="id3" name="Right Hand Button" value="Right" onclick
    ➥="buttonReport(this.id, this.name, this.value)"/>
</body>
</html>
```

Use your editor to create the file buttons.html and enter the preceding code. You should find that it generates output messages like the one shown in Figure 3.2, but with different message content depending on which button has been clicked.

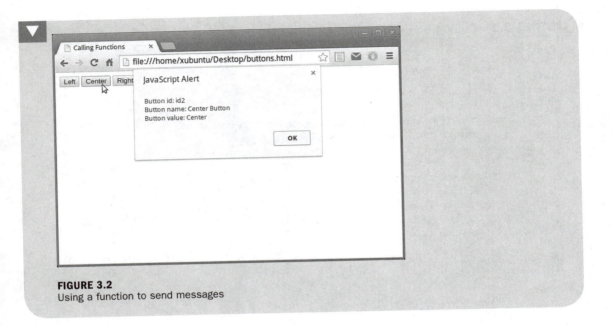

FIGURE 3.2
Using a function to send messages

Returning Values from Functions

OK, now you know how to pass information to functions so that they can act on that information for you. But how can you get information back from your function? You won't always want your functions to be limited to popping open a dialog!

Luckily, there is a mechanism to collect data from a function call—the *return value*. Let's see how it works:

```
function cube(x) {
    return x * x * x;
}
```

Instead of using an `alert()` dialog within the function, as in the previous example, this time we prefixed our required result with the `return` keyword. To access this value from outside the function, we simply assign to a variable the value *returned* by the function:

```
var answer = cube(3);
```

The variable `answer` will now contain the value 27.

NOTE

The values returned by functions are not restricted to numerical quantities as in this example. In fact, functions can return values having any of the data types supported by JavaScript. We discuss data types in Hour 5.

TIP

Where a function returns a value, we can use the function call to pass the return value directly to another statement in our code. For example, instead of

```
var answer = cube(3);
alert(answer);
```

we could simply use

```
alert(cube(3));
```

The value of 27 returned from the function call `cube(3)` immediately becomes the argument passed to the `alert()` method.

Scope of Variables

We have already seen how to declare variables with the `var` keyword. There is a golden rule to remember when using functions:

"Variables declared inside a function only exist inside that function."

This limitation is known as the *scope* of the variable. Let's see an example:

```
// Define our function addTax()
function addTax(subtotal, taxRate) {
    var total = subtotal * (1 + (taxRate/100));
    return total;
}
// now let's call the function
var invoiceValue = addTax(50, 10);
alert(invoiceValue); // works correctly
alert(total);  // doesn't work
```

If we run this code, we first see an `alert()` dialog with the value of the variable `invoiceValue` (which should be 55, but in fact will probably be something like 55.000000001 because we have not asked JavaScript to round the result).

We will not, however, then see an `alert()` dialog containing the value of the variable `total`. Instead, JavaScript simply produces an error. Whether you see this error reported depends on your browser settings—you learn more about error handling later in the book—but JavaScript will be unable to display an `alert()` dialog with the value of your variable `total`.

This is because we placed the declaration of the variable `total` *inside* the `addTax()` function. Outside the function the variable `total` simply doesn't exist (or, as JavaScript puts it, "is not defined"). We used the `return` keyword to pass back just the *value* stored in the variable `total`, and that value we then stored in another variable, `invoice`.

We refer to variables declared inside a function definition as being *local* variables; that is, *local to that function*. Variables declared outside any function are known as *global* variables. To add a little more confusion, local and global variables can have the same name, but still be different variables!

The range of situations where a variable is defined is known as the *scope* of the variable—we can refer to a variable as having *local scope* or *global scope*.

▼ TRY IT YOURSELF

Demonstrating the Scope of Variables

To illustrate the issue of a variable's scope, take a look at the following piece of code:

```
var a = 10;
var b = 10;
function showVars() {
    var a = 20; // declare a new local variable 'a'
    b = 20;     // change the value of global variable 'b'
    return "Local variable 'a' = " + a + "\nGlobal variable 'b' = " + b;
}
var message = showVars();
alert(message + "\nGlobal variable 'a' = " + a);
```

Within the `showVars()` function we manipulate two variables, `a` and `b`. The variable `a` we define inside the function; this is a local variable that only exists inside the function, quite separate from the global variable (also called a) that we declare at the very beginning of the script.

The variable `b` is not declared inside the function, but outside; it is a **global** variable.

Listing 3.3 shows the preceding code within an HTML page.

LISTING 3.3   Global and Local Scope

```
<!DOCTYPE html>
<html>
<head>
    <title>Variable Scope</title>
</head>
```

```
<body>
    <script>
        var a = 10;
        var b = 10;
        function showVars() {
            var a = 20; // declare a new local variable 'a'
            b = 20;      // change the value of global variable 'b'
            return "Local variable 'a' = " + a + "\nGlobal variable 'b' = " + b;
        }
        var message = showVars();
        alert(message + "\nGlobal variable 'a' = " + a);
    </script>
</body>
</html>
```

When the page is loaded, `showVars()` returns a message string containing information about the updated values of the two variables `a` and `b`, as they exist inside the function—a with local scope, and b with global scope.

A message about the current value of the other, *global* variable a is then appended to the message, and the message displayed to the user.

Copy the code into the file scope.html and load it into your browser. Compare your results with Figure 3.3.

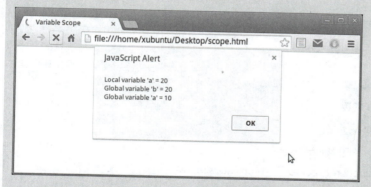

FIGURE 3.3
Local and global scope

Summary

In this hour you learned about what functions are, and how to create them in JavaScript. You learned how to call functions from within your code, and pass information to those functions in the form of arguments. You also found out how to return information from a function to its calling statement.

Finally, you learned about the local or global scope of a variable, and how the scope of variables affects how functions work with them.

Q&A

Q. Can one function contain a call to another function?

A. Most definitely; in fact, such calls can be nested as deeply as you need them to be.

Q. What characters can I use in function names?

A. Function names must start with a letter or an underscore and can contain letters, digits, and underscores in any combination. They cannot contain spaces, punctuation, or other special characters.

Workshop

Try to answer all the questions before reading the subsequent "Answers" section.

Quiz

1. Functions are called using

    a. The `function` keyword

    b. The `call` command

    c. The function name, with parentheses

2. What happens when a function executes a return statement?

    a. An error message is generated.

    b. A value is returned and function execution continues.

    c. A value is returned and function execution stops.

3. A variable declared inside a function definition is called

   a. A local variable

   b. A global variable

   c. An argument

Answers

1. c. A function is called using the function name.

2. c. After executing a return statement, a function returns a value and then ceases function execution.

3. a. A variable defined within a function has local scope.

Exercises

▶ Write a function to take a temperature value in Celsius as an argument, and return the equivalent temperature in Fahrenheit, basing it on the code from Hour 2.

▶ Test your function in an HTML page.

DOM Objects and Built-in Objects

What You'll Learn in This Hour:

▶ Talking to the user with `alert()`, `prompt()`, and `confirm()`
▶ Selecting page elements with `getElementById()`
▶ Accessing HTML content with `innerHTML`
▶ How to use the browser `history` object
▶ Reloading or redirecting the page using the `location` object
▶ Getting browser information via the `navigator` object
▶ Manipulating dates and times with the `Date` object
▶ Calculations made easier with the `Math` object

In Hour 1, "Introducing JavaScript," we talked a little about the DOM and introduced the top-level object in the DOM tree, the `window` object. We also looked at one of its child objects, `document`.

In this hour, we introduce some more of the utility objects and methods that you can use in your scripts.

Interacting with the User

Among the methods belonging to the `window` object, there are some designed specifically to help your page communicate with the user by assisting with the input and output of information.

alert()

You've already used the `alert()` method to pop up an information dialog for the user. You'll recall that this modal dialog simply shows your message with a single OK button. The term *modal* means that script execution pauses, and all user interaction with the page is suspended, until the user clears the dialog. The `alert()` method takes a message string as its argument:

```
alert("This is my message");
```

`alert()` does not return a value.

`confirm()`

The `confirm()` method is similar to `alert()`, in that it pops up a modal dialog with a message for the user. The `confirm()` dialog, though, provides the user with a choice; instead of a single OK button, the user may select between OK and Cancel, as shown in Figure 4.1. Clicking on either button clears the dialog and allows the calling script to continue, but the `confirm()` method returns a different value depending on which button was clicked—Boolean true in the case of OK, or false in the case of Cancel. We begin to look at JavaScript's data types in the next hour, but for the moment you just need to know that a Boolean variable can only take one of two values, *true* or *false*.

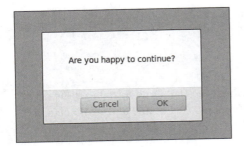

FIGURE 4.1
The `confirm()` dialog

The `confirm()` method is called in a similar way to `alert()`, passing the required message as an argument:

```
var answer = confirm("Are you happy to continue?");
```

Note that here, though, we pass the returned value of `true` or `false` to a variable so we can later test its value and have our script take appropriate action depending on the result.

`prompt()`

The `prompt()` method is yet another way to open up a modal dialog. In this case, though, the dialog invites the user to enter information.

A `prompt()` dialog is called in just the same manner as `confirm()`:

```
var answer = prompt("What is your full name?");
```

The `prompt` method also allows for an optional second argument, giving a default response in case the user clicks OK without typing anything:

```
var answer = prompt("What is your full name?", "John Doe");
```

The return value from a `prompt()` dialog depends on what option the user takes:

▶ If the user types in input and clicks OK or presses Enter, the user input string is returned.

▶ If the user clicks OK or presses Enter without typing anything into the prompt dialog, the method returns the default response (if any), as optionally specified in the second argument passed to `prompt()`.

▶ If the user dismisses the dialog (that is, by clicking Cancel or pressing Escape), then the prompt method returns *null*.

NOTE

The `null` value is used by JavaScript on certain occasions to denote an empty value. When treated as a number it takes the value 0, when used as a string it evaluates to the empty string (""), and when used as a Boolean value it becomes *false*.

The `prompt()` dialog generated by the previous code snippet is shown in Figure 4.2.

FIGURE 4.2
The `prompt()` dialog

Selecting Elements by Their ID

In Part III, "Objects," you'll learn a lot about navigating around the DOM using the various methods of the `document` object. For now, we limit ourselves to looking at one in particular—the `getElementById()` method.

To select an element of your HTML page having a specific ID, all you need to do is call the `document` object's `getElementById()` method, specifying as an argument the ID of the required element. The method returns the DOM object corresponding to the page element with the specified ID.

Let's look at an example. Suppose your web page contains a `<div>` element:

```
<div id="div1">
    ... Content of DIV element ...
</div>
```

In your JavaScript code, you can access this `<div>` element using `getElementById()`, passing the required ID to the method as an argument:

```
var myDiv = document.getElementById("div1");
```

We now have access to the chosen page element and all of its properties and methods.

CAUTION
_____

Of course, for this to work the page element must have its ID attribute set. Because ID values of HTML page elements are required to be unique, the method should always return a single page element, provided a matching ID is found.

_____

The `innerHTML` Property

A handy property that exists for many DOM objects, `innerHTML` allows us to get or set the value of the HTML content inside a particular page element. Imagine your HTML contains the following element:

```
<div id="div1">
    <p>Here is some original text.</p>
</div>
```

We can access the HTML content of the `<div>` element using a combination of `getElementById()` and `innerHTML`:

```
var myDivContents = document.getElementById("div1").innerHTML;
```

The variable `myDivContents` will now contain the string value:

```
"<p>Here is some original text.</p>"
```

We can also use `innerHTML` to *set* the contents of a chosen element:

```
document.getElementById("div1").innerHTML =
    "<p>Here is some new text instead!</p>";
```

Executing this code snippet erases the previous HTML content of the `<div>` element and replaces it with the new string.

Accessing Browser History

The browser's history is represented in JavaScript by the `window.history` object, which is essentially a list of the URLs previously visited. Its methods enable you to use the list, but not to manipulate the URLs explicitly.

The only property owned by the `history` object is its length. You can use this property to find how many pages the user has visited:

```
alert("You've visited " + history.length + " web pages in this browser session");
```

The `history` object has three methods.

`forward()` and `back()` are equivalent to pressing the Forward and Back buttons on the browser; they take the user to the next or previous page in the history list.

```
history.forward();
```

There is also the method `go`, which takes a single parameter. This can be an integer, positive or negative, and it takes the user to a relative place in the history list:

```
history.go(-3);  // go back 3 pages
history.go(2);  // go forward 2 pages
```

The method can alternatively accept a string, which it uses to find the first matching URL in the history list:

```
history.go("example.com");  // go to the nearest URL in the history
                // list that contains 'example.com'
```

Using the `location` Object

The `location` object contains information about the URL of the currently loaded page.

We can think of the page URL as a series of parts:

[protocol]//[hostname]:[port]/[pathname][search][hash]

Here's an example URL: http://www.example.com:8080/tools/display.php?section=435#list

The list of properties of the `location` object includes data concerning the various parts of the URL. The properties are listed in Table 4.1.

TABLE 4.1 Properties of the `location` Object

Property	Description
`location.href`	'http://www.example.com:8080/tools/display.php?section=435#list'
`location.protocol`	'http:'
`location.host`	'www.example.com:8080'
`location.hostname`	'www.example.com'
`location.port`	'8080'
`location.pathname`	'/tools/display.php'
`location.search`	'?section=435'
`location.hash`	'#list'

Navigating Using the `location` Object

There are two ways to take the user to a new page using the `location` object.

First, we can directly set the `href` property of the object:

```
location.href = 'www.newpage.com';
```

Using this technique to transport the user to a new page maintains the original page in the browser's history list, so the user can return simply by using the browser Back button. If you would rather the sending page were removed from the history list and replaced with the new URL, you can instead use the location object's `replace()` method:

```
location.replace('www.newpage.com');
```

This replaces the old URL with the new one both in the browser and in the history list.

Reloading the Page

To reload the current page into the browser—the equivalent to having the user click the "reload page" button—we can use the `reload()` method:

```
location.reload();
```

TIP

Using `reload()` without any arguments retrieves the current page from the browser's cache, if it's available there. To avoid this and get the page directly from the server, you can call `reload` with the argument `true`:

```
document.reload(true);
```

Browser Information—The navigator Object

While the `location` object stores information about the current URL loaded in the browser, the `navigator` object's properties contain data about the browser application itself.

TRY IT YOURSELF ▼

Displaying Information Using the navigator Object

We're going to write a script to allow you to find out what the `navigator` object knows about your own browsing setup. Use your editor to create the file navigator.html containing the code from Listing 4.1. Save the file and open it in your browser.

LISTING 4.1   Using the navigator Object

```
<!DOCTYPE html>
<html>
<head>
    <title>window.navigator</title>
    <style>
        td {border: 1px solid gray; padding: 3px 5px;}
    </style>
</head>
<body>
    <script>
        document.write("<table>");
        document.write("<tr><td>appName</td><td>"+navigator.appName +
        ➥"</td></tr>");
```

```
        document.write("<tr><td>appCodeName</td><td>"+navigator.appCodeName +
        ➥"</td></tr>");
        document.write("<tr><td>appVersion</td><td>"+navigator.appVersion +
        ➥"</td></tr>");
        document.write("<tr><td>language</td><td>"+navigator.language +
        ➥"</td></tr>");
        document.write("<tr><td>cookieEnabled</td><td>"+navigator.cookieEnabled +
        ➥"</td></tr>");
        document.write("<tr><td>cpuClass</td><td>"+navigator.cpuClass +
        ➥"</td></tr>");
        document.write("<tr><td>onLine</td><td>"+navigator.onLine + "</td></tr>");
        document.write("<tr><td>platform</td><td>"+navigator.platform +
        ➥"</td></tr>");
        document.write("<tr><td>No of Plugins</td><td>"+navigator.plugins.length +
        ➥"</td></tr>");
        document.write("</table>");
    </script>
</body>
</html>
```

Compare your results to mine, shown in Figure 4.3.

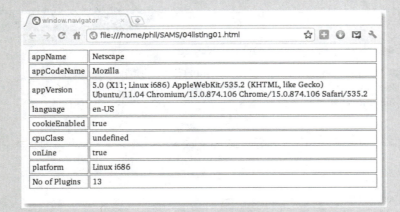

FIGURE 4.3
Browser information from the `navigator` object

Whoa, what's going on here? I loaded the page into the Chromium browser on my Ubuntu Linux PC. Why is it reporting the `appName` property as Netscape, and the `appCodeName` property as Mozilla? Also, the `cpuClass` property has come back as `undefined`; what's that all about?

There's a lot of history and politics behind the `navigator` object. The result is that the object provides, at best, an unreliable source of information about the user's platform. Not all properties are supported in all browsers (hence the failure to report the `cpuClass` property in the preceding example), and the names reported for browser type and version rarely match what one would intuitively expect. Figure 4.4 shows the same page loaded into Internet Explorer 9 on Windows 7.

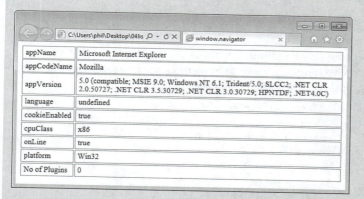

FIGURE 4.4
Browser information from the `navigator` object

We now have a value for `cpuClass`, but the `language` property is not supported in Internet Explorer, and has returned `undefined`.

Although cross-browser standards compliance is closer than it was a few years ago, there still remain occasions when you need to know the capabilities of your user's browser. Querying the `navigator` object is nearly always the *wrong* way to do it.

NOTE

Later in the book we talk about *feature detection*, a much more elegant and cross-browser way to have your code make decisions based on the capabilities of the user's browser.

Dates and Times

The Date object is used to work with dates and times. There is no Date object already created for you as part of the DOM, as was the case with the examples so far. Instead, we create our own Date objects as and when we need them. Each Date object we create can represent a different date and time.

Create a Date **Object with the Current Date and Time**

This is the simplest way to create a new Date object containing information about the date and time:

```
var mydate = new Date();
```

The variable mydate is an object containing information about the date and time at the moment the object was created. JavaScript has a long list of methods for retrieving, setting, and editing data within Date objects. Let's look at a few simple examples:

```
var year = mydate.getFullYear(); // four-digit year e.g. 2012
var month = mydate.getMonth(); // month number 0 - 11; 0 is Jan, etc.
var date = mydate.getDate(); // day of the month 1 - 31
var day = mydate.getDay(); // day of the week 0 - 6; Sunday = 0, etc.
var hours = mydate.getHours(); // hours part of the time, 0 - 23
var minutes = mydate.getMinutes(); // minutes part of time, 0 - 59
var seconds = mydate.getSeconds(); // seconds part of time, 0 - 59
```

Creating a Date **Object with a Given Date and Time**

We can easily create Date objects representing arbitrary dates and times by passing arguments to the Date() statement. There are several ways to do this:

```
new Date(milliseconds) //milliseconds since January 1st 1970
new Date(dateString)
new Date(year, month, day, hours, minutes, seconds, milliseconds)
```

Here are a few examples.

Using a date string:

```
var d1 = new Date("October 22, 1995 10:57:22")
```

When we use separate arguments for the parts, trailing arguments are optional; any missing will be replaced with zero:

```
var d2 = new Date(95,9,22) // 22nd October 1995 00:00:00
var d3 = new Date(95,9,22,10,57,0)  // 22nd October 1995 10:57:00
```

Setting and Editing Dates and Times

The `Date` object also has an extensive list of methods for setting or editing the various parts of the date and time:

```
var mydate = new Date();   // current date and time
document.write( "Object created on day number " + mydate.getDay() + "<br />");
mydate.setDate(15);      // change day of month to the 15th
document.write("After amending date to 15th, the day number is " +
➥mydate.getDay());
```

In the preceding code snippet, we initially created the object `mydate` representing the date and time of its creation, but with the day of the month subsequently changed to the 15th; if we retrieve the day of the week before and after this operation, we'll see that it has been correctly recalculated to take account of the changed date:

```
Object created on day number 5
After amending date to 15th, the day number is 0
```

So in this example, the object was created on a Friday; whereas the 15th of the month corresponded to a Sunday.

We can also carry out date and time arithmetic, letting the `Date` object do all the heavy lifting for us:

```
var mydate=new Date();
document.write("Created: " + mydate.toDateString() + " " + mydate.toTimeString() +
➥"<br/>");
mydate.setDate(mydate.getDate()+33); // add 33 days to the 'date' part
document.write("After adding 33 days: " + mydate.toDateString() + " " +
mydate.toTimeString());
```

The preceding example calculates a date 33 days in the future, automatically amending the day, date, month, and/or year as necessary. Note the use of `toDateString()` and `toTimeString()`; these are useful methods for converting dates into a readable format. The preceding example produces output like the following:

```
Created: Fri Jan 06 2012 14:59:24 GMT+0100 (CET)
After adding 33 days: Wed Feb 08 2012 14:59:24 GMT+0100 (CET)
```

The set of methods available for manipulating dates and times is way too large for us to explore them all here. A full list of the methods of the `Date` object is available in Appendix B, "JavaScript Quick Reference."

Simplifying Calculation with the `Math` Object

JavaScript's `Math` object can save you a lot of work when performing many sorts of calculations that frequently occur.

Unlike the `Date` object, the `Math` object does not need to be created before use; it already exists, and you can call its methods directly.

A full list of the available methods is available in Appendix B, but Table 4.2 shows some examples.

TABLE 4.2 Some Methods of the `Math` Object

Method	Description
`ceil(n)`	Returns n rounded up to the nearest whole number
`floor(n)`	Returns n rounded down to the nearest whole number
`max(a,b,c,...)`	Returns the largest number
`min(a,b,c,...)`	Returns the smallest number
`round(n)`	Returns n rounded up or down to the nearest whole number
`random()`	Returns a random number between 0 and 1

Let's work through some examples.

Rounding

The methods `ceil()`, `floor()`, and `round()` are useful for truncating the decimal parts of numbers:

```
var myNum1 = 12.55;
var myNum2 = 12.45;
alert(Math.floor(myNum1));  // shows 12
alert(Math.ceil(myNum1));   // shows 13
alert(Math.round(myNum1));  // shows 13
alert(Math.round(myNum2));  // shows 12
```

Note that when you use `round()`, if the fractional part of the number is .5 or greater, the number is rounded to the next highest integer. If the fractional part is less than .5, the number is rounded to the next lowest integer.

Finding Minimum and Maximum

We can use `min()` and `max()` to pick the largest and smallest number from a list:

```
var ageDavid = 23;
var ageMary = 27;
```

```
var ageChris = 31;
var ageSandy = 19;
document.write("The youngest person is "
    + Math.min(ageDavid, ageMary, ageChris, ageSandy)
    + " years old<br />");
document.write("The oldest person is "
    + Math.max(ageDavid, ageMary, ageChris, ageSandy)
    + " years old<br />");
```

The output as written to the page looks like this:

```
The youngest person is 19 years old
The oldest person is 31 years old
```

Random Numbers

To generate a random number, we can use `Math.random()`, which generates a random number between 0 and 1.

Normally we like to specify the possible range of our random numbers, for example, we might want to generate a random integer between 0 and 100.

As `Math.random()` generates a random number between 0 and 1, it's helpful to wrap it in a small function that suits our needs. The following function takes the `Math` object's randomly generated number, scales it up by multiplying by the variable range (passed to the function as an argument), and finally uses `round()` to remove any fractional part:

```
function myRand(range) {
    return Math.round(Math.random() * range);
}
```

To generate a random integer between 0 and 100, we can then simply call

```
myRand(100);
```

CAUTION

You always use `Math` methods directly, for example, `Math.floor()`, rather than as a method of an object you created. In other words, the following is wrong:

```
var myNum = 24.77;
myNum.floor();
```

The code would provoke a JavaScript error.

Instead you simply need

```
Math.floor(myNum);
```

Mathematical Constants

Various often-used mathematical constants are available as properties of `Math`. They are listed in Table 4.3.

TABLE 4.3 Mathematical Constants

Constant	Description
E	Base of natural logs, approximately 2.718.
LN2	Natural log of 2, approximately 0.693.
LN10	Natural log of 10, approximately 2.302.
LOG2E	Base 2 log of E, approximately 1.442.
LOG10E	Base 10 log of E, approximately 0.434.
PI	Approximately 3.14159.
SQRT1_2	1 over the square root of 2, approximately 0.707.
SQRT2	Square root of 2, approximately 1.414.

These constants can be used directly in your calculations:

```
var area = Math.PI * radius * radius;   // area of circle
var circumference = 2 * Math.PI * radius;   // circumference
```

The `with` Keyword

Although you can use the `with` keyword with any object, the `Math` object is an ideal object to use an example. By using `with` you can save yourself some tedious typing.

The keyword `with` takes an object as an argument, and is followed by a code block wrapped in braces. The statements within that code block can call methods without specifying an object, and JavaScript assumes that those methods belong to the object passed as an argument.

Here's an example:

```
with (Math) {
    var myRand = random();
    var biggest = max(3,4,5);
    var height = round(76.35);
}
```

In this example, we call `Math.random()`, `Math.max()`, and `Math.round()` simply by using the method names, because all method calls in the code block have been associated with the `Math` object.

Reading the Date and Time

We put into practice some of what we covered in this hour by creating a script to get the current date and time when the page is loaded. We also implement a button to reload the page, refreshing the time and date information.

Take a look at Listing 4.2.

LISTING 4.2   Getting Date and Time Information

```
<!DOCTYPE html>
<html>
<head>
    <title>Current Date and Time</title>
    <style>
        p {font: 14px normal arial, verdana, helvetica;}
    </style>
    <script>
        function telltime() {
            var out = "";
            var now = new Date();
            out += "<br />Date: " + now.getDate();
            out += "<br />Month: " + now.getMonth();
            out += "<br />Year: " + now.getFullYear();
            out += "<br />Hours: " + now.getHours();
            out += "<br />Minutes: " + now.getMinutes();
            out += "<br />Seconds: " + now.getSeconds();
            document.getElementById("div1").innerHTML = out;
        }
    </script>
</head>
<body>
    The current date and time are:<br/>
    <div id="div1"></div>
    <script>
        telltime();
    </script>
    <input type="button" onclick="location.reload()" value="Refresh" />
</body>
</html>
```

The first statement in the function `telltime()` creates a new `Date` object called `now`. As you will recall, since the object is created without passing any parameters to `Date()` it will have properties pertaining to the current date and time at the moment of its creation.

```
var now = new Date();
```

We can access the individual parts of the time and date using `getDate()`, `getMonth()`, and similar methods. As we do so, we assemble the output message as a string stored in the variable `out`.

```
out += "<br />Date: " + now.getDate();
out += "<br />Month: " + now.getMonth();
out += "<br />Year: " + now.getFullYear();
out += "<br />Hours: " + now.getHours();
out += "<br />Minutes: " + now.getMinutes();
out += "<br />Seconds: " + now.getSeconds();
```

Finally, we use `getElementById()` to select the (initially empty) `<div>` element having `id="div1"`, and write the contents of variable `out` into it using the `innerHTML` method.

```
document.getElementById("div1").innerHTML = out;
```

The function `telltime()` is called by a small script embedded in the `<body>` part of the page:

```
<script>
    telltime();
</script>
```

To refresh the date and time information, we simply need to reload the page into the browser. At that point the script runs again, creating a new instance of the `Date` object with the current date and time. We could just hit Refresh on the browser's menu, but since we know how to reload the page using the `location` object, we do that by calling

```
location.reload()
```

from a button's `onClick` method.

Figure 4.5 shows the script in action. Note that the month is displayed as 0. Remember that JavaScript counts months starting at 0 (January) and ending in 11 (December).

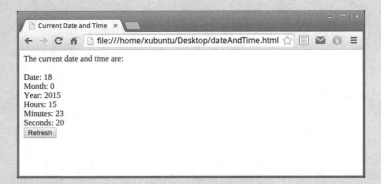

FIGURE 4.5
Getting date and time information

Summary

In this hour you looked at some useful objects either built into JavaScript or available via the DOM, and how their properties and methods can help you write code more easily.

You saw how to use the `window` object's modal dialogs to exchange information with the user.

You learned how to select page elements by their ID using the `document.getElementById` method, and how to get and set the HTML inside a page element using the `innerHTML` property.

You worked with browser information from the `navigator` object, and page URL information from the `location` object.

Finally, you saw how to use the `Date` and `Math` objects.

Q&A

Q. Does `Date()` have methods to deal with time zones?

A. Yes, it does. In addition to the `get...()` and `set...()` methods discussed in this hour (such as `getDate()`, `setMonth()`, etc.) there are UTC (Universal Time, previously called GMT) versions of the same methods (`getUTCDate()`, `setUTCMonth()`, and so on). You can retrieve the difference between your local time and UTC time by using the `getTimezoneOffset()` method. See Appendix B for a full list of methods.

Q. Why does `Date()` have the methods called `getFullYear()` and `setFullYear()` instead of just `getYear()` and `setYear()`?

A. The methods `getYear()` and `setYear()` do exist; they deal with two-digit years instead of the four-digit years used by `getFullYear()` and `setFullYear()`. Because of the potential problems with dates spanning the millennium, these functions have been deprecated. You should use `getFullYear()` and `setFullYear()` instead.

Workshop

Try to answer all the questions before reading the subsequent "Answers" section.

Quiz

1. What happens when a user clicks OK in a confirm dialog?

    a. A value of true is returned to the calling program.

    b. The displayed message is returned to the calling program.

    c. Nothing.

2. Which method of the `Math()` object always rounds a number up to the next integer?

   a. `Math.round()`

   b. `Math.floor()`

   c. `Math.ceil()`

3. If my loaded page is http://www.example.com/documents/letter.htm?page=2, what will the `location.pathname` property of the `location` object contain?

   a. `http`

   b. `www.example.com`

   c. `/documents/letter.htm`

   d. `page=2`

Answers

1. a. A value of true is returned when OK is clicked. The dialog is cleared and control is returned to the calling program.

2. c. `Math.ceil()` always rounds a number up to the next higher integer.

3. c. The `location.pathname` property contains `/documents/letter.htm`.

Exercises

▶ Modify Listing 4.2 to output the date and time as a single string, such as:

   `25 Dec 2011 12:35`

▶ Use the `Math` object to write a function to return the volume of a round chimney, given its radius and height in meters as arguments. The volume returned should be rounded up to the nearest cubic meter.

▶ Use the `history` object to create a few pages with their own Forward and Back buttons. After you've navigated to these pages (to put them in your browser's history list), do your Forward and Back buttons operate exactly like the browser's?

Numbers and Strings

- ▶ The numeric and string data types supported by JavaScript
- ▶ Conversion between data types
- ▶ How to manipulate strings

We use the term *data type* to talk about the nature of the data that a variable contains. A string variable contains a string, a number variable, a numerical value, and so forth. However, the JavaScript language is what's called a *loosely typed* language, meaning that JavaScript variables can be interpreted as different data types in differing circumstances.

In JavaScript, you don't have to declare the data type of a variable before using it, as the JavaScript interpreter will make its best guess. If you put a string into your variable and later want to interpret that value as a number, that's OK with JavaScript, provided that the variable actually contains a string that's "like" a numerical value (for example, "200px" or "50 cents", but not something such as your name). Later you can use it as a string again, if you want.

In this hour you learn about the JavaScript data types of number, string, and Boolean, and about some built-in methods for handling values of these types. We also mention *escape sequences* in strings, and two special JavaScript data types—*null* and *undefined*.

Numbers

Mathematicians have all sorts of names for different types of numbers. From the so-called *natural numbers* 1, 2, 3, 4 ..., you can add 0 to get the *whole numbers* 0, 1, 2, 3, 4 ..., and then include the negative values -1, -2, -3, -4 ... to form the set of *integers*.

To express numbers falling between the integers, we commonly use a decimal point with one or more digits following it:

3.141592654

Calling such numbers *floating point* indicates that they can have an arbitrary number of digits before and after the decimal point; that is, the decimal point can "float" to any location in the number.

JavaScript supports both integer and floating-point numbers.

Integers

An integer is a whole number—positive, negative, or zero. To put it another way, an integer is any numerical value without a fractional part.

All of the following are valid integers:

▶ 33

▶ -1,000,000

▶ 0

▶ -1

Floating-Point Numbers

Unlike integers, floating-point numbers have a fractional part, even if that fractional part is zero. They can be represented in the traditional way, like 3.14159, or in exponential notation, like 35.4e5.

NOTE

In exponential notation, e represents "times 10 to the power," so 35.4e5 can be read as 35.4×10^5. Exponential notation provides a compact way to express numbers from the very large to the very small.

All the following are valid floating-point numbers:

▶ 3.0

▶ 0.00001

▶ - 99.99

▶ 2.5e12

▶ 1e-12

TIP

JavaScript also has the ability to handle hexadecimal numbers. Hexadecimal numbers begin with 0x, for instance 0xab0080.

Not a Number (NaN)

NaN is the value returned when your script tries to treat something non-numerical as a number, but can't make any sense of it as a numerical value. For example, the result of trying to multiply a string by an integer is not numerical. You can test for non-numerical values with the isNaN() function:

```
isNaN(3);        // returns false
isNaN(3.14159);     // returns false
isNaN("horse");     // returns true;
```

Using parseFloat() and parseInt()

JavaScript offers us two functions with which we can force the conversion of a string into a number format.

The parseFloat() function parses a string and returns a floating-point number.

If the first character in the specified string is a number, it parses the string until it reaches the end of that number, and returns the value as a number, not a string:

```
parseFloat("21.4") // returns 21.4
parseFloat("76 trombones") // returns 76
parseFloat("The magnificent 7") // returns NaN
```

Using parseInt() is similar, but returns either an integer value or NaN. This function allows us to optionally include, as a second argument, the base (radix) of the number system we're using, and can therefore be used to return the base 10 values of binary, octal, or other number formats:

```
parseInt(18.95, 10); // returns 18
parseInt("12px", 10); // returns 12
parseInt("1110", 2); // returns 14
parseInt("Hello") // returns NaN
```

Infinity

Infinity is a value larger than the largest number that JavaScript can represent. In most JavaScript implementations, this is an integer of plus or minus 2^{53}. OK, that's not quite infinity, but it is pretty big.

There is also the keyword literal -Infinity to signify the negative infinity.

You can test for infinite values with the isFinite() function. The isFinite() function takes the value to test as an argument and tries to convert that argument into a number. If the result is NaN, positive infinity (Infinity), or negative infinity (-Infinity), the isFinite() function returns *false*; otherwise it returns *true*. (False and true are known as Boolean values, discussed later in this hour.)

```
isFinite(21); // true
isFinite("This is not a numeric value"); // false
isFinite(Math.sqrt(-1)); // false
```

Strings

A string is a sequence of characters from within a given character set (for example, the ASCII or Unicode character sets) and is usually used to store text.

You define a string by enclosing it in single or double quotes:

```
var myString = "This is a string";
```

You can define an empty string by using two quote marks with nothing between them:

```
var myString = "";
```

Escape Sequences

Some characters that you want to put in a string may not have associated keys on the keyboard, or may be special characters that for other reasons can't occur in a string. Examples include the tab character, the new line character, and the single or double quotes that enclose the string itself. To use such a character in a string, it must be represented by the character preceded by a backslash (\ ), a combination that JavaScript interprets as the desired special character. Such a combination is known as an *escape sequence*.

Suppose that you wanted to enter some "new line" characters into a string, so that when the string is shown by a call to the `alert()` method, it will be split into several lines:

```
var message = "IMPORTANT MESSAGE:\n\nError detected!\nPlease check your data";
alert(message);
```

The result of inserting these escape sequences is shown in Figure 5.1.

FIGURE 5.1
Using escape sequences in a string

The more common escape sequences are shown in Table 5.1.

TABLE 5.1 Some Common Escape Sequences

Escape Sequence	Character
\t	Tab
\n	New line; inserts a line break at the point where it appears in the string
\"	Double quote
\'	Single quote or apostrophe
\\	The backslash itself
\x99	Two-digit number specifying the hexadecimal value of an ASCII character
\u9999	Four-digit hexadecimal number specifying a Unicode character

String Methods

A full list of the properties and methods of the `string` object is given in Appendix B, "JavaScript Quick Reference," but for now let's look at some of the important ones, listed in Table 5.2.

TABLE 5.2 Some Popular Methods of the `string` Object

Method	Description
concat	Joins strings and returns a copy of the joined string
indexOf	Returns the position of the first occurrence of a specified value in a string
lastIndexOf	Returns the position of the last occurrence of a specified value in a string
replace	Searches for a match between a substring and a string, and replaces the substring with a new substring
split	Splits a string into an array of substrings, and returns the new array
substr	Extracts a substring from a string, beginning at a specified start position, and through the specified number of characters
toLowerCase	Converts a string to lowercase letters
toUpperCase	Converts a string to uppercase letters

concat()

You've already had experience in earlier hours of joining strings together using the + operator. This is known as string concatenation, and JavaScript strings have a `concat()` method offering additional capabilities:

```
var string1 = "The quick brown fox ";
var string2 = "jumps over the lazy dog";
var longString = string1.concat(string2);
```

indexOf()

We can use `indexOf()` to find the first place where a particular substring of one or more characters occurs in a string. The method returns the index (the position) of the searched-for substring, or -1 if it isn't found anywhere in the string:

```
var string1 = "The quick brown fox ";
string1.indexOf('fox') // returns 16
string1.indexOf('dog') // returns -1
```

TIP

Remember that the index of the first character in a string is 0, not 1.

lastIndexOf()

As you'll have guessed, `lastIndexOf()` works just the same way as `indexOf()`, but finds the last occurrence of the substring, rather than the first.

replace()

Searches for a match between a substring and a string, and returns a new string with the substring replaced by a new substring:

```
var string1 = "The quick brown fox ";
var string2 = string1.replace("brown", "orange"); // string2 is now "the quick
orange fox"
```

split()

Used to split a string into an array of substrings and return the new array:

```
var string1 = "The quick brown fox ";
var newArray = string1.split(" ")
```

TIP

You learn about arrays in the next hour. Make a note to refer back to this method after you've read about arrays.

`substr()`

The `substr()` method takes one or two arguments.

The first is the starting index—`substr()` extracts the characters from a string, beginning at the starting index, for the specified number of characters, returning the new substring. The second parameter (number of characters) is optional, and if omitted, all of the remaining string will be extracted:

```
var string1 = "The quick brown fox ";
var sub1 = string1.substr(4, 11); // extracts "quick brown"
var sub2 = string1.substr(4); // extracts "quick brown fox"
```

`toLowerCase()` and `toUpperCase()`

Puts the string into all uppercase or all lowercase:

```
var string1 = "The quick brown fox ";
var sub1 = string1.toLowerCase(); // sub1 contains "the quick brown fox "
var sub2 = string1.toUpperCase(); // sub2 contains "THE QUICK BROWN FOX "
```

Boolean Values

Data of the `Boolean` type can have one of only two values, *true* or *false*. Boolean variables are most often used to store the result of a logical operation in your code that returns a true/false or yes/no result:

```
var answer = confirm("Do you want to continue?"); // answer will contain
                                                   true or false
```

CAUTION

When you want to assign a Boolean value of `true` or `false`, it's important to remember NOT to enclose the value in quotes, or the value will be interpreted as a string literal:

```
var success = false;   // correct
var success = "false"; // incorrect
```

If you write code that expects Boolean values in computations, JavaScript automatically converts
true to 1 and false to 0.

```
var answer = confirm("Do you want to continue?"); // answer will contain
                                                   //      true or false
alert(answer * 1); // will display either 0 or 1
```

It works the other way, too. JavaScript interprets any nonzero value as *true*, and zero as *false*.
JavaScript interprets all of the following values as false:

► Boolean false (you don't say?)

► undefined

► null

► 0 (zero)

► NaN

► "" (empty string)

TIP

The preceding values are often referred to as "falsy," meaning "not exactly false, but can be interpreted as false." Values that JavaScript interprets as true are likewise referred to as "truthy."

▼ TRY IT YOURSELF

A Simple Spam Detector Function

We'll use two of these methods to write a simple function that detects the presence in a given
string of a particular word. In the example, we'll use the word "fake" as our target word. The
function should return a zero or positive value if it detects the word "fake" anywhere in a string
passed in as a parameter; otherwise, it should return a negative number. Here's the "empty"
function:

```
function detectSpam(input) {
}
```

You might use a function like this to examine email subject lines, for example, to detect spam
email selling "fake" designer items. In a practical application, the code would be much more
complex, but it's the string manipulation that's important here.

First, we want to convert the string to lowercase:

```
function detectSpam(input) {
    input = input.toLowerCase();
}
```

This is necessary because we'll then use `indexOf()` to look for the word "fake," and `indexOf()` differentiates between upper- and lowercase.

```
function detectSpam(input) {
    input = input.toLowerCase();
    return input.indexOf("fake");
}
```

Enter the code of Listing 5.1 into your editor and save it as an HTML file.

LISTING 5.1 Spam Detector Function

```
<!DOCTYPE html>
<html>
<head>
    <title>Spam Detector</title>
</head>
<body>
<script>
    function detectSpam(input) {
        input = input.toLowerCase();
        return input.indexOf("fake");
    }

    var mystring = prompt("Enter a string");
    alert(detectSpam(mystring));
</script>
</body>
</html>
```

Open the page in your browser, and enter a string into the prompt dialog, as depicted in Figure 5.2.

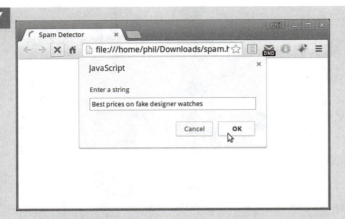

FIGURE 5.2
Entering a string

A new dialog will open, displaying the location in the input string where the word "fake" was found, or "-1" if the word did not appear anywhere.

Figure 5.3 shows the target word being found at position 15, i.e. the 16th character in the string.

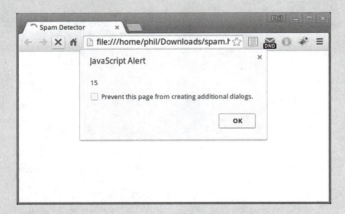

FIGURE 5.3
Output from spam detection script

TIP

In Hour 7, "Program Control," you'll learn how to make decisions in your code based on the results of tests such as this one.

The Negation Operator (!)

JavaScript interprets the ! character, when placed before a Boolean variable, as "not," that is, "the opposite value." Take a look at this code snippet:

```
var success = false;
alert(!success);  // alerts 'true'
```

In Hour 7 we use this and other operators to test the values of JavaScript variables, and have our programs make decisions based on the results.

NOTE

JavaScript also has two keywords called *object literals*—null and undefined.

Normally you assign the value null to something when you want it to have a valid but nonexistent value. For a numeric value, null is equivalent to zero, for a string it equates to the empty string (""), and for a Boolean value it means *false*.

Unlike null, undefined is not a keyword. It is a predefined global variable used to store the value of a variable whose name has been used in a statement, but that does not have a value assigned to it. This means that it is not zero or null, but it is *undefined*—JavaScript does not recognize it.

Summary

In this hour, you learned about the number and string data types supported by JavaScript and saw some examples of how to manipulate data of these types using a variety of JavaScript's numerical and string methods.

Q&A

Q. What is the maximum length of a string in JavaScript?

A. The JavaScript Specification does not specify a maximum string length; instead, it will be specific to your browser and operating system. For certain implementations, it will be a function of available memory.

Q. Does JavaScript have a data type to represent a single character?

A. No, unlike some other languages JavaScript doesn't have a specific data type to represent a single character. To do this in JavaScript, you create a string that consists of only one character.

Workshop

Try to answer all the questions before reading the subsequent "Answers" section.

Quiz

1. What statement would return a new string created by appending one string called `string2` to another string called `string1`?

   a. `concat(string1) + concat(string2);`

   b. `string1.concat(string2);`

   c. `join(string1, string2);`

2. Which statement sets the value of variable `paid` to Boolean true?

   a. `var paid = true;`

   b. `var paid = "true";`

   c. `var paid.true();`

3. For a string called `myString` containing the value "stupid is as stupid does," which of the following would return a value of -1?

   a. `myString.indexOf("stupid");`

   b. `myString.lastIndexOf("stupid");`

   c. `myString.indexOf("is stupid");`

Answers

1. b. `string1.concat(string2);` returns a new string created by joining `string2` to the end of `string1`.

2. a. Boolean values should not be enclosed in quotes.

3. c. The substring "is stupid" does not appear in `myString`.

Exercises

▶ Write a JavaScript function to remove a given number of characters from the end of a string.

▶ Write a JavaScript function to capitalize the first letter of each word in a given string.

HOUR 6
Arrays

What You'll Learn in This Hour:

▶ What we mean by the *array* data type
▶ How to declare and populate arrays
▶ How to manage array contents

Sometimes it makes sense to store multiple variable values under a single variable name. JavaScript has the *array* data type to help you do this.

In this hour you'll see how JavaScript arrays are created and how the data stored in these arrays can be manipulated in code.

Arrays

An array is a type of object used for storing multiple values in a single variable. Each value has a numeric index that may contain data of any data type—Booleans, numbers, strings, functions, objects, and even other arrays.

Creating a New Array

The syntax used for creating an array will already be familiar to you; after all, an array is simply another object:

```
var myArray = new Array();
```

However, for arrays there is a shorthand version—simply use square brackets ([]) like this:

```
var myArray = [];
```

Initializing an Array

You can optionally preload data into your array at the time it is created:

```
var myArray = ['Monday', 'Tuesday', 'Wednesday'];
```

Alternatively, items can be added after the array has been created:

```
var myArray = [];
myArray[0] = 'Monday';
myArray[1] = 'Tuesday';
myArray[2] = 'Wednesday';
```

array.length

All arrays have a `length` property that tells how many items the array contains. The `length` property is automatically updated when you add items to or remove items from the array. The following code returns the length of the preceding array:

```
myArray.length  // returns 3
```

CAUTION

The length is always 1 higher than the highest index, even if there are actually fewer items in the array. Suppose we add a new item to the preceding array:

```
myArray[50] = 'Ice cream day';
```

`myArray.length` now returns 51, even though the array only has four entries.

Array Methods

CAUTION

Some of the array methods have the same name—and almost the same function—as string methods of the same name. Be aware of what data type you are working with, or your script might not function as you would like.

Table 6.1 contains some of the more commonly used methods of the array object.

TABLE 6.1 Some Useful Array Methods

Method	Description
concat	Joins multiple arrays.
join	Joins all the array elements together into a string.
toString	Returns the array as a string.
indexOf	Searches the array for specific elements.
lastIndexOf	Returns the last item in the array that matches the search criteria.

Method	Description
slice	Returns a new array from the specified index and length.
sort	Sorts the array alphabetically or by the supplied function.
splice	Adds or deletes the specified index(es) to or from the array.

concat()

You've already had experience with string concatenation, and JavaScript arrays have a concat() method too:

```
var myOtherArray = ['Thursday','Friday'];
var myWeek = myArray.concat(myOtherArray);
// myWeek will contain 'Monday', 'Tuesday', 'Wednesday', 'Thursday', 'Friday'
```

join()

To join all of an array's elements together into a single string, we can use the join() method:

```
var longDay = myArray.join(); // returns MondayTuesdayWednesday
```

Optionally, we can pass a string argument to this method; the passed string will then be inserted as a separator in the returned string:

```
var longDay = myArray.join("-"); // returns Monday-Tuesday-Wednesday
```

toString()

toString() is almost a special case of join()—it returns the array as a string with the elements separated by commas:

```
var longDay = myArray.toString(); // returns Monday,Tuesday,Wednesday
```

indexOf()

We can use indexOf() to find the first place where a particular element occurs in an array. The method returns the index of the searched-for element, or -1 if it isn't found anywhere in the array:

```
myArray.indexOf('Tuesday')  // returns 1 (remember, arrays start with index 0)
myArray.indexOf('Sunday') // returns -1
```

lastIndexOf()

As you might expect, lastIndexOf() works just the same way as indexOf(), but finds the last occurrence in the array of the search term, rather than the first occurrence.

slice()

When we need to create an array that is a subset of our starting array, we can use `slice()`, passing to it the starting index and the number of elements we want to retrieve:

```
var myShortWeek = myWeek.slice(1, 3);
//myShortWeek contains 'Tuesday', 'Wednesday', 'Thursday'
```

sort()

We can use `sort()` to carry out an alphabetical sort:

```
myWeek.sort()  // returns 'Friday', 'Monday', 'Thursday', 'Tuesday', 'Wednesday'
```

splice()

To add or delete specific items from the array, we can use `splice()`.

The syntax is a little more complex than that of the previous examples:

```
array.splice(index, howmany, [new elements]);
```

The first element sets the location in the array where we want to perform the splice; the second element, how many items to remove (if set to 0, none are deleted), and thereafter, an optional list of any new elements to be inserted.

```
myWeek.splice(2,1,"holiday")
```

The preceding line of code moves to the array item with index 2 ('Wednesday'), removes one element ('Wednesday'), and inserts a new element ('holiday'); so `myWeek` now contains 'Monday', 'Tuesday', 'holiday', 'Thursday', 'Friday'. The method returns any removed elements.

CAUTION

Using `splice()` changes the original array! If you need to preserve the array for use elsewhere in your code, copy the array to a new variable before executing `splice()`.

▼ TRY IT YOURSELF

Array Manipulation

Let's put some of these methods to work. In your text editor, create the script listed in Listing 6.1 and save it as array.html.

LISTING 6.1 Array Manipulation ▼

```html
<!DOCTYPE html>
<html>
<head>
<title>Strings and Arrays</title>
<script>
    function wrangleArray() {
        var sentence = "JavaScript is a really cool language";
        var newSentence = "";
        //Write it out
        document.getElementById("div1").innerHTML = "<p>" + sentence + "</p>";
        //Convert to an array
        var words = sentence.split(" ");
        // Remove 'really' and 'cool', and add 'powerful' instead
        var message = words.splice(3,2,"powerful");
        // use an alert to say what words were removed
        alert('Removed words: ' + message);
        // Convert the array to a string, and write it out
        document.getElementById("div2").innerHTML = "<p>" + words.join(" ") +
        ➡"</p>";
    }
</script>
</head>
<body>
    <div id="div1"></div>
    <div id="div2"></div>
    <script>wrangleArray();</script>
</body>
</html>
```

As we work through this listing, you may want to refer to the definitions of the individual string and array methods given earlier in the hour, and the discussion of `getElementById()` and `innerHTML` from Hour 4, "DOM Objects and Built-in Objects."

Stepping through the function `wrangleArray()`, we first define a string:

```
var sentence = "JavaScript is a really cool language";
```

After writing it out to any empty `<div>` element using `innerHTML`, we apply the `split()` method to the string, passing to it a single space as an argument. The method returns an array of elements, created by splitting the string wherever a space occurs—that is to say, splits it into individual words. We store that array in the variable `words`.

We next apply the `splice()` array method to the `words` array, removing two words at array index 3, "really" and "cool". Since the `splice()` method returns any deleted words, we can display these in an `alert()` dialog:

```
var message = words.splice(3,2,"powerful");
alert('Removed words: ' + message);
```

Finally, we apply the `join()` method to the array, once more collapsing it into a string. Since we supply a single space as the argument to `join()`, the individual words are once more separated by spaces. Finally we output the revised sentence to a second `<div>` element by using `innerHTML`.

The `wrangleArray()` function is called by a small script in the body of the document:

```
<script>wrangleArray();</script>
```

The script operation is shown in Figure 6.1.

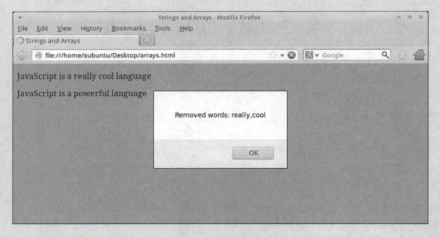

FIGURE 6.1
Output from array manipulation script

Summary

An array is a convenient means of storing multiple values in a single variable. In this hour, you learned about some of the methods of creating and working with JavaScript array objects.

Q&A

Q. Does JavaScript allow associative arrays?

A. JavaScript does not directly support associative arrays (arrays with named indexes). However, there are ways to simulate their behavior by using objects. You see examples of this later in the book.

Q. Can I create a multidimensional array in JavaScript?

A. You can create an array of arrays, which amounts to the same thing:

```
var myArray = [[1,2], [3,4], [5,6]];

alert(myArray[1][0]);        // alerts '3'
```

Workshop

Try to answer all the questions before reading the subsequent "Answers" section.

Quiz

1. If the element with highest index in array `Foo` is `Foo[8]`, what value will be returned by `Foo.length`?

2. You have an array called `monthNames` containing the names of all the months of the year. How would you use `join()` to create a string name containing all of these month names with a single space between names?

3. What value will be returned by `indexOf()` if it is passed a value that does not appear in the array to which it is applied?

Answers

1. `Foo.length` will return 9.

2. `var names = monthNames.join(" ");`

3. It will return -1.

Exercise

▶ Review the array and string methods that share a method name. Familiarize yourself with how the syntax and operation changes depending on whether these methods are applied to a string or an array.

Program Control

What You'll Learn in This Hour:

▶ Using conditional statements
▶ Comparing values with comparison operators
▶ Applying logical operators
▶ Writing loops and control structures
▶ Setting Timers in JavaScript

In Hour 5, "Numbers and Strings," and Hour 6, "Arrays," you took a quick trip through the data types that JavaScript variables can contain. To create anything but the simplest scripts, though, you're going to need your code to make decisions based on those values. In this hour we examine ways to recognize particular conditions and have our program act in a prescribed way as a result.

Conditional Statements

Conditional statements, as the name implies, are used to detect particular conditions arising in the values of the variables you are using in your script. JavaScript supports various such conditional statements, as outlined in the following sections.

The `if()` Statement

In the previous hour we discussed Boolean variables, which we saw could take one of only two values—*true* or *false*.

JavaScript has several ways to test such values, the simplest of which is the `if` statement. It has the following general form:

```
if(this condition is true) then do this;
```

Let's look at a trivial example:

```
var message = "";
var bool = true;
if(bool) message = "The test condition evaluated to TRUE";
```

First we declare a variable `message`, and assign an empty string to it as a value. We then declare a new variable, `bool`, which we set to the Boolean value of *true*. The third statement tests the value of the variable `bool` to see whether it is true; if so (as in this case) the value of the variable `message` is set to a new string. Had we assigned a value of *false* to `bool` in the second line, the test condition would not have been fulfilled, and the instruction to assign a new value to `message` would have been ignored, leaving the variable `message` containing the empty string.

Remember, we said that the general form of an `if` statement is

```
if(this condition is true) then do this.
```

In the case of a Boolean value, as in this example, we have replaced the condition with the variable itself; since its value can only be *true* or *false*, the contents of the parentheses passed back to `if` accordingly evaluate to `true` or `false`.

We can test for the Boolean value `false` by using the negation character (`!`):

```
if(!bool) message = "The value of bool is FALSE";
```

Clearly, for `!bool` to evaluate to true, `bool` must be of value `false`.

Comparison Operators

The `if()` statement is not limited to testing the value of a Boolean variable; instead, we can enter a condition in the form of an expression into the parentheses of our `if` statement, and JavaScript evaluates the expression to determine whether it is true or false:

```
var message = "";
var temperature = 60;
if(temperature < 64) message = "Turn on the heating!";
```

The less-than operator (`<`) is one of a range of comparison operators available in JavaScript. Some of the comparison operators are listed in Table 7.1.

NOTE

A more comprehensive list of comparison operators appears in Appendix B, "JavaScript Quick Reference."

TABLE 7.1   JavaScript Comparison Operators

Operator	Meaning
==	is equal to
===	is equal to in both value and type
!=	is not equal to
>	is greater than
<	is less than
>=	is greater than or equal to
<=	is less than or equal to

TRY IT YOURSELF ▼

Extending Our Spam Detector

In Hour 5, you developed a simple function to detect the word "fake" in a given input string.

Now you can further develop that function using the `if()` statement.

Here's the function from Hour 5:

```
function detectSpam(input) {
    input = input.toLowerCase();
    return input.indexOf("fake");
}
```

The function, you'll recall, currently returns a number corresponding with the location in the input string where the word "fake" has been located.

Let's modify the function to instead return `true` or `false` depending on whether the target word was found:

```
if(input.indexOf("fake") < 0) {
    return false;
}
return true;
```

Now we can see that, if the condition

```
input.indexOf("fake") < 0
```

is met, the function will terminate, returning `false`; otherwise, execution will continue to the next line after the `if()` block, and the function will terminate, returning `true`.

Listing 7.1 shows the modified code in a complete HTML file. Create this file in your editor.

LISTING 7.1   Spam Detector Function

```
<!DOCTYPE html>
<html>
<head>
    <title>Spam Detector</title>
</head>
<body>
<script>
    function detectSpam(input) {
        input = input.toLowerCase();
        if(input.indexOf("fake") < 0) {
            return false;
        }
        return true;
    }

    var mystring = prompt("Enter a string");
    alert(detectSpam(mystring));
</script>
</body>
</html>
```

Now let's see how the program performs when given the same string we used in Hour 5, as shown in Figure 7.1.

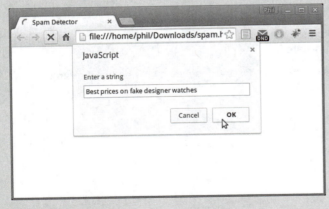

FIGURE 7.1
Entering a string

As you can see from Figure 7.2, the alert dialog now simply reports `true`, rather than showing the location in the string where the target word was found. Reload the file in the browser and try it again with a string that doesn't contain the word "fake" to confirm that the detector returns `false`.

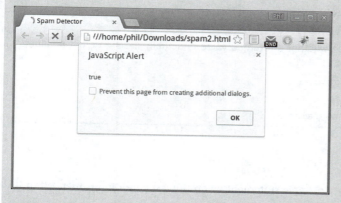

FIGURE 7.2
The spam detector reports `true`

Testing for Equality

In the previous example, how could we test to see whether the temperature *exactly equals* 64 degrees? Remember that we use the equals sign (=) to *assign* a value to a variable, so this code won't work as might be expected:

```
if(temperature = 64) ....
```

Were we to use this statement, the expression within the parentheses would be evaluated by JavaScript and our variable `temperature` would be *assigned* the value of 64. If this value assignment terminates successfully—and why shouldn't it?—then the value assignment would return a value of *true* back to the `if()` statement, and the rest of the statement would therefore be executed. This isn't the behavior we want at all.

Instead, to test for equality we must use a double equals sign (==):

```
if(temperature == 64) message = "64 degrees and holding!";
```

CAUTION

If you need to test whether two items are equal *both in value and in type*, JavaScript has an operator, ===, to perform this test. For example:

```
var x = 2; // assign a numeric value
if(x == "2") ... // true, as the string "2" is interpreted
if(x === "2") ...// false, a string is not numeric
```

This can be useful when testing to see whether a returned value is actually false, or just a value that is "falsy" (can be *interpreted* as false):

```
var x = 0; // assign a value of zero
if(!x) ... // evaluates to true
if(x === false)..// evaluates to false
```

More about `if()`

The previous examples carry out only a single statement when the test condition is met. What if we want to do more than this; for instance, carry out several statements?

To achieve this, we simply enclose in curly braces ({ }) all of the code statements that we want to execute if the condition is fulfilled:

```
if(temperature < 64) {
    message = "Turn on the heating!";
    heatingStatus = "on";
    // ... more statements can be added here
}
```

We can also add a clause to our `if` statement that contains code we want to execute if the condition is *not* fulfilled. To achieve this we use the `else` construct:

```
if(temperature < 64) {
    message = "Turn on the heating!";
    heatingStatus = "on";
    // ... more statements can be added here
} else {
    message = "Temperature is high enough";
    heatingStatus = "off";
    // ... more statements can be added here too
}
```

There exists a shorthand form of the syntax for the `if()` statement:

```
(condition is true)? [do if true] : [do if false];
```

Here's an example:

```
errorMessage = count + ((count == 1)? " error ":" errors ") + "found.";
```

In this example, if the number of errors stored in variable `count` is exactly 1, the message variable will contain

1 error found.

If the value in `count` is 0 or a number greater than 1, the message variable will contain a string such as

3 errors found.

Testing Multiple Conditions

You can use "nested" combinations of `if` and `else` to test multiple conditions before deciding how to act. Let's return to our heating system example, and have it switch on the cooling fan if the temperature is too high:

```
if(temperature < 64) {
    message = "Turn on the heating!";
    heatingStatus = "on";
    fanStatus = "off";
} else if(temperature > 72){
    message = "Turn on the fan!";
    heatingStatus = "off";
    fanStatus = "on";
} else {
    message = "Temperature is OK";
    heatingStatus = "off";
    fanStatus = "off";
}
```

The `switch` Statement

When we're testing for a range of different possible outcomes of the same conditional statement, a concise syntax we can use is that of JavaScript's `switch` statement:

```
switch(color) {
    case "red" :
        message = "Stop!";
        break;
    case "yellow" :
        message = "Pass with caution";
        break;
    case "green" :
        message = "Come on through";
        break;
```

```
    default :
        message = "Traffic light out of service. Pass only with great care";
}
```

The keyword `switch` has in parentheses the name of the variable to be tested.

The tests themselves are listed within the braces, { and }. Each `case` statement (with its value in quotes) is followed by a colon, then the list of actions to be executed if that case has been matched. There can be any number of code statements in each section.

Note the `break` statement after each case. This jumps us to the end of the `switch` statement after having executed the code for a matching case. If `break` is omitted, it's possible that more than one case will have its code executed.

The optional `default` case has its code executed if none of the specified cases were matched.

Logical Operators

There will be occasions when we want to test a combination of criteria to determine whether a test condition has been met, and doing so with `if ... else` or `switch` statements becomes unwieldy.

Let's return once more to our temperature control program. JavaScript allows us to combine conditions using logical AND (`&&`) and logical OR (`||`). Here's one way:

```
if(temperature >= 64 && temperature <= 72) {
    message = "The temperature is OK";
} else {
    message = "The temperature is out of range!";
}
```

We can read the preceding condition as "If the temperature is greater than or equal to 64 AND the temperature is less than or equal to 72."

We can achieve exactly the same functionality using OR instead of AND:

```
if(temperature < 64 || temperature > 72) {
    message = "The temperature is out of range!";
} else {
    message = "The temperature is OK";
}
```

Here we have reversed the way we carry out the test; our conditional statement is now fulfilled when the temperature is *out of* range, and can be read as "If the temperature is less than 64 OR greater than 72."

Loops and Control Structures

The `if` statement can be thought of as a *junction* in program execution. Depending on the result of the test performed on the data, the program may go down one route or another with its execution of statements.

There are many occasions, though, when we might want to execute some operation a number of times before continuing with the rest of our program. If the number of repeats is fixed, we could perhaps achieve this with multiple `if` statements and incrementing counter variables, though the code would be messy and hard to read. But what if we don't know how many times we need to repeat our piece of code, because the number of repeats depends upon, for example, the changing value of a variable?

JavaScript has various built-in loop structures that allow us to achieve such goals.

while

The syntax of the `while` statement is very much like the syntax for the `if` statement:

```
while(this condition is true) {
    carry out these statements ...
}
```

The `while` statement *works* just like `if`, too. The only difference is that, after completing the conditional statements, `while` goes back and tests the condition again. All the time the condition keeps coming up `true`, `while` keeps right on executing the conditional code. Here's an example:

```
var count = 10;
var sum = 0;
while(count > 0) {
    sum = sum + count;
    count--;
}
alert(sum);
```

Each time `while` evaluates the condition as *true*, the statements in the curly braces are executed over and over, adding the current value of `count` to the variable `sum` on each trip around the loop.

When `count` has been decremented to zero, the condition fails and the loop stops; program operation then continues from after the closing brace. By this time, the variable `sum` has a value of

```
10 + 9 + 8 + 7 + 6 + 5 + 4 + 3 + 2 + 1 = 55
```

do ... while

The do ... while structure is similar in operation to while, but with one important difference. Here's the syntax:

```
do {
    ... these statements ...
} while(this condition is true)
```

The only real difference here is that, since the while clause appears *after* the braces, the list of
conditional statements is executed once *before* the while clause is evaluated. The statements in
a do ... while clause will therefore always be executed at least once.

for

The for loop is another loop similar in operation to while, but with a more comprehensive
syntax. With the for loop, we can specify an initial condition, a test condition (to end the loop),
and a means of changing a counter variable for each pass through the loop, all in one statement. Have a look at the syntax:

```
for(x=0; x<10; x++) {
    ... execute these statements ...
}
```

We interpret this as follows:

"For x initially set to zero, and while x is less than 10, and incrementing x by 1 on each pass
through the loop, carry out the conditional statements."

Let's rewrite the example we gave when looking at the while loop, but this time using a for
loop:

```
var count;
var sum = 0;
for(count = 10; count > 0; count--) {
    sum = sum + count;
}
```

If the counter variable has not previously been declared, it is often convenient to declare it with
the var keyword within the for statement instead of outside:

```
var sum = 0;
for(var count = 10; count > 0; count--) {
    sum = sum + count;
}
alert(sum);
```

As in the previous example, after the loop terminates the variable sum has a value of

```
10 + 9 + 8 + 7 + 6 + 5 + 4 + 3 + 2 + 1 = 55
```

Leaving a Loop with `break`

The `break` command works within a loop pretty much as it does in a `switch` statement—it kicks us out of the loop and returns operation to the line of code immediately after the closing brace.

Here's an example:

```
var count = 10;
var sum = 0;
while(count > 0) {
    sum = sum + count;
    if(sum > 42) break;
    count--;
}
alert(sum);
```

We saw previously that, without the break instruction, the value of sum evolved like this:

```
10 + 9 + 8 + 7 + 6 + 5 + 4 + 3 + 2 + 1 = 55
```

Now, we find that when the value of sum reaches

```
10 + 9 + 8 + 7 + 6 + 5 = 45
```

the conditional clause of the `if(sum > 42)` statement will come up *true*, and cause the loop to terminate due to the `break` command.

CAUTION

Beware accidentally creating an infinite loop. Here's a loop we used earlier:

```
while(count > 0) {
    sum = sum + count;
    count--;
}
```

Imagine, for example, that we omitted the line

```
count--;
```

Now every time `while` tests the variable `count`, it finds it to be greater than zero, and the loop never ends. An infinite loop can stop the browser from responding, cause a JavaScript error, or cause the browser to crash.

Looping Through Objects with `for ... in`

The `for...in` loop is a special sort of loop intended for stepping through the properties of an object. Let's see it in action applied to an array object in Listing 7.2.

LISTING 7.2   The `for ... in` Loop

```
<!DOCTYPE html>
<html>
<head>
    <title>Loops and Control</title>
</head>
<body>
    <script>
        var days = ['Sun','Mon','Tue','Wed','Thu','Fri','Sat'];
        var message = "";
        for (i in days) {
            message += 'Day ' + i + ' is ' + days[i] + '\n';
        }
        alert(message);
    </script>
</body>
</html>
```

In this sort of loop, we don't need to worry about maintaining a loop counter or devising a test to see when the loop should complete. The loop will occur once for every property of the supplied object (in our example, once for every array item) and then terminate.

The result of running this example is shown in Figure 7.3.

FIGURE 7.3
Result of running our `for ... in` loop

NOTE

You'll recall that an array is one type of JavaScript object. You can use the `for ... in` loop to investigate the properties of any object, whether it's a DOM object, a JavaScript built-in object, or one you've created yourself (as you'll be doing in Hour 8, "Object-Oriented Programming").

Setting and Using Timers

There are some situations in which you'll want to program a specific delay into the execution of your JavaScript code. This is especially common when writing user interface routines; for instance, you may want to display a message for a short period before removing it.

To help you, JavaScript provides two useful methods, `setTimeout()` and `setInterval()`.

> **NOTE**
>
> `setTimeout()` and `clearTimeout()` are both methods of the HTML DOM `window` object.

setTimeout()

The `setTimeout(action, delay)` method calls the function (or evaluates the expression) passed in its first argument after the number of milliseconds specified in its second argument. You can use it, for example, to display an element in a given configuration for a fixed period of time:

```
<div id="id1">I'm about to disappear!</div>
```

Let's suppose your page contains the preceding `<div>` element. If you put the following code into a `<script>` element in the page `<head>` section, the function `hide()` will be executed 3 seconds after the page finishes loading, making the `<div>` element invisible:

```
function hide(elementId) {
    document.getElementById(elementId).style.display = 'none';
}
window.onload = function() {
    setTimeout("hide('id1')", 3000);
}
```

The `setTimeout()` method returns a value. If later you want to cancel the timer function, you can refer to it by passing that returned value to the `clearTimeout()` method:

```
var timer1 = setTimeout("hide('id1')", 3000);
clearTimeout(timer1);
```

setInterval()

The `setInterval(action, delay)` method works similarly to `setTimeout()`, but instead of imposing a single delay before executing the statement passed to it as its first argument, it executes it repeatedly, with a delay between executions corresponding to the number of milliseconds specified in the second argument.

Like `setTimeout()`, `setInterval()` returns a value that you can later pass to the `clear-Interval()` method to stop the timer:

```
var timer1 = setInterval("updateClock()", 1000);
clearInterval(timer1);
```

Summary

In this hour you learned a lot about testing conditions and controlling program flow based on the values of variables, and how to write various kinds of program loops controlled by conditions.

You also learned a little about using timers in your programs.

Q&A

Q. Is there any particular reason why I should use one sort of loop over another?

A. It's true that there is usually more than one type of loop that will solve any particular programming problem. You can use the one you feel most comfortable with, though it's usually good practice to use whichever loop makes the most sense (in conjunction with your chosen variable names) in the context of what your code sets out to do.

Q. Is there a way to stop the current trip around a loop and move straight to the next iteration?

A. Yes, you can use the `continue` command. It works pretty much like `break`, but instead of canceling the loop and continuing code execution from after the closing brace, `continue` only cancels the current trip around the loop and moves on to the next one.

Workshop

Try to answer all the questions before reading the subsequent "Answers" section.

Quiz

1. How is "greater than or equal to" expressed in JavaScript?

    a. `>`

    b. `>=`

    c. `>==`

2. What command forces the cancellation of a loop, and moves code operation to the statement after the closing brace?

   a. `break;`

   b. `loop;`

   c. `close;`

3. Which of the following is likely to cause an infinite loop to occur?

   a. The wrong sort of loop has been used.

   b. The condition to terminate the loop is never met.

   c. There are too many statements in the loop.

Answers

1. b. JavaScript interprets `>=` as "greater than or equal to."

2. a. The `break` command ends loop execution.

3. b. An infinite loop occurs if the condition to terminate the loop is never met.

Exercises

▶ In Hour 4, "DOM Objects and Built-in Objects," you learned how to get the current day of the week. Write a program using a switch statement to output a different message to the user, depending on what day it is today.

▶ Modify Listing 7.2 to list the months of the year rather than the days of the week. How can you modify the code to list the months starting with January as Month 1 rather than Month 0?

Object-Oriented Programming

What You'll Learn in This Hour:

▶ What object-oriented programming is

▶ Two ways to create objects

▶ Instantiating an object

▶ Extending and inheriting objects using `prototype`

▶ Accessing object methods and properties

▶ Using feature detection

As your programs become more complex, you need to use coding techniques that help you to maintain control and ensure that your code remains efficient, readable, and maintainable. In this hour you learn the basics of object-oriented programming (OOP), an important technique for writing clear and reliable code that you can reuse over and over.

What Is Object-Oriented Programming?

The code examples to date have been so-called *procedural* programming. Procedural programming is characterized by having data stored in variables, which are operated on by lists of instructions. Each instruction (or list of instructions, such as a function) can create, destroy, or modify the data, yet the data always remains somehow "separate" from the program code.

In object-oriented programming (OOP), the program instructions and the data on which they operate are more intertwined. OOP is a way of conceptualizing a program's data into discrete "things" referred to as *objects*—each having its own *properties* (data) and *methods* (instructions).

Suppose, for example, you wanted to write a script to help manage a car rental business. You might design a general-purpose object called `Car`. The `Car` object would have certain properties (`color`, `year`, `odometerReading`, and `make`) and perhaps a few methods (e.g., a method `setOdometer(newMiles)` to update the `odometerReading` property to the current figure `newMiles`).

For each car in the rental fleet, you would create an *instance* of the `Car` object.

NOTE

An instance of an object is a particular application of an object "template" to create a working object based on specific data. For example, the general object template `Car` might have a specific instance where a `Car` object has been created with specific data identifying it as a "blue 1998 Ford," and another instance describing a "yellow 2004 Nissan." In most discussions of object-oriented programming, such an object template is referred to as a *class*. I've resisted the temptation to use that term, as JavaScript doesn't really use classes, but the JavaScript concept called a *constructor function* is similar. You learn about constructor functions during this hour.

Writing OOP code offers several advantages over procedural methods:

▶ **Code reuse**—First, OOP allows you to reuse your code in a variety of scripts. You could achieve this with regular functions, but it would soon become difficult to keep track of all the variables that needed to be passed, their scope, and meaning. For objects, in contrast, you only need to document the properties and methods for each object. Providing they adhere to these rules, other programs—and even other programmers—can easily use your object definitions.

▶ **Encapsulation**—You can define the way objects interact with other parts of your scripts by carefully controlling the properties and methods that the rest of the program can "see." The *internal* workings of the object can be hidden away, forcing code external to the object to access that object's data only through the documented interfaces that the object offers.

▶ **Inheritance**—Often when coding you will have a need for some code that is nearly, but not quite, the same as something that's been coded before—maybe even something already coded in the same application. Using *inheritance*, new objects can be created based on the design of previously defined objects, optionally with additions or modifications to their methods and properties; the new object *inherits* properties and methods from the old.

In the previous hours you often used objects; either those built into JavaScript, or those that make up the DOM. However, you can also create your own objects, with their own properties and functions, to use in your programs.

NOTE

Some programming languages such as C++ and Smalltalk lean heavily toward OOP, and are often referred to as object-oriented languages. JavaScript is not one of these, but it does support enough of the essentials to allow you to write useful OOP code. We could easily fill the whole book with theory and practice of OOP, but we just look at the basics here.

Object Creation

JavaScript offers several ways to create an object. Let's look first at how to declare a *direct instance* of an object; later we create an object by using a *constructor function.*

Create a Direct Instance

JavaScript has a built-in object simply called `Object` that you can use as a kind of blank canvas for creating your own objects:

```
myNewObject = new Object();
```

OK, you now have a brand new object, `myNewObject`. For the moment, it doesn't actually do anything, as it doesn't have any properties or methods. You can begin to rectify that by adding a property:

```
myNewObject.info = 'I am a shiny new object';
```

Now your object owns a property—in this case a text string containing some information about the object and called `info`. You can also easily add a method to the object too, by first defining a function, and then attaching it to `myNewObject` as one of the object's methods:

```
function myFunc() {
        alert(this.info);
    };
myNewObject.showInfo = myFunc;
```

CAUTION

Notice that you use just the name of the function here without the parentheses. You do so because you are trying to assign to method `newObject.showInfo` the *definition* of the function `myFunc()`.

Had you used the code

```
myNewObject.showInfo = myFunc();
```

you would have been asking JavaScript to *execute* `myFunc()` and assign its *return value* to `newObject.showInfo`.

To call the new method, you can simply use the now-familiar dot notation:

```
myNewObject.showInfo();
```

Using the `this` Keyword

Note the use of the `this` keyword in the previous function definition. You may recall that you used such a keyword in Hour 2, "Writing Simple Scripts," and Hour 3, "Using Functions." In those previous examples, you used `this` in an inline event handler:

```
<img src="tick.gif" alt="tick" onmouseover="this.src='tick2.gif';"  />
```

When used in that way, `this` refers to the HTML element itself—in the preceding case the `<img>` element. When you use `this` inside a function (or method), the keyword `this` refers to the function's *parent* object.

Upon the first declaration of the function `myFunc()`, its parent is the global object; that is, the `window` object. The `window` object does not have a property called `info`, so if you were to call the `myFunc()` function directly, an error would occur.

However, you go on to create a method called `showInfo` of `myNewObject` and you assign `myFunc()` to that method:

```
myNewObject.showInfo = myFunc;
```

In the context of the `showInfo()` method, `myNewObject` is the parent object, so `this.info` refers to the property `myNewObject.info`.

Let's see if we can clarify this a little with the code in Listing 8.1.

LISTING 8.1   Creating an Object

```
<!DOCTYPE html>
<html>
<head>
    <title>Object Oriented Programming</title>
    <script>
        myNewObject = new Object();
        myNewObject.info = 'I am a shiny new object';
        function myFunc(){
                alert(this.info);
            }
        myNewObject.showInfo = myFunc;
    </script>
</head>
<body>
    <input type="button" value="Good showInfo Call" onclick="myNewObject.
    ➥showInfo()" />
    <input type="button" value="myFunc Call" onclick="myFunc()" />
    <input type="button" value="Bad showInfo Call" onclick="showInfo()" />
</body>
</html>
```

Notice that in the `<head>` section of the page, you create the object `myNewObject` and assign it the property `info` and the method `showInfo`, as described earlier.

Loading this page into your browser, you are confronted with three buttons.

Clicking on the first button makes a call to the `showInfo` method of the newly created object:

```
<input type="button" value="Good showInfo Call" onclick="myNewObject.showInfo()" />
```

As you would hope, the value of the `info` property is passed to the `alert()` dialog, as shown in Figure 8.1.

FIGURE 8.1
The `info` property is correctly called

The second button attempts to make a call directly to the function `myFunc()`:

```
<input type="button" value="myFunc Call" onclick="myFunc()" />
```

Because `myFunc()` is a method of the global object (having been defined without reference to any other object as parent), it attempts to pass to the `alert()` dialog the value of a nonexistent property `window.info`, with the result shown in Figure 8.2.

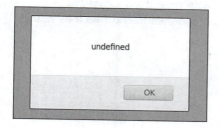

FIGURE 8.2
The global object has no property called `info`

Finally, your third button attempts to call `showInfo` without reference to its parent object:

```
<input type="button" value="Bad showInfo Call" onclick="showInfo()" />
```

Because the method does not exist outside the object `myNewObject`, JavaScript reports an error, as shown in Figure 8.3.

NOTE

We'll talk more about showing JavaScript errors using your browser's JavaScript Console or Error Console later in the book.

FIGURE 8.3
JavaScript reports that `showInfo` is not defined

Anonymous Functions

There is a more convenient and elegant way to assign a value to your object's `showInfo` method, without having to create a separate, named function and then later assign it by name to the required method. Instead of this code:

```
function myFunc() {
        alert(this.info);
    };
myNewObject.showInfo = myFunc;
```

you could simply have written the following:

```
myNewObject.showInfo = function() {
    alert(this.info);
}
```

Because you haven't needed to give a name to your function prior to assigning it, this technique is referred to as using an *anonymous function*.

By using similar assignment statements you can add as many properties and methods as you need to your instantiated object.

TIP

JavaScript offers a further way to create a direct instance of an object; the technique uses JSON (JavaScript Object Notation). It isn't covered here, as we explore JSON in detail in Hour 10, "Meet JSON."

Using a Constructor Function

Directly creating an instance of an object is fine if you think you'll only need one object of that type. Unfortunately, if you need to create another instance of the same type of object, you'll have to go through the same process again—creating the object, adding properties, defining methods, and so on.

TIP

An object with only one global instance is sometimes called a *singleton* object. These objects are useful sometimes; for example, a user of your program might have only one associated user-Profile object, perhaps containing his or her user name, URL of last page viewed, and similar properties.

A better way to create objects that will have multiple instances is by using an *object constructor function*. An object constructor function creates a kind of "template" from which further objects can be instantiated.

Take a look at the following code. Instead of using new Object(), you first declare a function, myObjectType(), and in its definition you can add properties and methods using the this keyword.

```
function myObjectType(){
    this.info = 'I am a shiny new object';
    this.showInfo = function(){
        alert(this.info);  // show the value of the property info
    }
    this.setInfo = function (newInfo) {
        this.info = newInfo; // overwrite the value of the property info
    }
}
```

In the preceding code you added a single property, info, and two methods: showInfo, which simply displays the value currently stored in the info property, and setInfo. The setInfo method takes an argument, newInfo, and uses its value to overwrite the value of the info property.

Instantiating an Object

You can now create as many instances as you want of this object type. All will have the properties and methods defined in the myObjectType() function. Creating an object instance is known as *instantiating* an object.

Having defined your constructor function, you can create an instance of your object simply by using the constructor function:

```
var myNewObject = new myObjectType();
```

NOTE

Note that this syntax is identical to using new Object(), except you use your purpose-designed object type in place of JavaScript's general-purpose Object(). In doing so, you instantiate the object complete with the properties and methods defined in the constructor function.

Now you can call its methods and examine its properties:

```
var x = myNewObject.info  // x now contains 'I am a shiny new object'
myNewObject.showInfo();  // alerts 'I am a shiny new object'
myNewObject.setInfo("Here is some new information");  // overwrites the info
property
```

Creating multiple instances is as simple as calling the constructor function as many times as you need to:

```
var myNewObject1 = new myObjectType();
var myNewObject2 = new myObjectType();
```

Let's see this in action. The code in Listing 8.2 defines an object constructor function the same as the one described previously.

Two instances of the object are instantiated; clearly, both objects are initially identical. You can examine the value stored in the info property for each object by clicking on one of the buttons labeled Show Info 1 or Show Info 2.

A third button calls the setInfo method of object myNewObject2, passing a new string literal as an argument to the method. This overwrites the value stored in the info property of object myNewObject2, but of course leaves myNewObject unchanged. The revised values can be checked by once again using Show Info 1 and Show Info 2.

LISTING 8.2   Creating Objects with a Constructor Function

```
<!DOCTYPE html>
<html>
<head>
    <title>Object Oriented Programming</title>
    <script>
        function myObjectType(){
            this.info = 'I am a shiny new object';
            this.showInfo = function(){
                alert(this.info);
            }
            this.setInfo = function (newInfo) {
                this.info = newInfo;
            }
        }
        var myNewObject1 = new myObjectType();
        var myNewObject2 = new myObjectType();
    </script>
</head>
<body>
    <input type="button" value="Show Info 1" onclick="myNewObject1.showInfo()" />
    <input type="button" value="Show Info 2" onclick="myNewObject2.showInfo()" />
    <input type="button" value="Change info of object2"
    ➥onclick="myNewObject2.setInfo('New Information!')" />
</body>
</html>
```

Using Constructor Function Arguments

There is nothing to stop you from customizing your objects at the time of instantiation, by passing one or more arguments to the constructor function. In the following code, the definition of the constructor function includes one argument, personName, which is assigned to the name property by the constructor function. As you instantiate two objects, you pass a name as an argument to the constructor function for each instance.

```
function Person(personName){
    this.name = personName;
    this.info = 'I am called ' + this.name;
    this.showInfo = function(){
        alert(this.info);
    }
}
var person1 = new Person('Adam');
var person2 = new Person('Eve');
```

You can define the constructor function to accept as many or as few arguments as you want:

```
function Car(Color, Year, Make, Miles) {
    this.color = Color;
    this.year = Year;
    this.make = Make;
    this.odometerReading = Miles;
    this.setOdometer = function(newMiles) {
        this.odometerReading = newMiles;
    }
}
var car1 = new Car("blue", "1998", "Ford", 79500);
var car2 = new Car("yellow", "2004", "Nissan", 56350);
car1.setOdometer(82450);
```

Extending and Inheriting Objects Using `prototype`

A major advantage of using objects is the capability to reuse already written code in a new context. JavaScript provides a means to modify objects to include new methods and/or properties or even to create brand-new objects based on ones that already exist.

These techniques are known, respectively, as *extending* and *inheriting* objects.

Extending Objects

What if you want to extend your objects with new methods and properties after the objects have already been instantiated? You can do so using the keyword `prototype`. The prototype object allows you to quickly add a property or method that is then available for all instances of the object.

▼ TRY IT YOURSELF

Extend an Object Using `prototype`

Let's extend the `Person` object of the previous example with a new method, `sayHello`:

```
Person.prototype.sayHello = function() {
    alert(this.name + " says hello");
}
```

Create a new HTML file in your editor, and enter the code from Listing 8.3.

LISTING 8.3   Adding a New Method with `prototype`

```
<!DOCTYPE html>
<html>
<head>
<title>Object Oriented Programming</title>
    <script>
        function Person(personName){
            this.name = personName;
            this.info = 'This person is called ' + this.name;
            this.showInfo = function(){
                alert(this.info);
            }
        }
        var person1 = new Person('Adam');
        var person2 = new Person('Eve');
        Person.prototype.sayHello = function() {
            alert(this.name + " says hello");
        }
    </script>
</head>
<body>
    <input type="button" value="Show Info on Adam" onclick="person1.showInfo()" />
    <input type="button" value="Show Info on Eve" onclick="person2.showInfo()" />
    <input type="button" value="Say Hello Adam" onclick="person1.sayHello()" />
    <input type="button" value="Say Hello Eve" onclick="person2.sayHello()" />
</body>
</html>
```

Let's walk through this code and see what's happening.

First, you define a constructor function that takes a single argument, `personName`. Within the constructor, two properties, `name` and `info`, and one method, `showInfo`, are defined.

You create two objects, instantiating each with a different `name` property. Having created these two person objects, you then decide to add a further method, `sayHello`, to the `person` object definition. You do so using the `prototype` keyword.

Load the HTML file into your browser. Clicking on the four buttons visible on the page shows that the initially defined `showInfo` method is still intact, but the new `sayHello` method operates too, and is available for both of the existing instances of the object type.

Inheritance

Inheritance is the capability to create one object type from another; the new object type inherits the properties and methods of the old, as well as optionally having further properties and methods of its own. This can save you a lot of work, as you can first devise "generic" classes of objects and then refine them into more specific classes by inheritance.

JavaScript uses the `prototype` keyword to emulate inheritance, too.

Because `object.prototype` is used to add new methods and properties, you can utilize it to add ALL of the methods and properties of an existing constructor function to your new object.

Let's define another simple object:

```
function Pet() {
    this.animal = "";
    this.name = "";
    this.setAnimal = function(newAnimal) {
        this.animal = newAnimal;
    }
    this.setName = function(newName) {
        this.name = newName;
    }
}
```

A `Pet` object has properties that contain the type of animal and the name of the pet, and methods to set these values:

```
var myCat = new Pet();
myCat.setAnimal = "cat";
myCat.setName = "Sylvester";
```

Now suppose you want to create an object specifically for dogs. Rather than starting from scratch, you want to inherit the `Dog` object from `Pet`, but add an additional property, `breed`, and an additional method, `setBreed`.

First, let's create the `Dog` constructor function and in it define the new property and method:

```
function Dog() {
    this.breed = "";
    this.setBreed = function(newBreed) {
        this.breed = newBreed;
    }
}
```

Having added the new property, `breed`, and the new method, `setBreed`, you can now additionally inherit all the properties and methods of `Pet`. You do so using the `prototype` keyword:

```
Dog.prototype = new Pet();
```

You can now access the properties and methods of `Pet` in addition to those of `Dog`:

```
var myDog = new Dog();
myDog.setName("Alan");
```

```
myDog.setBreed("Greyhound");
alert(myDog.name + " is a " + myDog.breed);
```

Extending JavaScript's Own Objects

Prototype can also be used to extend JavaScript's built-in objects. You can implement the
`String.prototype.backwards` method, for instance, that will return a reversed version of any
string you supply, as in Listing 8.4.

LISTING 8.4 Extending the String Object

```
<!DOCTYPE html>
<html>
<head>
    <title>Object Oriented Programming</title>
    <script>
        String.prototype.backwards = function(){
            var out = '';
            for(var i = this.length-1; i >= 0; i--){
                out += this.substr(i, 1);
            }
            return out;
        }
    </script>
</head>
<body>
    <script>
        var inString = prompt("Enter your test string:");
        document.write(inString.backwards());
    </script>
</body>
</html>
```

Save the code of Listing 8.4 as an HTML file and open it in your browser. The script uses a
`prompt()` dialog to invite you to enter a string, and then shows the string reversed on the page.

Let's see how the code works.

```
String.prototype.backwards = function(){
    var out = '';
    for(var i = this.length-1; i >= 0; i--){
        out += this.substr(i, 1);
    }
    return out;
}
```

First, you declare a new variable, `out`, within the anonymous function that you are creating. This variable will hold the reversed string.

You then begin a loop, starting at the end of the input string (remember that JavaScript string character indexing starts at 0, not 1, so you need to begin at `this.length - 1`) and decrementing one character at a time. As you loop backwards through the string, you add characters one at a time to your output string stored in `out`.

When you reach the beginning of the input string, the reversed string is returned. The result is shown in Figure 8.4.

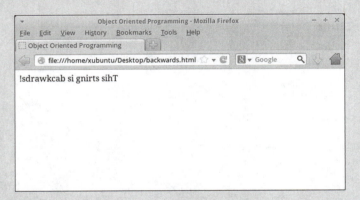

FIGURE 8.4
Method to reverse a string

Encapsulation

Encapsulation is the name given to OOP's capability to hide data and instructions inside an object. How this is achieved varies from language to language, but in JavaScript any variables declared inside the constructor function are available only from within the object; they are invisible from outside. The same is true of any function declared inside the constructor function.

Such variables and functions become accessible to the outside world only when they are assigned with the `this` keyword; they then become properties and methods of the object.

Let's look at an example:

```
function Box(width, length, height) {
    function volume(a,b,c) {
        return a*b*c;
    }
    this.boxVolume = volume(width, length, height);
}
```

```
var crate = new Box(5,4,3);
alert("Volume = " + crate.boxVolume); // works correctly
alert(volume(5,4,3)); // fails as function volume() is invisible
```

In the preceding example, the function `volume(a,b,c)` cannot be called from any place outside the constructor function as it has not been assigned to an object method by using `this`. However, the property `crate.boxVolume` *is* available outside the constructor function; even though it uses the function `volume()` to calculate its value, it only does so inside the constructor function.

If you don't "register" methods and properties using `this`, they are not available outside. Such methods and properties are referred to as *private*.

Using Feature Detection

Back in the dark days before the W3C DOM evolved to its current state, JavaScript developers were forced into horrible code contortions to try to cope with browsers' different DOM implementations. It was not uncommon for scripts to be written almost as two or more separate programs, the version to be executed only being decided after an attempt to detect the browser in use.

As you saw in your work with the `navigator` object in Hour 4, "DOM Objects and Built-in Objects," browser detection is a tricky business. The `navigator` object contains information that can be misleading at best (and sometimes downright incorrect). Also, when a new browser or version is introduced with new capabilities and features, your browser-detecting code is usually broken once again.

Thankfully a much better way to write cross-browser code has emerged, based on objects. Instead of attempting browser detection, it's a much better idea to have JavaScript examine whether the particular feature you need is supported. You can do this by testing for the availability of a specific object, method, or property. In many cases it's sufficient to try to use the object, method, or property in question, and detect the value JavaScript returns.

Here's an example of testing for browser support of the `document.getElementById()` method, which you've already met. While `getElementById()` has been supported by all new browsers for some time now, very early browsers do not support this method. You can test for the availability of the `getElementById()` method (or any similar method or property) by using `if()`:

```
if(document.getElementById) {
    myElement = document.getElementById(id);
} else {
    // do something else
}
```

If `document.getElementById` is not available, the `if()` conditional statement will switch code operation to avoid using that method.

Another, related method uses the `typeof` operator to check whether a JavaScript function exists before calling it:

```
if(typeof document.getElementById == 'function') {
    // you can use getElementById()
} else {
    // do something else
}
```

A number of possible values can be returned by `typeof`, as listed in Table 8.1.

TABLE 8.1 Values Returned by `typeof`

Evaluates to	Indicates
"number"	Operand is a number.
"string"	Operand is a string.
"boolean"	Operand is a Boolean.
"object"	Operand is an object.
null	Operand is null.
undefined	Operand is not defined.

You can use this technique to check for the existence not only of DOM and built-in objects, methods, and properties, but also those created within your scripts.

Note that at no point in this exercise have you tried to determine what browser your user has—you simply want to know whether it supports the objects, properties, or methods you are about to try to use. Not only is such *feature detection* much more accurate and elegant than so-called *browser sniffing* (trying to infer the browser in use by interpreting properties of the `navigator` object), but it's also much more future proof—the introduction of new browsers or browser versions won't break anything in your code's operation.

Summary

In this hour you learned about object-oriented programming (OOP) in JavaScript, starting with the basic concepts behind OOP, and how it can help your code development, especially for more complex applications.

You learned a way to directly instantiate an object and add properties and methods to it. You then learned to create an object constructor function, from which you can instantiate multiple similar objects.

You also learned about the `prototype` keyword, and how it can be used to extend objects or create new objects via inheritance.

Q&A

Q. Should I always write object-oriented code?

A. It's a matter of personal preference. Some coders prefer to always think in terms of objects, methods, and properties, and write all their code with those principles in mind. Others feel that, particularly for smaller and simpler programs, the level of abstraction provided by OOP is too much, and that procedural coding is OK.

Q. How would I use my objects in other programs?

A. An object's constructor function is quite a portable entity. If you link into your page a JavaScript file containing an object constructor function, you have the means to create objects and use their properties and methods throughout your code.

Workshop

Try to answer all the questions before reading the subsequent "Answers" section.

Quiz

1. A new object created from a constructor function is known as:

    a. an instance of the object

    b. a method of the object

    c. a prototype

2. Deriving new objects by using the design of currently existing objects is known as:

    a. Encapsulation

    b. Inheritance

    c. Instantiation

3. Which of the following is a valid way to create a direct instance of an object?

    a. `myObject.create();`

    b. `myObject = new Object;`

    c. `myObject = new Object();`

Answers

1. a. A new object created from a constructor function is known as an instance.

2. b. New objects are derived from existing ones through inheritance.

3. c. `myObject = new Object();`

Exercises

▶ Write a constructor function for a `Card` object with properties of `suit` (diamonds, hearts, spades, or clubs) and `face` (ace, 2, 3 ...king). Add methods to set the values of `suit` and `face`.

Can you include a `shuffle` method to set the `suit` and `face` properties to represent a random card from the deck? (Hint: Use the `Math.random()` method described in Hour 4, "DOM Objects and Built-in Objects.")

▶ Extend JavaScript's `Date` object using the `prototype` keyword to add a new method, `getYesterday()`, that returns the name of the previous day to that represented by the `Date` object.

Scripting with the DOM

What You'll Learn in This Hour:

▶ The concept of nodes
▶ The different types of nodes
▶ Using `nodeName`, `nodeType`, and `nodeValue`
▶ Using the `childNodes` collection
▶ Selecting elements with `getElementsByTagName()`
▶ How to use Mozilla's DOM Inspector
▶ How to create new elements
▶ Ways to add, edit, and remove child nodes
▶ Dynamically loading JavaScript files
▶ Changing element attributes

You've already learned about the W3C DOM and, in the code examples of previous hours, you used various DOM objects, properties, and methods.

In this hour you begin exploring how JavaScript can directly interact with the DOM. In particular, you learn some new ways to navigate around the DOM, selecting particular DOM objects that represent parts of the page's HTML contents. You see how to create new elements, how to add, edit, and remove nodes of the DOM tree, and how to manipulate elements' attributes.

DOM Nodes

In Part I, "First Steps with JavaScript," you were introduced to the W3C Document Object Model (DOM) as a hierarchical tree of parent-child relationships that together form a model of the current web page. By using appropriate methods, you can navigate to any part of the DOM and retrieve details about it.

You probably recall that the top-level object in the DOM hierarchy is the `window` object, and that one of its children is the `document` object. In this hour we mainly deal with the `document` object and its properties and methods.

Take a look at the simple web page of Listing 9.1.

LISTING 9.1   A Simple Web Page

```
<!DOCTYPE html>
<html>
<head>
    <title>To-Do List</title>
</head>
<body>
    <h1>Things To Do</h1>
    <ol id="toDoList">
        <li>Mow the lawn</li>
        <li>Clean the windows</li>
        <li>Answer your email</li>
    </ol>
    <p id="toDoNotes">Make sure all these are completed by 8pm so you can watch the
    ➥game on TV!</p>
</body>
</html>
```

Figure 9.1 shows the page displayed in Mozilla Firefox.

FIGURE 9.1
Our simple web page displayed in Firefox

When page loading has completed, the browser has a full, hierarchical DOM representation of this page available for us to examine. Figure 9.2 shows a simplified version of how part of that representation might look.

Remember, the DOM is not available until the page has finished loading. Don't try to execute any statements that use the DOM until then, or your script is likely to produce errors.

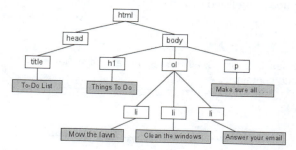

FIGURE 9.2
The DOM's tree model of our page

Look at how the tree diagram of Figure 9.2 relates to the code in Listing 9.1.

The `<html>` element contains all the other markup of the page. It is the *parent* element to two immediate *child* elements, the `<head>` and `<body>` elements. These two elements are *siblings*, as they share a parent. They are also parents themselves; the `<head>` element has one child element, `<title>`, and the `<body>` element three children: the `<h1>` heading, the ordered list `<ol>`, and a paragraph, `<p>`. Of these three siblings, only `<ol>` has children, those being three `<li>` line item elements. Various of these elements of the tree contain text, shown represented in the gray boxes in Figure 9.2.

The DOM is constructed as a hierarchy of such relationships. The boxes that make up the junctions and terminating points of the tree diagram are known as *nodes*.

Types of Nodes

Figure 9.2 shows various *element nodes*, each of which represents an HTML element such as a paragraph element, `<p>`, along with some *text nodes*, representing the text content of such page elements.

TIP

Where they exist, text nodes are always contained within element nodes. However, not every element node contains a text node.

There are a number of other node types, representing such information as each element's attributes, HTML comments, and other information relevant to the page. Many node types can, of course, contain other nodes as children.

Each different type of node has an associated number known as its `nodeType` property. The `nodeType` properties for the various types of nodes are listed in Table 9.1.

TIP

You'll likely do most of your work using node types 1, 2, and 3, as you manipulate page elements, their attributes, and the text that those elements contain.

TABLE 9.1 `nodeType` Values

nodeType	Type of Node
1	element
2	attribute
3	text (including whitespace)
4	CDATA section
5	entity reference
6	entity
7	processing instruction
8	HTML comment
9	document
10	document type (DTD)
11	document fragment
12	notation

The `childNodes` Property

A useful DOM property for each node is a collection of its immediate children. This array-like list is called `childNodes`, and it enables you to access information about the children of any DOM node.

The `childNodes` collection is a so-called *NodeList*, in which the items are numerically indexed. A collection looks and (for the most part) behaves like an array—you can refer to its members like those of an array, and you can iterate through them like you would for an array. However, there are a few array methods you can't use, such as push() and pop(). For all the examples here, you can treat the collection like you would a regular array.

A node list is a live collection, which means that any changes to the collection to which it refers are immediately reflected in the list; you don't have to fetch it again when changes occur.

Using the childNodes Property

You can use the collection returned by the childNodes property to examine the ordered list element <ol> that appears in Listing 9.1. You're going to write a small function to read the child nodes of the <ol> element and return the total number present in the list.

First, you can retrieve the <ol> element via its ID.

```
var olElement = document.getElementById("toDoList");
```

The child nodes of the <ol> element will now be contained in the object

```
olElement.childNodes
```

You only want to select the <li> elements in the list, so you now want to step through the childNodes collection, counting just those nodes for which nodeType==1 (i.e., those corresponding to HTML elements), ignoring anything else contained in the ordered list element such as comments and whitespace. Remember, you can treat the collection pretty much like an array; here you use the length property as you would for an array:

```
var count = 0;
for (var i=0; i < olElement.childNodes.length; i++) {
    if(olElement.childNodes[i].nodeType == 1) count++;
}
```

CAUTION

Whitespace (such as the space and tab characters) in HTML code is generally ignored by the browser when rendering the page. However, the presence of whitespace within a page element—for example, within your ordered list element—will in many browsers create a child node of type text (nodeType == 3) within the element. This makes simply using childNodes.length a risky business.

Let's cook up a little function to carry out this task when the page has loaded, and output the result with an alert dialog:

```
function countListItems() {
    var olElement = document.getElementById("toDoList");
    var count = 0;
    for (var i=0; i < olElement.childNodes.length; i++) {
        if(olElement.childNodes[i].nodeType == 1) count++;
    }
    alert("The ordered list contains " + count + " items");
}
window.onload = countListItems;
```

Create a new HTML page in your editor and enter the code of Listing 9.1. Incorporate the preceding JavaScript code into a `<script>` element in the page head, and load the page into the browser.

Figure 9.3 shows the result of loading the page in Mozilla Firefox.

FIGURE 9.3
Using the `childNodes` array

`firstChild` and `lastChild`

There is a handy shorthand for selecting the first and last elements in the `childNodes` array.

`firstChild` is, unsurprisingly, the first element in the `childNodes` array. Using `firstChild` is equivalent to using `childNodes[0]`.

To access the last element in the collection, you gain a big advantage by using `lastChild`. To access this element you would otherwise have to do something like this:

```
var lastChildNode = myElement.childNodes[myElement.childNodes.length - 1];
```

That's pretty ugly. Instead, you can simply use

```
var lastChildNode = myElement.lastChild;
```

The `parentNode` Property

The `parentNode` property, unsurprisingly, returns the parent node of the node to which it's applied. In the previous example, you used

```
var lastChildNode = myElement.lastChild;
```

Using `parentNode` you can go one step back up the tree. The line

```
var parentElement = lastChildNode.parentNode;
```

would return the parent element of `lastChildNode`, which is, of course, the object `myElement`.

`nextSibling` and `previousSibling`

Sibling nodes are nodes that share a parent node. When applied to a specified parent node, these read-only properties return the next and previous sibling nodes, respectively, or `null` if there is no such node.

```
var olElement = document.getElementById("toDoList");
var firstOne = olElement.firstChild;
var nextOne = firstOne.nextSibling;
```

CAUTION

Remember that, depending on which browser you use, whitespace in your HTML code may create text nodes in the DOM. The node you're working with may have more siblings than you thought!

Node Value

In addition to `nodeType`, the DOM offers the property `nodeValue` to return the value stored in a node. You generally want to use this to return the text stored in a text node.

Let's suppose that instead of counting the list items in the previous example, you wanted to extract the text contained in the `<p>` element of the page. To do this you need to access the relevant `<p>` node, find the text node that it contains, and then use `nodeValue` to return the information:

```
var text = '';
var pElement = document.getElementById("toDoNotes");
for (var i=0; i < pElement.childNodes.length; i++) {
    if(pElement.childNodes[i].nodeType == 3) {
```

```
        text += pElement.childNodes[i].nodeValue;
    };
}
alert("The paragraph says:\n\n" + text );
```

Node Name

The nodeName property returns the name of the specified node as a string value. The values returned by the nodeName value are summarized in Table 9.2. The nodeName property is read-only—you can't change its value.

Where nodeName returns an element name, it does so without the surrounding < and > that you would use in HTML source code:

```
var pElement = document.getElementById("toDoNotes");
alert( pElement.nodeName);  // alerts 'P'
```

TABLE 9.2   Values Returned by the nodeName Property

nodeType	Node Type	nodeName
1	element	element (tag) name
2	attribute	attribute name
3	text	the string "#text"

Selecting Elements with getElementsByTagName()

You already know how to access an individual page element using the document object's getElementById() method. Another method of the document object, getElementsByTag-Name(), allows you to build an array populated with all of the occurrences of a particular tag.

Like getElementById(), the getElementsByTagName() method accepts a single argument. However, in this case it's not the element ID but the required tag name that is passed to the method as an argument.

CAUTION

Make careful note of the spelling. *Elements* (plural) is used in getElementsByTagName(), whereas *Element* (singular) is used in getElementById().

As an example, suppose you wanted to work with all of the `<div>` elements in a particular document. You can populate a variable with an array-like collection called `myDivs` by using

```
var myDivs = document.getElementsByTagName("div");
```

TIP

Even if there is only one element with the specified tag name, `getElementsByTagName()` still returns a collection, although it will contain only one item.

You don't have to use `getElementsByTagName()` on the entire document. It can be applied to any individual object and return a collection of elements with the given tag name contained within that object.

TRY IT YOURSELF ▼

Using `getElementsByTagName()`

Earlier you wrote a function to count the list items (`<li>`) inside an ordered list (`<ol>`) element:

```
function countListItems() {
    var olElement = document.getElementById("toDoList");
    var count = 0;
    for (var i=0; i < olElement.childNodes.length; i++) {
        if(olElement.childNodes[i].nodeType == 1) count++;
    }
alert("The ordered list contains " + count + " items");
}
```

You used the `childNodes` array to get all the child nodes and then selected those corresponding to elements by testing for `nodeType == 1`.

You can easily implement the same function by using `getElementsByTagName()`.

You start the same way by selecting the `<ol>` element based on its `id`:

```
var olElement = document.getElementById("toDoList");
```

Now you can create an array called `listItems` and populate it with all if the `<li>` elements contained in your `<ol>` object `olElement`:

```
var listItems = olElement.getElementsByTagName("li");
```

All that remains is to display how many items are in the array:

```
alert("The ordered list contains " + listItems.length + " items");
```

Listing 9.2 contains the complete code for the page, including the revised function
`countListItems()`.

LISTING 9.2   Using `getElementsByTagName()`

```
<!DOCTYPE html>
<html>
<head>
    <title>To-Do List</title>
    <script>
        function countListItems() {
            var olElement = document.getElementById("toDoList");
            var listItems = olElement.getElementsByTagName("li");
            alert("The ordered list contains " + listItems.length + " items");
        }
        window.onload = countListItems;
    </script>
</head>
<body>
    <h1>Things To Do</h1>
    <ol id="toDoList">
        <li>Mow the lawn</li>
        <li>Clean the windows</li>
        <li>Answer your email</li>
    </ol>
    <p id="toDoNotes">Make sure all these are completed by 8pm so you can watch the
    ➥game on TV!</p>
</body>
</html>
```

Save this listing as an HTML file and load it into your browser. Check that the result is the same
as in Figure 9.3.

NOTE

A further useful method for getting a collection of elements is

`document.getElementsByClassName()`

As you'll have worked out from the method name, this method returns all the page elements
having a particular value of the `class` attribute. However, this was not supported in Internet Explorer
until IE9.

Reading an Element's Attributes

HTML elements often contain a number of attributes with associated values:

```
<div id="id1" title="report">Here is some text.</div>
```

The attributes are always placed within the opening tag, each attribute being of the form `attribute=value`. The attributes themselves are child nodes of the element node in which they appear, as depicted in Figure 9.4.

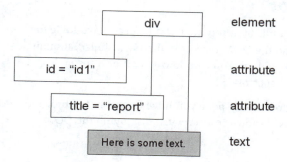

FIGURE 9.4
Attribute nodes

Having navigated to the element node of interest, you can read the value of any of its attributes using the `getAttribute()` method:

```
var myNode = document.getElementById("id1");
alert(myNode.getAttribute("title"));
```

The previous code snippet would display "report" within the `alert` dialog. If you try to retrieve the value of a nonexistent attribute, `getAttribute()` will return `null`. You can use this fact to efficiently test whether an element node has a particular attribute defined:

```
if(myNode.getAttribute("title")) {
  ... do something ...
}
```

The `if()` condition will only be met if `getAttribute()` returns a non-null value, since `null` is interpreted by JavaScript as a "falsy" value (not Boolean false, but considered as such).

CAUTION

There also exists a property simply called `attributes` that contains an array of all of a node's attributes. In theory you can access the attributes as `name=value` pairs in the order they appear in the HTML code, by using a numerical key; so `attributes[0].name` would be `id` and `attributes[1].value` would be `'report'`. However, its implementation in Internet Explorer and some versions of Firefox is buggy. It's safer to use `getAttribute()` instead.

Mozilla's DOM Inspector

One of the easiest ways to view node information is by using the DOM Inspector available for Mozilla Firefox. If you use Firefox, you may find the DOM Inspector already installed, though since Firefox 3 it's been available as a separate add-on. You can download it at https://addons.mozilla.org/en-US/firefox/addon/dom-inspector-6622/.

Once installed, you can open the DOM Inspector for any page you have loaded in the browser by pressing Ctrl+Shft+I. The window that opens is shown in Figure 9.5, displaying the DOM representation of the web page of Listing 9.1.

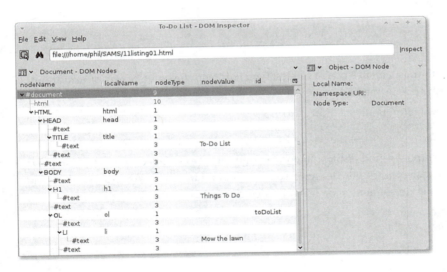

FIGURE 9.5
Mozilla's DOM Inspector

A DOM node is selected from the tree structure in the left-hand display pane, and details about it can be examined in the right-hand pane. As well as the viewer for the DOM tree, other viewers are included for viewing CSS rules, style sheets, computed style, JavaScript objects, and more.

The interface can seem a little daunting at first, but it's well worth exploring the program's capabilities.

TIP

When you amend the DOM using the methods described in this hour, you change the way a page appears in the browser. Bear in mind, though, that you're not changing the document itself. If you ask your browser to display the source code of the page, you won't see any changes there.

That's because the browser is actually displaying the current DOM representation of the document. Change that, and you change what appears onscreen.

Creating New Nodes

Adding new nodes to the DOM tree is a two-stage process:

1. First, you create a new node. Once created, the node is initially in a kind of "limbo"; it exists, but it's not actually located anywhere in the DOM tree, and therefore doesn't appear on the visible page in the browser window.

2. Next, you add the new node to the tree, in the desired location. At this point it becomes part of the visible page.

Let's look at some of the methods of the `document` object that are available for creating nodes.

createElement()

You can call on the `createElement()` method to create new HTML elements having any of the standard HTML element types—paragraphs, spans, tables, lists, and so on.

Let's suppose you've decided to create a new `<div>` element for your document. To do so, you simply need to pass the relevant `nodeName` value—in this case `"div"`—to the `createElement` method:

```
var newDiv = document.createElement("div");
```

The new `<div>` element now exists, but currently has no contents, no attributes, and no location in the DOM tree. You see how to solve these issues shortly.

createTextNode()

Many of the HTML elements in your page need some content in the form of text. The `create-TextNode()` method takes care of that. It works pretty much like `createElement()`, except that the argument it accepts is not a `nodeName` value, but a string containing the desired text content of the element:

```
var newTextNode = document.createTextNode("Here is some text content.");
```

As with `createElement()`, the newly created node is not yet located in the DOM tree; JavaScript has it stored in the `newTextNode` variable while it waits for you to place it in its required position.

`cloneNode()`

There's no point in reinventing the wheel. If you already have a node in your document that's just like the new one you want to create, you can use `cloneNode()` to do so.

Unlike `createElement()` and `createTextNode()`, `cloneNode()` takes a single argument—a Boolean value of *true* or *false*.

Passing true to the `cloneNode()` function tells JavaScript that you want to clone not only the node, but all of its child nodes:

```
var myDiv = document.getElementById("id1");
var newDiv = myDiv.cloneNode(true);
```

In this example, I've asked JavaScript to clone the element's child nodes too; for example, any text that `myDiv` contained (which would be contained in a child text node of the element) will be faithfully reproduced in the new `<div>` element.

Had I called

```
var newDiv = myDiv.cloneNode(false);
```

then the new `<div>` element would be identical to the original, except that it would have no child nodes. It would, for instance, have any attributes belonging to the original element (provided that the original node was an element node, of course).

CAUTION

Remember that the `id` of an element is one of its attributes. When you clone a node, remember to then change the `id` of your new element, since `id` values should be unique within a document.

As with new nodes created by `createElement()` and `createTextNode()`, the new node created by `cloneNode()` is initially floating in space; it does not yet have a place in the DOM tree.

You see how to achieve that next.

Manipulating Child Nodes

The new nodes you've created aren't yet of any practical value, as they don't yet appear anywhere in the DOM. A few methods of the `document` object are specifically designed for placing nodes in the DOM tree, and they are described in the following sections.

appendChild()

Perhaps the simplest way of all to attach a new node to the DOM is to append it as a child node to a node that already exists somewhere in the document. Doing so is just a matter of locating the required parent node and calling the `appendChild()` method:

```
var newText = document.createTextNode("Here is some text content.");
var myDiv = document.getElementById("id1");
myDiv.appendChild(newText);
```

In the preceding code snippet, a new text node has been created and added as a child node to the currently existing `<div>` element having an `id` of `id1`.

TIP

Remember that `appendChild()` always adds a child node after the last child node already present, so the newly appended node becomes the new `lastChild` of the parent node.

Of course, `appendChild()` works equally well with all types of nodes, not just text nodes. Suppose you needed to add another `<div>` element within the parent `<div>` element:

```
var newDiv = document.createElement("div");
var myDiv = document.getElementById("id1");
myDiv.appendChild(newDiv);
```

Your originally existing `<div>` element now contains a further `<div>` element as its last child; if the parent `<div>` element already contained some text content in the form of a child text node, then the parent `div` (as represented in the newly modified DOM, not in the source code) would now have the following form:

```
<div id="id1">
    Original text contained in text node
    <div></div>
</div>
```

insertBefore()

Whereas `appendChild()` always adds a child element to the end of the list of children, with `insertBefore()` you can specify a child element and insert the new node immediately before it.

The method takes two arguments: the new node, and the child before which it should be placed. Let's suppose that your page contains the following HTML snippet:

```
<div id="id1">
    <p id="para1">This paragraph contains some text.</p>
    <p id="para2">Here's some more text.</p>
</div>
```

To insert a new paragraph between the two that are currently in place, first create the new paragraph:

```
var newPara = document.createElement("p");
```

Identify the parent node, and the child node before which you want to make the insertion:

```
var myDiv = document.getElementById("id1");
var para2 = document.getElementById("para2");
```

Then pass these two as arguments to `insertBefore()`:

```
myDiv.insertBefore(newPara, para2);
```

`replaceChild()`

You can use `replaceChild()` when you want to replace a current child node of a specific parent element with another node. The method takes two arguments—a reference to the new child element followed by a reference to the old one.

▼ TRY IT YOURSELF

Replacing Child Elements

Take a look at the code of Listing 9.3.

LISTING 9.3   Replacing Child Elements

```
<!DOCTYPE html>
<html>
<head>
    <title>Replace Page Element</title>
</head>
<body>
    <div id="id1">
        <p id="para1">Welcome to my web page.</p>
        <p id="para2">Please take a look around.</p>
        <input id="btn" value="Replace Element" type="button" />
    </div>
</body>
</html>
```

Suppose that you want to use the DOM to remove the first paragraph in the `<div>` and replace it instead with an `<h2>` heading as follows:

```
<h2>Welcome!</h2>
```

First create the new node representing the `<h2>` heading:

```
var newH2 = document.createElement("h2");
```

This new element needs to contain a text node for the heading text. You can either create it and add it now, or do it later when you've added your new `<h2>` element to the DOM. Let's do it now:

```
var newH2Text = document.createTextNode("Welcome!");
newH2.appendChild(newH2Text);
```

Now you can swap out the unwanted child node of the `<div>` element and replace it with the new one:

```
var myDiv = document.getElementById("id1");
var oldP = document.getElementById("para1");
myDiv.replaceChild(newH2, oldP);
```

Finally, you need to add an `onclick` event handler to the button element, so that when the button is clicked, your element replacement function is executed. We do that with an anonymous function assigned to the `window.onload` method:

```
window.onload = function() {
    document.getElementById("btn").onclick = replaceHeading;
}
```

Listing 9.4 shows the code for the page with the JavaScript added.

LISTING 9.4   **The Completed Code to Replace Child Elements**

```
<!DOCTYPE html>
<html>
<head>
    <title>Replace Page Element</title>
    <script>
        function replaceHeading() {
            var newH2 = document.createElement("h2");
            var newH2Text = document.createTextNode("Welcome!");
            newH2.appendChild(newH2Text);
            var myDiv = document.getElementById("id1");
            var oldP = document.getElementById("para1");
            myDiv.replaceChild(newH2, oldP);
        }
        window.onload = function() {
            document.getElementById("btn").onclick = replaceHeading;
        }
    </script>
</head>
<body>
```

```
        <div id="id1">
            <p id="para1">Welcome to my web page.</p>
            <p id="para2">Please take a look around.</p>
            <input id="btn" value="Replace Element" type="button" />
        </div>
    </body>
</html>
```

Create a new HTML file with your editor and insert the code listed in Listing 9.4. On loading the page into your browser, you should see the two single-line paragraphs of text with the button beneath. If all has gone according to plan, clicking the button should swap the first <p> element for your <h2> heading, as depicted in Figure 9.6.

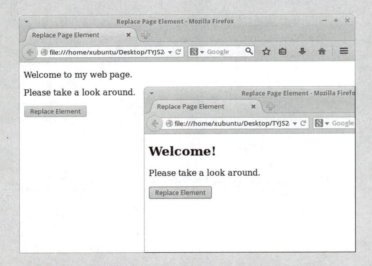

FIGURE 9.6
The element-replacement script in action

removeChild()

There is a DOM method specifically provided for removing child nodes from the DOM tree.

Referring once more to Listing 9.3, if you wanted to remove the <p> element with id="para2" you can just use

```
var myDiv = document.getElementById("id1");
var myPara = document.getElementById("para2");
myDiv.removeChild(myPara);
```

If you don't have a handy reference to the element's parent, just use the `parentNode` property:

```
myPara.parentNode.removeChild(myPara);
```

The return value from the `removeChild()` method contains a reference to the removed node. If you need to, you can use this to further process the child node that has just been removed:

```
var removedItem = myDiv.removeChild(myPara);
alert('Item with id ' + removedItem.getAttribute("id") + ' has been removed.');
```

Editing Element Attributes

In the previous hour you saw how to read element attributes using the `getAttribute()` method.

There is a corresponding method named `setAttribute()` to allow you to create attributes for element nodes and assign values to those attributes. The method takes two arguments; unsurprisingly, these are the attribute to be added and the value it should have.

In the following example, the title attribute is added to a `<p>` element and assigned the value "Opening Paragraph":

```
var myPara = document.getElementById("para1");
myPara.setAttribute("title", "Opening paragraph");
```

Setting the value of an attribute that already exists effectively overwrites the value of that attribute. You can use that knowledge to effectively edit existing attribute values:

```
var myPara = document.getElementById("para1");
myPara.setAttribute("title", "Opening paragraph"); // set 'title' attribute
myPara.setAttribute("title", "New title");  // overwrite 'title' attribute
```

Dynamically Loading JavaScript Files

On occasion you'll want to load JavaScript code on the fly to a page that's already loaded in the browser. You can use `createElement()` to dynamically create a new `<script>` element containing the required code, and then add this element to the page's DOM:

```
var scr = document.createElement("script");
scr.setAttribute("src", "newScript.js");
document.head.appendChild(scr);
```

Remember that the `appendChild()` method places the new child node after the last child currently present, so the new `<script>` element will go right at the end of the `<head>` section of the page.

Take note, though, that if you dynamically load JavaScript source files using this method, the JavaScript code contained in those files will not be available to your page until the external file has finished loading.

You would be well advised to have your program check that this is so before attempting to use the additional code.

Nearly all modern browsers implement an `onload` event when the script has downloaded. This works just like the `window.onload` event you've already met, but instead of firing when the main page has finished loading, it does so when the external resource (in this case a JavaScript source file) is fully downloaded and available for use:

```
src.onload = function() {
    ... things to do when new source code is downloaded ...
}
```

CAUTION

This won't work in older versions of Internet Explorer, but `onload` has been supported for script elements since IE8. To be sure, you may prefer to use object detection of the resources contained in your newly loaded file instead.

▼ TRY IT YOURSELF

A Dynamically Created Menu

In this exercise you're going to use the techniques learned in this and the previous hour to create page menus on the fly.

Our example HTML page has a top-level `<h1>` heading, followed by a number of short articles each consisting of an `<h2>` heading followed by some paragraphs of text. This is similar to a format you might see in a blog, a news page, or the output from an RSS reader, among other examples.

What you are going to do is employ DOM methods to automatically generate a menu at the page head, having links that allow the user to jump to any of the articles on the page. The HTML file is shown in Listing 9.5. Create your own HTML file based on this script. Feel free to use your own content for the headings and text, so long as the section titles are contained in `<h2>` elements.

LISTING 9.5   HTML File for Dynamic Menu Creation

```
<!DOCTYPE html>
<html>
<head>
    <meta charset="utf-8" />
```

```
    <title>Scripting the DOM</title>
    <script src="menu.js"></script>
    <script>window.onload = makeMenu;</script>
</head>
<body>
    <h1>The Extremadura Region of Western Spain</h1>
    <h2>Geography Of The Region</h2>
    <p>The autonomous community of Extremadura is in western Spain alongside the
Portuguese border. It borders the Spanish regions of Castilla y Leon, Castilla La
Mancha and Andalucía as well as Portugal (to the West). Covering over 40,000 square
kilometers it has two provinces: Cáceres in the North and Badajoz in the South.</p>
    <h2>Where To Stay</h2>
    <p>There is a wide range of accommodation throughout Extremadura including
small inns and guest houses ('Hostals') or think about renting a 'casa rural'
(country house)if you are traveling in a group.</p>
    <h2>Climate</h2>
    <p>Generally Mediterranean, except for the north, where it is continental.
Generally known for its extremes, including very hot and dry summers with frequent
droughts, and its long and mild winters.</p>
    <h2>What To See</h2>
    <p>Extremadura hosts major events all year round including theater, music,
cinema, literature and folklore. Spectacular venues include castles, medieval town
squares and historic centers. There are special summer theater festivals in the
Mérida, Cáceres, Alcántara and Alburquerque.</p>
    <h2>Gastronomy</h2>
    <p>The quality of Extremaduran food arises from the fine quality of the local
ingredients. In addition to free-range lamb and beef, fabulous cheeses, red and
white wines, olive oil, honey and paprika, Extremadura is particularly renowned for
Iberian ham. The 'pata negra' (blackfoot) pigs are fed on acorns in the cork-oak
forests, the key to producing the world's best ham and cured sausages. .</p>
</body>
</html>
```

The page is shown in Figure 9.7.

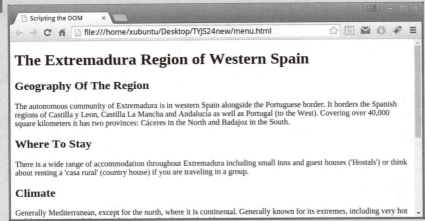

FIGURE 9.7
Page that is to have a dynamically created menu

The first thing to do is make a collection of all the `<h2>` elements from the page. These will form the items in your menu. For each of these headings make a link to an anchor element that you place right next to the corresponding `<h2>` element.

The menu links will be arranged as links in an unordered list (`<ul>`) element. This list will be placed in a `<div>` container that you insert at the page head.

First, get the collection of `<h2>` elements:

```
var h2s = document.getElementsByTagName("h2");
```

You need to create the `<div>` container to hold your menu; inside that `<div>`, there'll be a `<ul>` list element to contain the menu items:

```
var menu = document.createElement("div");
var menuUl = document.createElement("ul");
menu.appendChild(menuUl);
```

Now you can cycle through the collection of `<h2>` headings:

```
for(var i = 0; i < h2s.length; i++) {
    ... do things for each heading ...
}
```

For each heading you find in the document, you have a number of tasks to perform:

▶ Collect the content of the heading's child text node, which forms the text of the heading:

```
var itemText = h2s[i].childNodes[0].nodeValue;
```

▶ Create a new list item (`<li>`) element for the menu:

```
var menuLi = document.createElement("li");
```

▶ Add that `<li>` element to the menu:

```
menuUl.appendChild(menuLi);
```

▶ Each list item must contain a link to an anchor located next to the heading to which the menu item points:

```
var menuLiA = document.createElement("a");
menuLiA = menuLi.appendChild(menuLiA);
```

▶ Set an appropriate `href` attribute of the link (remember that variable `i` increments as you count through the headings in the array). These links will have the form

```
<a href="#itemX">[Title Text]</a>
```

where X is the index number of the menu item:

```
menuLiA.setAttribute("href", "#item" + i);
```

▶ Create a matching anchor element just before each `<h2>` heading. The anchor elements have the form

```
<a name="itemX">
```

so you need to add the `name` attribute, and locate the link just before the associated heading:

```
var anc = document.createElement("a");
anc.setAttribute("name", "item" + i);
document.body.insertBefore(anc, h2s[i]);
```

When all that has been completed for each `<h2>` heading, you can add your new menu to the page:

```
document.body.insertBefore(menu, document.body.firstChild);
```

The content of the JavaScript source file menu.js is shown in Listing 9.6. The code has been incorporated into a function named `makeMenu()` that is called by the `window.onload` event handler, building your menu as soon as the page has loaded and the DOM is therefore available.

LISTING 9.6   JavaScript Code for menu.js

```
function makeMenu() {
    // get all the H2 heading elements
    var h2s = document.getElementsByTagName("h2");
    // create a new page element for the menu
```

```
var menu = document.createElement("div");
// create a UL element and append to the menu div
var menuUl = document.createElement("ul");
menu.appendChild(menuUl);
// cycle through h2 headings
for(var i = 0; i < h2s.length; i++) {
    // get text node of h2 element
    var itemText = h2s[i].childNodes[0].nodeValue;
    // add a list item
    var menuLi = document.createElement("li");
    // add it to the menu list
    menuUl.appendChild(menuLi);
    // the list item contains a link
    var menuLiA = document.createElement("a");
    menuLiA = menuLi.appendChild(menuLiA);
    // set the href of the link
    menuLiA.setAttribute("href", "#item" + i);
    // set the text of the link
    var menuText = document.createTextNode(itemText);
    menuLiA.appendChild(menuText);
    // create matching anchor element
    var anc = document.createElement("a");
    anc.setAttribute("name", "item" + i);
    // add anchor before the heading
    document.body.insertBefore(anc, h2s[i]);
}
// add menu to the top of the page
document.body.insertBefore(menu, document.body.firstChild);
}
```

Figure 9.8 shows the script in action.

By examining the modified DOM using your browser tools, you can see the additional DOM elements added to the page to form the menu and the anchors. Figure 9.9 shows how this is displayed in Google Chromium's Developer Tools, highlighting the additional elements.

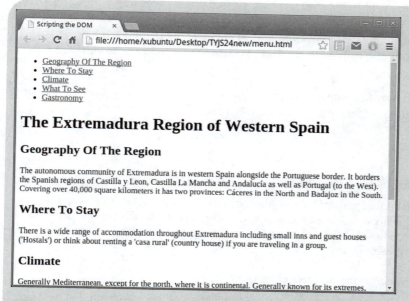

FIGURE 9.8
The automatic menu script in action

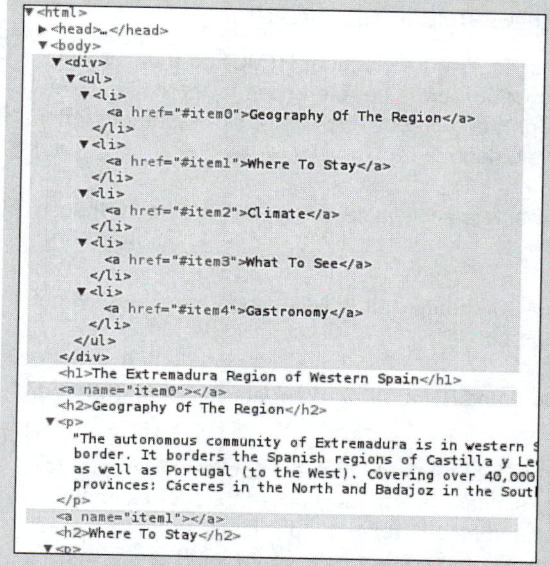

FIGURE 9.9
The additional DOM elements

Summary

In this hour you learned about DOM nodes and how to navigate the DOM using a variety of node-related methods. You also learned about using Mozilla's DOM Inspector to examine the DOM of your page.

In addition, you learned how to create new nodes to add to the DOM, and how to edit page content dynamically by adding, editing, and removing DOM nodes.

Q&A

Q. Is there a quick way to determine whether a node has any child nodes?

A. Yes, you can use the `hasChildNodes()` method. This method returns a Boolean value of `true` if the node has one or more child nodes, or `false` if not. Remember that attribute nodes and text nodes cannot have child nodes, so the method will always return false if applied to these types of node.

Q. Is Mozilla's DOM Inspector the only tool of its type?

A. Not at all. Just about every browser has some DOM inspection tools built into the developer tools. However, Mozilla's DOM Inspector gives a particularly clear view of the DOM hierarchy and the parameters of individual nodes; that's why I presented it here.

Q. Is it better to use the DOM to insert and retrieve HTML, or `innerHTML`?

A. Each has its advantages and disadvantages. To insert a chunk of HTML into a document, using `innerHTML` is quick and easy. However, it returns no references to the code you've inserted, so you can't carry out operations on that content very easily. DOM methods offer finer-grained control for manipulating page elements.

Wherever you use `innerHTML`, the same result is achievable using DOM methods, though usually with a little more code.

Remember, too, that `innerHTML` is not a W3C standard. It is well supported currently, but there's no guarantee that that will always be so.

Q. I've seen references on the Web to DOM Core and HTML DOM. What are these, and what are the differences between them?

A. The DOM Core describes a basic nucleus of DOM methods that are applicable not just to HTML pages, but also pages written in any similar markup language—XML, for example. HTML DOM is a larger collection of additional methods relating specifically to HTML pages. They do offer some shorthand ways of carrying out certain tasks, at the expense of making your code a little less portable to non-HTML applications.

The examples in this book generally use DOM Core methods to be more general. In Listing 9.6, for example, I used the statement

```
menuLiA.setAttribute("href", "#item" + i);
```

I could equally have used the HTML DOM statement

```
menuLiA.href = "#item" + i;
```

which is a little shorter.

Workshop

Try to answer all the questions before reading the subsequent "Answers" section.

Quiz

1. Which of the following is NOT a type of node?

   a. Element

   b. Attribute

   c. Array

2. The `getElementsByTagName()` method returns:

   a. An array-like collection of element objects

   b. An array-like collection of `nodeType` values

   c. An array-like collection of tag names

3. In some browsers the whitespace within a page element will cause the creation of

   a. A text node

   b. A JavaScript error

   c. An attribute node

4. To create a new `<span>` element, you could use

   a. `document.createElement("span");`

   b. `document.createElement(span);`

   c. `document.appendChild("span");`

5. To copy a node, including all of its child nodes, you could use

   a. `cloneNode(false);`

   b. `copyNode();`

   c. `cloneNode(true);`

6. To set the `alt` attribute of an `<img>` element to "Company Logo," you can use

   a. `setAttribute(alt, "Company Logo");`

   b. `setAttribute("alt", "Company Logo");`

   c. `setAttribute(alt = "Company Logo");`

Answers

1. c. An array is not a type of node.

2. a. An array-like collection of element objects is returned.

3. a. Whitespace within an element usually creates a text node as a child node of the element.

4. a. Use `document.createElement("span");`

5. c. Use `cloneNode(true);`

6. b. Use `setAttribute("alt", "Company Logo");`

Exercises

▶ Using the `nodeType` information listed in Table 9.1, write a function to find all the HTML comments in the body section of a page, and concatenate them into a single string. Add some comments to the code listed in Listing 9.2; then introduce and test your new function.

▶ If you have Firefox, download and install the DOM Inspector and familiarize yourself with its interface. Use the program to investigate the DOM of some of your favorite web pages.

▶ Having used the `insertBefore()` method, you might reasonably expect that there would be an `insertAfter()` method available. Unfortunately, that's not so. Can you write an `insertAfter()` function to do this task? Use similar arguments to `insertBefore()`; that is, `insertAfter(newNode, targetNode)`.

   (Hint: Use `insertBefore()` and the `nextSibling` property.)

▶ When you click on a menu item generated by the code in Listing 9.6, the page scrolls to the relevant item. To return to the menu, you have to manually scroll back up.

   Can you modify the script such that, as well as inserting an anchor, it inserts a Back to Top link before each H2 element? (Hint: You don't need to add a new link, just add an `href` and some link text to each anchor.)

Meet JSON

What You'll Learn in This Hour:

▶ What JSON is

▶ How to simulate associative arrays

▶ About JSON and objects

▶ Accessing JSON data

▶ Data serialization with JSON

▶ How to keep JSON secure

Earlier in the book you saw how to directly instantiate an object using the `new Object()` syntax. In this hour you learn about JavaScript Object Notation (JSON), which, as its name implies, offers another way to create object instances, and which can also act as a general-purpose data exchange syntax.

NOTE

The official home of JSON is at http://json.org/, which also has links to a wide variety of JSON resources on the Web.

What Is JSON?

JSON (pronounced "Jason") is a simple and compact notation for JavaScript objects. Once expressed in JSON, objects can easily be converted to strings to be stored and transmitted (across networks or between applications, for instance).

However, the real beauty of JSON is that an object expressed in JSON is really just expressed in normal JavaScript code. You therefore take advantage of "automatic" parsing in JavaScript; you can just have JavaScript interpret the contents of a JSON string as code, with no extra parsers or converters.

JSON Syntax

JSON data is expressed as a sequence of parameter and value pairs, each pair using a colon character to separate parameter from value. These `"parameter":"value"` pairs are themselves separated by commas:

```
"param1":"value1", "param2":"value2", "param3":"value3"
```

Finally, the whole sequence is enclosed between curly braces to form a JSON object representing your data:

```
var jsonObject = {
    "param1":"value1",
    "param2":"value2",
    "param3":"value3"
}
```

The object `jsonObject` defined here uses a subset of standard JavaScript notation—it's just a little piece of valid JavaScript code.

Objects written using JSON notation can have properties and methods accessed directly using the usual dot notation:

```
alert(jsonObject.param1); // alerts 'value1'
```

More generally, though, JSON is a general-purpose syntax for exchanging data in a string format. Not only objects, but ANY data that can be expressed as a series of `parameter:value` pairs can be expressed in JSON notation. It is then easy to convert the JSON object into a string by a process known as serialization; serialized data is convenient for storage or transmission around networks. You'll see how to serialize a JSON object later in this hour.

NOTE

As a general-purpose data exchange syntax, JSON can be used somewhat like XML, though JSON can be simpler for humans to read. Also, the parsing of large XML files can be a slow process, whereas JSON gives your script a JavaScript object, ready to use.

JSON has gathered momentum recently because it offers several important advantages. JSON is

- ▶ Easy to read for both people and computers

- ▶ Simple in concept—a JSON object is nothing more than a series of `parameter:value` pairs enclosed by curly braces

- ▶ Largely self-documenting

- ▶ Fast to create and parse

▶ A subset of JavaScript, meaning that no special interpreters or other additional packages are necessary

A number of leading online services and APIs including Flickr, Twitter, and several services from Google and Yahoo! now offer data encoded using JSON notation.

NOTE

See http://www.flickr.com/services/api/response.json.html for details of how Flickr supports JSON.

Accessing JSON Data

To recover the data encoded into the JSON string, you need to somehow convert the string back to JavaScript code. This is usually referred to as *deserializing* the string.

Using `eval()`

Only more recent browsers have native support for JSON syntax (we talk about using native browser support in just a moment). However, since JSON syntax is a subset of JavaScript, the JavaScript function `eval()` can be used to convert a JSON string into a JavaScript object.

NOTE

The JavaScript `eval()` function evaluates or executes whatever is passed as an argument. If the argument is an expression, `eval()` evaluates the expression; for example,

```
var x = eval(4 * 3); // x=12
```

If the argument comprises one or more JavaScript statements, `eval()` executes those statements:

```
eval("a=1; b=2; document.write(a+b);"); // writes 3 to the page
```

The `eval()` function uses the JavaScript interpreter to parse the JSON text and produce a JavaScript object:

```
var myObject = eval ('(' + jsonObjectString + ')');
```

You can then use the JavaScript object in your script:

```
var user = '{"username" : "philb1234","location" : "Spain","height" : 1.80}';
var myObject = eval ('(' + user + ')');
alert(myObject.username);
```

CAUTION

The string must be enclosed in parentheses like this to avoid falling foul of an ambiguity in the JavaScript syntax.

Using Native Browser Support

All recent browsers offer native support for JSON, making the use of `eval()` unnecessary.

NOTE

Browsers natively supporting JSON include

▶ Firefox (Mozilla) 3.5+

▶ Internet Explorer 8+

▶ Google Chrome

▶ Opera 10+

▶ Safari 4+

Browsers with native JSON support create a JavaScript object called `JSON` to manage JSON encoding and decoding. The `JSON` object has two methods, `stringify()` and `parse()`.

JSON.parse()

You can interpret a JSON string using the method `JSON.parse()`, which takes a string containing a JSON-serialized object and breaks it up, creating an object with properties corresponding to the `"parameter":"value"` pairs found in the string:

```
var Mary = '{ "height":1.9, "age":36, "eyeColor":"brown" }';
var myObject = JSON.parse(Mary);
var out = "";
for (i in myObject) {
    out += i + " = " + myObject[i] + "\n";
}
alert(out);
```

You can see the result in Figure 10.1.

FIGURE 10.1
Using `JSON.parse()`

Data Serialization with JSON

In the context of data storage and transmission, *serialization* is the name given to the process of converting data into a format that can be stored or transmitted across a network and recovered later into the same format as the original.

In the case of JSON, a string is the chosen format of the serialized data. To serialize your JSON object (for instance, to send it across a network connection), you need to express it as a string.

In later browsers, those having JSON support, you can simply use the `JSON.stringify()` method.

JSON.stringify()

You can create a JSON-encoded string of an object using the `JSON.stringify()` method.

Let's create a simple object and add some properties:

```
var Dan = new Object();
Dan.height = 1.85;
Dan.age = 41;
Dan.eyeColor = "blue";
```

Now you can serialize the object using `JSON.stringify`:

```
alert( JSON.stringify(Dan) );
```

The serialized object is shown in Figure 10.2.

FIGURE 10.2
Using `JSON.stringify()`

TRY IT YOURSELF ▼

Parsing a JSON String

Create an HTML file using your editor, and enter the code of Listing 10.1.

LISTING 10.1   Parsing a JSON String

```
<!DOCTYPE html>
<html>
<head>
    <title>Parsing JSON</title>
    <script>
        function jsonParse() {
            var inString = prompt("Enter JSON object");
            var out = "";
            myObject = JSON.parse(inString);
            for (i in myObject) {
                out += "Property: " + i + " = " + myObject[i] + '\n';
            }
            alert(out);
        }
    </script>
</head>
<body onload="jsonParse()">
</body>
</html>
```

The function `jsonParse()` is called when the page finishes loading, by using the `onload` event handler of the `window` object attached to the `<body>` element of the page.

The first line of code inside the function invites you to enter a string corresponding to a JSON object:

```
var inString = prompt("Enter JSON object");
```

Type it carefully, remembering to enclose any strings in quotation marks, as in Figure 10.3.

FIGURE 10.3
Entering a JSON string

The script then declares an empty string variable called `out`, which later holds the output message:

```
var out = "";
```

The `JSON.parse()` method is then used to create an object based on the input string:

```
myObject = JSON.parse(inString);
```

You can now build your output message string by looping around the object methods:

```
for (i in myObject) {
    out += "Property: " + i + " = " + myObject[i] + '\n';
}
```

Finally, display the result:

```
alert(out);
```

The output message should look like the one in Figure 10.4.

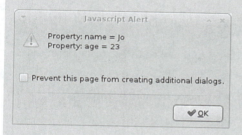

FIGURE 10.4
The object created by parsing a JSON string

Reload the page and retry the script with a different number of `"parameter":"value"` pairs.

JSON Data Types

The parameter part of each `parameter:value` pair must follow a few simple grammatical rules:

- ▶ It must not be a JavaScript reserved keyword.
- ▶ It must not start with a number.
- ▶ It must not include any special characters except the underscore or dollar sign.

The values in JSON objects can contain any of the following data types:

- ▶ Number
- ▶ String

▶ Boolean

▶ Array

▶ Object

▶ null (empty)

CAUTION

JavaScript syntax has several data types that are not included in the JSON standard, including Date, Error, Math, and Function. These data types must be represented as some other data format, with the encoding and decoding programs following the same encoding and decoding rules.

Simulating Associative Arrays

In Hour 6, "Arrays," we discussed the JavaScript array object and looked at its various properties and methods.

You may recall that the elements in JavaScript arrays have unique numeric identifiers:

```
var myArray = [];
myArray[0] = 'Monday';
myArray[1] = 'Tuesday';
myArray[2] = 'Wednesday';
```

In many other programming languages, you can use textual keys to make the arrays more descriptive:

```
myArray["startDay"] = "Monday";
```

Unfortunately, JavaScript does not directly support such so-called *associative* arrays.

However, using objects it is easy to go some way toward simulating their behavior. Using JSON notation makes the code easy to read and understand:

```
var conference = { "startDay" : "Monday",
    "nextDay"  : "Tuesday",
    "endDay"   : "Wednesday"
}
```

You can now access the object properties as if the object were an associative array:

```
alert(conference["startDay"]);  // outputs "Monday"
```

This works because the two syntaxes

```
object["property"]
```

and

```
object.property
```

are equivalent in JavaScript.

Remember that this is not really an associative array, although it looks like one. If you loop through the object, you will get, in addition to these three properties, any methods that have been assigned to the object.

Creating Objects with JSON

You might recall from Hour 6 that one convenient way to express an array is with square brackets:

```
var categories = ["news", "sport", "films", "music", "comedy"];
```

JSON provides us with a somewhat similar shorthand for defining JavaScript objects.

Although it was developed for describing JavaScript objects, JSON is independent of any language or platform. JSON libraries and tools exist for many programming languages, including Java, PHP, C, and others.

Properties

As you've already seen, to express an object in JSON notation, you enclose the object in curly braces, rather than square ones, and list object properties as `"property":"value"` pairs:

```
var user = {
    "username" : "philb1234",
    "location" : "Spain",
    "height" : 1.80
}
```

You may recall that using the statement

```
var myObject = new Object();
```

creates an "empty" instance of an object with no properties or methods. The equivalent in JSON notation, unsurprisingly, is

```
var myObject = {};
```

The object properties are immediately available to access in the usual fashion:

```
var name = user.username; //  variable 'name' contains 'philb1234'
```

Methods

You can add methods this way too, by using anonymous functions within the object definition:

```
var user = {
    "username" : "philb1234",
    "location" : "Spain",
    "height" : 1.80,
    "setName":function(newName){
        this.username=newName;
    }
}
```

Then you can call the `setName` method in the usual way:

```
var newname = prompt("Enter a new username:");
user.setName(newname);
```

While adding methods in this manner works fine in a JavaScript context, it is not permitted when using JSON as a general-purpose data interchange format. Functions declared this way will not be parsed correctly in a browser using native JSON parsing, though `eval()` will work. However, if you simply need to instantiate objects for use within your own script, you can add methods this way.

See the following section on JSON security.

Arrays

Property values themselves can be JavaScript arrays:

```
var bookListObject = {
    "booklist": ["Foundation",
            "Dune",
```

```
        "Eon",
        "2001 A Space Odyssey",
        "Stranger In A Strange Land"]
}
```

In the preceding example, the object has a property named `booklist`, the value of which is an array. You can access the individual items in the array by passing the required array key (remember that the array keys begin at zero):

```
var book = bookListObject.booklist[2]; // variable book has value "Eon"
```

The preceding line of code assigns to the variable `book` the second item in the `booklist` array object, which is a property of the object named `bookListObject`.

Objects

The JSON object can even incorporate other *objects*. By making the array elements themselves JSON encoded objects, you can access them using dot notation.

In the following example code, the value associated with the property `booklist` is an array of JSON objects. Each JSON object has two `"parameter":"value"` pairs, holding the title and author respectively of the book in question.

After retrieving the array of books, as in the previous example, it is easy to then access the `title` and `author` properties:

```
var bookListObject = {
    "booklist": [{"title":"Foundation", "author":"Isaac Asimov"},
        {"title":"Dune", "author":"Frank Herbert"},
        {"title":"Eon", "author":"Greg Bear"},
        {"title":"2001 A Space Odyssey", "author":"Arthur C. Clarke"},
        {"title":"Stranger In A Strange Land", "author":"Robert A. Heinlein"}]
}
    //show the author of the third book
    alert(bookListObject.booklist[2].author); // displays "Greg Bear"
```

TRY IT YOURSELF ▼

Manipulating JSON Objects

Let's take the previous JSON object `bookListObject` and construct a user message that lists the books and authors in an easily read format. Create an HTML file and enter the code from Listing 10.2. Your JSON object is identical to the one in the previous example, but this time you're going to access the array of books, and step through it with a loop, building a message string by appending the books and authors as you go. Finally you'll display the book information to the user.

▼ **LISTING 10.2**   Handling JSON Multilevel Objects

```
<!DOCTYPE html>
<html>
<head>
    <title>Understanding JSON</title>
    <script>
    var booklistObject = {
        "booklist": [{"title":"Foundation", "author":"Isaac Asimov"},
            {"title":"Dune", "author":"Frank Herbert"},
            {"title":"Eon", "author":"Greg Bear"},
            {"title":"2001 A Space Odyssey", "author":"Arthur C. Clarke"},
            {"title":"Stranger In A Strange Land", "author":"Robert A. Heinlein"}]
    }

        // a variable to hold our user message
        var out = "";

        // get the array
        var books = booklistObject.booklist;

        //Loop through array, getting the books one by one
        for(var i =0; i<books.length;i++) {
            var booknumber = i+1;
            out += "Book "   + booknumber +
                " is: '" + books[i].title +
                "' by " + books[i].author +
                "\n";
        }
    </script>
</head>
<body onload="alert(out)">
</body>
</html>
```

After designing the JSON object, you declare a variable and assign an empty string. This variable will hold the output message as you build it:

```
var out = "";
```

Now you extract the array of books, assigning this array to a new variable, books, to avoid a lot of long-winded typing later:

```
var books = booklistString.booklist;
```

Afterward, you simply need to loop through the books array, reading the `title` and `author` properties of each book object, and constructing a string to append to your output message:

```
for(var i =0; i<books.length;i++) {
    var booknumber = i+1; // array keys start at zero!
    out += "Book "  + booknumber +
        " is: '" + books[i].title +
        "' by " + books[i].author +
        "\n";
}
```

Finally, show your message to the user:

```
alert(out);
```

The result of running this script is shown in Figure 10.5.

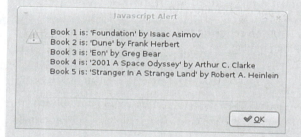

FIGURE 10.5
Your book information is displayed to the user

JSON Security

Using JavaScript's `eval()` function can execute any JavaScript command. This could represent a potential security problem, especially when working with JSON data from untrusted sources.

It is safer to use a browser with a native JSON parser to convert a JSON string into a JavaScript object. A JSON parser will recognize only JSON text and will not execute script commands. Native JSON parsers are generally faster than using `eval()`, too.

Native JSON support is implemented in the newer browsers and in the latest ECMAScript (JavaScript) standard.

Summary

In this hour you learned about JSON notation, a simple data interchange syntax that can also be used to create instances of JavaScript objects.

You learned how to use the native JSON support of modern browsers to serialize objects into JSON strings, and parse JSON strings into JavaScript objects.

Q&A

Q. Where can I read the official JSON documentation?

A. The JSON syntax is formally described in RFC 4627. You can read it at http://www.ietf.org/rfc/rfc4627. There is also a good deal of information at the official home of JSON, http://json.org/.

Q. How can I find out whether my browser supports JSON natively?

A. You can check for the existence of the JSON object using the `typeof` operator, as described in Hour 8, "Object-Oriented Programming."

```
if(typeof JSON == 'object') {
    // you have JSON support, go ahead!
} else {
    // find another way to work, e.g. using eval()
}
```

Of course, you must be sure that your script hasn't defined its own object called JSON, or this won't work as expected.

Workshop

Try to answer all the questions before reading the subsequent "Answers" section.

Quiz

1. JSON is an acronym standing for

    a. JavaScript Object Notation

    b. Java String Object Notation

    c. JavaScript Serial Object Notation

2. Which of these can you do with JSON?

    a. Create a constructor function.

    b. Parse XML data.

    c. Directly instantiate an object.

3. What character is normally used to enclose the series of parameter:value pairs in a JSON object?

    a. Curly braces, `{}`

    b. Square braces, `[]`

    c. Parentheses, `()`

Answers

1. a. JavaScript Object Notation

2. c. Directly instantiate an object

3. a. Curly braces, `{}`

Exercises

▶ Load your file containing Listing 10.1 back into your browser. Try entering some JSON strings using arrays as property values, for example:

```
{"days":["Mon","Tue","Wed"] }
```

How does the program react? Is its behavior as you would expect?

▶ Instantiate an object using the `new Object()` syntax you learned in Hour 8, and add some properties with values of type array. Use the `stringify()` method to turn the object into a JSON string and display it.

HOUR 11
JavaScript and HTML5

What You'll Learn in This Hour:

▶ About the new HTML5 markup tags

▶ How to handle video and audio

▶ Using the `<canvas>` element

▶ Drag and drop in HTML5

▶ Working with local storage

▶ How to interface with the local file system

The previous version of HTML, HTML 4.01, has been around since 1999.

The XML-based version of HTML, XHTML, had been the subject of various recent W3C efforts, the latest having been moves toward XHTML2. In 2009 the W3C announced that XHTML2 was to be dumped in favor of diverting resources to a new version of HTML, HTML5.

TIP

Note how it's written: HTML5. There's no space between the L and the 5.

This latest incarnation of HTML concentrates on developing HTML as a front end for web applications, extending the markup language via semantically rich elements, introducing some new attributes, and adding the possibility to use brand-new APIs in conjunction with JavaScript.

The HTML5 standard was finalized as the new standard for HTML in the fall of 2014, and the major browsers already support many of the new HTML5 elements and APIs.

In this hour, you learn how to control some of these powerful new features with JavaScript.

New Markup for HTML5

Even HTML pages that are well-formed are more difficult to read and interpret than they could be, because the markup contains very little semantic information.

Page sections such as sidebars, headers and footers, and navigation elements are all contained in general-purpose page elements such as divs, and only identifiable by the ID and class names invented by the page's developer.

HTML5 adds new elements to more easily identify each of these, and more, types of content. Some of the new tags are listed in Table 11.1.

TABLE 11.1   Some New HTML5 Tags

Tag	Description
`<section>`	Used to define sections of pages
`<header>`	The header of a page
`<footer>`	The footer of a page
`<nav>`	The navigation on a page
`<article>`	The article or primary content on a page
`<aside>`	Extra content, such as a sidebar on a page
`<figure>`	Images that annotate an article
`<figcaption>`	A caption for a `<figure>` element
`<summary>`	A visible heading for a `<details>` element

Some Important New Elements

While HTML5 introduces a wide variety of interesting new capabilities, this section concentrates on the new tags that help ease some long-standing difficulties.

Video Playback with `<video>`

Video on the Web is extremely popular. However, the methods for implementing video are generally proprietary, reproduction happening via plug-ins such as Flash, Windows Media, and Apple QuickTime. Markup that works for embedding these elements in one browser doesn't always work in the others.

HTML5 contains a new `<video>` element, the aim of which is to enable the embedding of any and all video formats.

Using the new `<video>` tag, you can implement your favorite QuickTime movie like this:

```
<video src="video.mov" />
```

So far there has been much debate about which video formats (codecs) should be supported by the video element; at the time of writing, the search continues for a codec that requires no special licensing terms, though WebM (http://www.webmproject.org/) is currently looking like the favorite. For the time being, quoting multiple sources gets around the problem and avoids the need for browser sniffing; there are currently three widely supported video formats—MP4, WebM, and Ogg.

```
<video id="vid1" width="400" height="300" controls="controls">
    <source src="movie.mp4" type="video/mp4" />
    <source src="movie.ogg" type="video/ogg" />
    <source src="movie.webm" type="video/webm" />
    <p>Video tag not supported.</p>
</video>
```

It is also a good practice to include width and height attributes for the `<video>` element. If height and width are not set, the browser doesn't know how much screen space to reserve, resulting in the page layout changing as the video loads.

You are also recommended to place some suitable text between the `<video>` and `</video>` tags to display in browsers that don't support the `<video>` tag.

Some important properties of the `<video>` tag are listed in Table 11.2.

TABLE 11.2   Some Attributes of the `<video>` Element

Attribute	Description
`loop`	Play in a loop
`autoplay`	Start video on load
`controls`	Display playback controls for playback (how they look is browser dependent)
`ended`	Boolean `true` if playback has finished (read-only)
`paused`	Boolean `true` if playback is paused (read-only)
`poster`	An optional image that will be displayed while the movie is loading
`volume`	Audio volume from 0 (silent) to 1 (maximum)

Note that the appearance of the controls added using the `controls` property will depend on the browser in use, as shown in Figure 11.1.

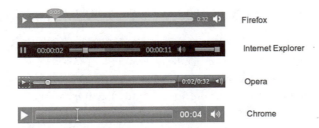

Firefox

Internet Explorer

Opera

Chrome

FIGURE 11.1
The appearance of controls varies between browsers

You can access these properties in the same way as any other JavaScript or DOM object. For the previous video definition, you might use

```
var myVideo = document.getElementById("vid1").volume += 0.1;
```

to marginally increase the volume, or

```
if(document.getElementById("vid1").paused) {
    alert(message);
}
```

to pass a message to the user indicating that video playback is currently paused.

Testing Format Support with `canPlayType()`

You can check for support for a particular codec using the JavaScript method

```
media.canPlayType(type)
```

In the preceding example, `type` is a string containing the media type, for example, "video/ webm". This method must return an empty string if the browser knows it cannot play the content. The method might also return "probably" if the browser is confident it can support the format, or "maybe" otherwise.

Controlling Playback

Playback can also be controlled programmatically using the `pause()` and `play()` commands, as in the following code snippet:

```
var myVideo = document.getElementById("vid1").play();
var myVideo = document.getElementById("vid1").pause();
```

Playing Sound with the `<audio>` Tag

Pretty much everything stated previously about the `<video>` tag applies equally well to the `<audio>` tag. The simple way to use the `<audio>` tag is like this:

```
<audio src="song.mp3"></audio>
```

You can add further attributes to achieve more control over playback, such as `loop` and `autoplay`:

```
<audio src="song.mp3" autoplay loop></audio>
```

TIP

Don't abuse `loop` and `autoplay`, or you may find that many of your site visitors don't return!

As with the earlier examples for video files, you can include alternative formats to help ensure that a user's browser will find one that it can play, as in the following code:

```
<audio controls="controls">
    <source src="song.ogg" type="audio/ogg" />
    <source src="song.mp3" type="audio/mpeg" />
    Your browser does not support the audio element.
</audio>
```

MP3, WAV, and Ogg are typically supported file formats for the `<audio>` element. Controlling an audio file in JavaScript uses the same methods as for the `<video>` tag.

To add and play an audio file via JavaScript, you can treat it just like any other JavaScript or DOM object:

```
var soundElement = document.createElement('audio');
soundElement.setAttribute('src', 'sound.ogg');
soundElement.play();
soundElement.pause();
```

The `<audio>` and `<video>` tags have many useful properties that you can access via JavaScript. Here are a few useful ones, the meaning of which will be immediately apparent:

```
mediaElement.duration
mediaElement.currentTime
mediaElement.playbackRate
mediaElement.muted
```

For example, to move to a point 45 seconds into a song you might use

```
soundElement.currentTime = 45;
```

Drawing on the Page with `<canvas>`

The new `<canvas>` tag gives you just that: a rectangular space in your page where you can draw shapes and graphics, as well as load and display image files and control their display via JavaScript. The many practical uses for the element include dynamic charts, JavaScript/HTML games, and instructional animations.

Using the `<canvas>` tag simply allows you to define a region by setting its `width` and `height` parameters; everything else related to creating the graphical content is done via JavaScript. There is an extensive set of drawing methods known as the Canvas 2D API.

▼ TRY IT YOURSELF

Moving a Ball Using `<canvas>`

You're going to make a simple animation in a `<canvas>` element—just a red disc (to represent a ball) moving in a circle on the page.

The only HTML markup required in the body of the page is the `<canvas>` element itself:

```
<canvas id="canvas1" width="400" height="300"></canvas>
```

All the drawing and animation will be done in JavaScript.

TIP

If you don't set `width` and `height` parameters, the canvas defaults to 300 pixels wide by 150 pixels high.

You first need to specify the *rendering context*. At the time of writing, 2D is the only widely supported context, though a 3D context is under development.

```
context = canvas1.getContext('2d');
```

The only primitive shapes supported by `<canvas>` are rectangles:

```
fillRect(x,y,width,height);        //draw a filled rectangle
strokeRect(x,y,width,height);      //draw an outlined rectangle
clearRect(x,y,width,height);       // clear the rectangle
```

All other shapes must be created by using one or more path-drawing functions. Since you want to draw a colored disc, that's what you need here.

Several different path-drawing functions are offered by `<canvas>`.

Move to x, y without drawing anything:

```
moveTo(x, y)
```

Draw a line from the current location to x, y:

```
lineTo(x, y)
```

Draw a circular arc of radius r, having circle center x, y, from `startAngle` to `endAngle`.

```
arc(x, y, r, startAngle, endAngle, anti)
```

Setting the last parameter to Boolean `true` makes the arc draw counterclockwise instead of the default clockwise.

To create shapes using these basic commands, you need some additional methods:

```
object.beginPath();
object.closePath();          //complete a partial shape
object.stroke();             //draw an outlined shape
object.fill();               //draw a filled shape
```

TIP
_____

If you use the `fill` method, an open shape will be closed automatically without you having to use `closePath()`.
_____

To make the ball you're going to generate a filled circle. Let's make it red, of radius 15, and centered on canvas coordinates 50, 50:

```
context.beginPath();
context.fillStyle="#ff0000";
context.arc(50, 50, 15, 0, Math.PI*2, true);
context.closePath();
```

To animate the ball, you need to alter the x and y coordinates of the ball center using a timer. Take a look at the `animate()` function:

```
function animate() {
    context.clearRect(0,0, 400,300);
    counter++;
    x += 20 * Math.sin(counter);
    y += 20 * Math.cos(counter);
    paint();
}
```

This function is called repeatedly via the `setInterval()` method. Each time it's called, the canvas is cleared by using the `clearRect()` method across the full size of the canvas element. The variable counter is incremented on each loop, and its new value is then used to redefine the position of the disc's center.

The complete code is listed in Listing 11.1.

LISTING 11.1 Moving a Ball Using `<canvas>`

```
<!DOCTYPE HTML>
<html>
<head>
    <title>HTML5 canvas</title>
<script>
    var context;
    var x=50;
    var y=50;
    var counter = 0;
    function paint()    {
        context.beginPath();
        context.fillStyle="#ff0000";
        context.arc(x, y, 15, 0, Math.PI*2, false);
        context.closePath();
        context.fill();
    }
    function animate() {
        context.clearRect(0,0, 400,300);
        counter++;
        x += 20 * Math.sin(counter);
        y += 20 * Math.cos(counter);
        paint();
    }
    window.onload = function() {
        context= canvas1.getContext('2d');
        setInterval(animate, 100);
    }
</script>
</head>
<body>
    <canvas id="canvas1" width="400" height="300">
        <p>Your browser doesn't support the canvas element.</p>
    </canvas>
</body>
</html>
```

Create this file and load it into your browser. If your browser supports the `<canvas>` element, you should see a red disc following a circular route on the page, as in Figure 11.2.

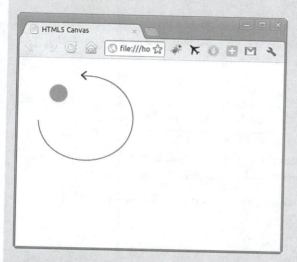

FIGURE 11.2
An animation using `<canvas>`

Drag and Drop

Drag and drop is a part of the HTML5 standard. Just about any element can be made draggable.

To make an element draggable, all that's required is to set its `draggable` attribute to true:

```
<img draggable="true" />
```

Dragging something, though, isn't much use by itself. To employ a draggable object to achieve something useful, you're probably going to want to be able to drop it somewhere.

To define where an object can be dropped, and control the dragging and dropping process, you need to write event listeners to detect and control the various parts of the drag-and-drop process.

There are a few different events you can utilize to control your drag and drop:

▶ `dragstart`

▶ `drag`

▶ `dragenter`

▶ `dragleave`

▶ dragover

▶ drop

▶ dragend

To control your drag and drop, you need to define a source element (where the drag starts), the data payload (what it is you're dragging), and a drop target (an area to catch the dropped item).

TIP

Not all items can be drop targets—an `<img>`, for example, cannot accept drops.

The `dataTransfer` property contains a piece of data sent in a drag action. The value of `dataTransfer` is usually set in the `dragstart` event and read/handled in the `drop` event.

Calling `setData(format, data)` or `getData(format, data)` will (respectively) set or read this piece of data.

▼ TRY IT YOURSELF

Drag and Drop in HTML5

You're going to build a demonstrator for the HTML5 drag-and-drop interface.

Fire up your editor and create a file containing the code listed in Listing 11.2.

LISTING 11.2   HTML5 Drag and Drop

```
<!DOCTYPE HTML>
<html>
<head>
    <title>HTML5 Drag and Drop</title>
    <style>
        body {background-color: #ddd; font-family: arial, verdana, sans-serif;}
        #drop1 {width: 200px;height: 200px;border: 1px solid black;background-
        ➥color:white}
        #drag1 {width: 50px;height: 50px;}
    </style>
    <script>
        function allowDrop(ev) {
            ev.preventDefault();
        }

        function drag(ev) {
```

```
                ev.dataTransfer.setData("Text",ev.target.id);
        }

        function drop(ev) {
            var data = ev.dataTransfer.getData("Text");
            ev.target.appendChild(document.getElementById(data));
            ev.preventDefault();
        }

        window.onload = function() {
            var dragged = document.getElementById("drag1");
            var drophere = document.getElementById("drop1");
            dragged.ondragstart = drag;
            drophere.ondragover = allowDrop;
            drophere.ondrop = drop;
        }
    </script>
</head>
<body>
    <div id="drop1" ></div>
    <p>Drag the image below into the box above:</p>
    <img id="drag1" src="drag.gif" draggable="true" />
</body>
</html>
```

To get the party started, you define a couple of HTML elements on your page. The `<div>` element with ID of `drop1` is the target area for catching the drop, and the image with ID of `drag1` is to become your draggable item.

Three important functions are defined in the code. Each of these functions is passed the current event to process. Behind the scenes, `ev.target` changes automatically for each type of event, depending on where you are in the drag-and-drop process:

▶ A function named `drag(ev)` is executed when the drag starts. This function sets the value of the `dataTransfer` property for the drag to the ID of the dragged object:

```
function drag(ev) {
    ev.dataTransfer.setData("Text",ev.target.id);
}
```

▶ Another function named `allowDrop(ev)` is executed when the drag passes over the intended drop area. All that this function must achieve is to prevent the drop area's default behavior from taking place (as the default behavior prevents dropping):

```
function allowDrop(ev) {
    ev.preventDefault();
}
```

▶ Finally, a function named `drop(ev)` is executed when the dragged item is dropped. In this function, the value of the `dataTransfer` property is read to determine the ID of the dragged object; then that object is appended as a child object to the drop area object. Once again, the default operation needs to be prevented from taking place:

```
function drop(ev) {
    var data = ev.dataTransfer.getData("Text");
    ev.target.appendChild(document.getElementById(data));
    ev.preventDefault();
}
```

The loaded page should look something like the one shown in Figure 11.3; dragging the small image and dropping it over the white drop area, you should see it "dock" into the `<div>` element, as shown in the figure.

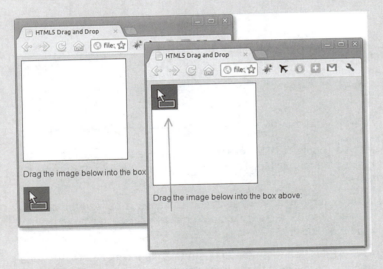

FIGURE 11.3
HTML5 drag and drop

Local Storage

HTML5 pages can store even large amounts of data within the user's browser, without any negative effect on the website's performance. Web storage is more secure and faster than doing this via cookies. Like when using cookies, the data is stored in key/value pairs, and a web page can only access the data it has itself stored.

The two new objects for storing data locally in the browser are

- ▶ `localStorage`—Stores data with no expiration date

- ▶ `sessionStorage`—Stores data just for the current session

If you're unsure about your browser's support for local storage, once again you can use feature detection:

```
if(typeof(Storage)!=="undefined") {
    ... both objects are available ...
}
```

To store a value you can invoke the `setItem` method, passing to it a key and a value:

```
localStorage.setItem("key", "value");
```

Alternatively, you can use the `localStorage` object like an associative array:

```
localStorage["key"] = "value";
```

Retrieving the values can use either of these methods too:

```
alert(localStorage.getItem("key"));
```

or

```
alert(localStorage["key"]);
```

Working with Local Files

At last HTML provides a standard way to interact with the user's local files, using HTML5's File API specification. There are several ways to access external files:

- ▶ `File` provides information including name, size, and MIME type, and gives a reference to the file handle.

- ▶ `FileList` is an array-like sequence of `File` objects.

- ▶ The `FileReader` interface uses `File` and `FileList` to asynchronously read a file. You can check on read progress, catch any errors, and find out when a file is completely loaded.

Checking for Browser Support

Once more, you can check whether your browser supports the File API by the usual feature-detection method:

```
if (window.File && window.FileReader && window.FileList) {
    // we're good
}
```

Interacting with the Local File System

In this example you're going to modify the previous drag-and-drop example to allow a list of files to be dragged into a web page from the local file system. To do so, you're going to use the `FileList` data structure.

Take a look at the modified `drop(ev)` function:

```
function drop(ev) {
        var files = ev.dataTransfer.files;
        for (var i = 0; i < files.length; i++) {
            var f = files[i];
            var pnode = document.createElement("p");
            var tnode = document.createTextNode(f.name + " (" + f.type + ") " +
            ➥f.size + " bytes");
            pnode.appendChild(tnode);
            ev.target.appendChild(pnode);
        }
        ev.preventDefault();
    }
```

Here, the array-like `FileList` containing information about the dragged files is extracted from the `dataTransfer` object:

```
var files = ev.dataTransfer.files;
```

Then, each file is processed in turn by iterating through them individually:

```
for (var i = 0; i < files.length; i++) {
    var f = files[i];
    ...statements to process each file ...
}
```

The complete listing is shown in Listing 11.3.

LISTING 11.3   Interacting with the Local File System

```html
<!DOCTYPE HTML>
<html>
<head>
    <title>HTML5 Local Files</title>
    <style>
        body {background-color: #ddd; font-family: arial, verdana, sans-serif;}
        #drop1 {
            width: 400px;
            height: 200px;
            border: 1px solid black;
            background-color: white;
            padding: 10px;
        }
    </style>
    <script>
        function allowDrop(ev) {
            ev.preventDefault();
        }

        function drop(ev) {
            var files = ev.dataTransfer.files;
            for (var i = 0; i < files.length; i++) {
                var f = files[i]
                var pnode = document.createElement("p");
                var tnode = document.createTextNode(f.name
                ➥+ " (" + f.type + ") " + f.size + " bytes");
                pnode.appendChild(tnode);
                ev.target.appendChild(pnode);
            }
            ev.preventDefault();
        }

        window.onload = function() {
            var drophere = document.getElementById("drop1");
            drophere.ondragover = allowDrop;
            drophere.ondrop = drop;
        }
    </script>
</head>
<body>
    <div id="drop1" ></div>
</body>
</html>
```

After creating this file in your editor and loading the resulting page into the browser, you should be able to drag files into the drop area from your local system, and see filename, MIME type, and size listed, as shown in Figure 11.4.

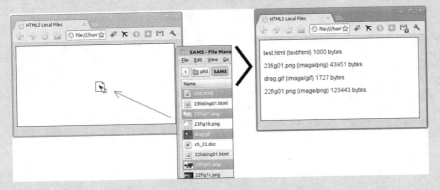

FIGURE 11.4
Interfacing with local files

Summary

HTML5 offers a whole array of new facilities to HTML, enabling the markup language to be used as a much better basis for web applications and allowing JavaScript to exploit some brand-new APIs.

In this hour, you had a whistle-stop tour of these new capabilities, including some hands-on coding experience using some of these new APIs.

Q&A

Q. **What is the best way for me to learn HTML5?**

A. Learn HTML5 by using it. Jump right in and start building pages using HTML5 features. Use the semantic tags; try video and audio playback; play with drag and drop, and the file API; and build animations using `<canvas>`. When you have questions, many Internet-based tutorials, blogs, and code examples are available.

Q. **Are there already real live sites using HTML5?**

A. Sure, lots of them. Take a look at http://html5gallery.com/ for some examples.

Workshop

Try to answer all the questions before reading the subsequent "Answers" section.

Quiz

1. Which of the following is NOT a valid HTML5 semantic element?

   a. `<header>`

   b. `<sidebar>`

   c. `<nav>`

2. Which of the following is NOT a valid method for `<audio>` and `<video>` elements?

   a. `play()`

   b. `pause()`

   c. `stop()`

3. Which of the following is NOT a standard drag-and-drop event?

   a. `drag`

   b. `dragover`

   c. `dragout`

Answers

1. b. `<sidebar>` is not a valid HTML5 element.

2. c. There is no `stop()` method.

3. c. There is no `dragout` event; use `dragleave`.

Exercises

▶ Review some of the examples of previous hours, and try to rewrite them using some of the new HTML5 interfaces.

▶ HTML5 is pretty new at the time of writing. Check out the current state of browser support for the various aspects of HTML5 at http://caniuse.com/ or http://html5readiness.com/.

HOUR 12

JavaScript and CSS

What You'll Learn in This Hour:

► Separating style from content
► The DOM style property
► Retrieving styles
► Setting styles
► Accessing classes using `className`
► The DOM `styleSheet` object
► Enabling, disabling, and switching stylesheets in JavaScript
► Changing the mouse cursor

In the early days of the World Wide Web, pages were all about their text content. Early browsers had rudimentary support for graphic effects—some didn't even support images. Styling a web page was largely a matter of using the few style-related attributes and tags allowed by the early incarnations of HTML.

Things improved markedly with the introduction of browser support for Cascading Style Sheets (CSS), which allowed the styling of a page to be treated independently from its HTML markup.

Earlier in the book, you learned how to edit the structure of your page using JavaScript's DOM methods. However, JavaScript can also be used to access and amend CSS styles for the current page. In this hour you learn how.

A Ten-Minute CSS Primer

If you've decided to learn JavaScript there's a pretty good chance that you're already familiar with CSS styling. Just in case it's managed to pass you by, let's review the basics.

Separating Style from Content

Before CSS came along, most styling in HTML pages was carried out using HTML tags and/or their attributes. To change the font color of a piece of text, for example, you would have used something like this:

```
<p><font color="red">This text is in red!</font></p>
```

This was pretty awful for a number of reasons:

▶ Every single piece of text in the page that we wanted to be colored red had to be marked up with these extra tags.

▶ The created style could not be carried over to other pages; they too had to be marked up individually with additional HTML.

▶ To later change pages' styles, you had to edit each and every page and sift through the HTML, changing every style-related tag and attribute individually.

▶ With all this extra markup, the HTML became very hard to read and maintain.

CSS attempts to separate the styling of an HTML element from the markup function of that element. This is done by defining individual *style declarations* and then applying these to HTML elements or collections of elements.

You can use CSS to style the visual properties of a page element, such as color, font, and size, as well as format-related properties such as positioning, margins, padding, and alignment.

Separating style from content in this way brings with it a lot of benefits:

▶ Style declarations can be applied to more than one element or even (when using external stylesheets) more than one page.

▶ Changes to style declarations affect all associated HTML elements, making updating your site's style more accurate, quick, and efficient.

▶ Sharing styles encourages more consistent styling through your site.

▶ HTML markup is clearer to read and maintain.

CSS Style Declarations

The syntax of CSS style declarations is not unlike that of JavaScript functions. Suppose you want to declare a style for all paragraph elements in a page, causing the font color inside the paragraphs to be colored red:

```
p {
    color: red
}
```

You can apply more than one style rule to your chosen element or collection of elements, separating them with semicolons:

```
p {
    color: red;
    text-decoration: italic;
}
```

Since you have used the selector p, the preceding style declarations affect every paragraph element on the page. To select just one specific page element, you can do so by using its ID. To do so, the selector you use for your CSS style declaration is not the name of the HTML element, but the ID value prefixed by a hash character. For instance, the HTML element

```
<p id="para1">Here is some text.</p>
```

could be styled by the following style declaration:

```
#para1 {
    font-weight: bold;
    font-size: 12pt;
    color: black;
}
```

To style multiple page elements using the same style declaration, you can simply separate the selectors with commas. The following style declaration affects all <div> elements on the page, plus whatever element has the id value para1:

```
div, #para1 {
    color: yellow;
    background-color: black;
}
```

Alternatively, you can select all elements sharing a particular class attribute, by prefixing the class name with a dot to form your selector:

```
<p class="info">Welcome to my website.</p>
<span class="info">Please log in or register using the form below.</span>
```

We can style these elements with one declaration:

```
.info {
    font-family: arial, verdana, sans-serif;
    color: green;
}
```

Where to Place Style Declarations

Somewhat similarly to JavaScript statements, CSS style declarations can either appear within the page or be saved in an external file and referenced from within the HTML page.

To reference an external stylesheet, normal practice is to add a line to the page `<head>` like this:

```
<link rel="stylesheet" type="text/css" href="style.css" />
```

Alternatively, you can place style declarations directly in the `<head>` of your page between `<style>` and `</style>` tags:

```
<style>
    p {
        color: black;
        font-family: tahoma;
    }
    h1 {
        color: blue;
        font-size: 22pt;
    }
</style>
```

Finally, it's possible to add style declarations directly into an HTML element by using the `style` attribute:

```
<p style="color:red; font-size: 12px;">Please see our terms of service.</p>
```

TIP

Styles defined in external stylesheets have the advantage that they can easily be applied to multiple pages, whereas styles defined within the page can't.

The DOM `style` Property

You saw in previous hours how the HTML page is represented by the browser as a DOM tree. The DOM *nodes*—individual "leaves and branches" making up the DOM tree—are objects, each having its own properties and methods.

You've seen various methods that allow you to select individual DOM nodes, or collections of nodes, such as `document.getElementById()`.

Each DOM node has a property called `style`, which is itself an object containing information about the CSS styles pertaining to its parent node. Let's see an example:

```
<div id="id1" style="width:200px;">Welcome back to my site.</div>
<script>
    var myNode = document.getElementById("id1");
    alert(myNode.style.width);
</script>
```

In this case the alert would display the message "200px."

NOTE
___

In addition to the syntax
```
myNode.style.width
```

you can also use the equivalent
```
myNode.style["width"]
```

This is sometimes necessary, such as when passing a property name as a variable:
```
var myProperty = "width";
myNode.style[myProperty] = "200px";
```

Unfortunately, while this method works fine with *inline* styles, if you apply a style to a page element via a `<style>` element in the head of your page, or in an external stylesheet, the DOM style object won't be able to access it.

NOTE
___

In Hour 13, "Introducing CSS3," you'll read about another way to access style properties in JavaScript that avoids the limitation of only working for inline styles.
___

The DOM `style` object, though, is not read-only; you can set the values of style properties using the `style` object, and properties you've set this way *will* be returned by the DOM `style` object.

NOTE
___

CSS contains many properties with names that contain hyphens, such as `background-color`, `font-size`, `text-align`, and so on. Since the hyphen is not allowed in JavaScript property and method names, we need to amend the way these properties are written. To access such a property in JavaScript, remove the hyphen from the property name and capitalize the character that follows, so `font-size` becomes `fontSize`, `text-align` becomes `textAlign`, and so on.
___

TRY IT YOURSELF ▼

Setting Style Properties

Let's write a function to toggle the background color and font color of a page element between two values, using the DOM `style` object:
```
function toggle() {
    var myElement = document.getElementById("id1");
    if(myElement.style.backgroundColor == 'red') {
        myElement.style.backgroundColor = 'yellow';
```

```
      myElement.style.color = 'black';
   } else {
      myElement.style.backgroundColor = 'red';
      myElement.style.color = 'white';
   }
}
```

The function `toggle()` first finds out the current `background-color` CSS property of a page element, and then compares that color to `red`.

If the `background-color` property currently has the value of `red`, it sets the style properties of the element to show the text in black on a yellow background; otherwise, it sets the style values to show white text on a red background.

We use this function to toggle the colors of a `<span>` element in an HTML document.

The complete listing is shown in Listing 12.1.

LISTING 12.1   Styling Using the DOM `style` Object

```
<!DOCTYPE html>
<html>
<head>
   <title>Setting the style of page elements</title>
   <style>
      span {
         font-size: 16pt;
         font-family: arial, helvetica, sans-serif;
         padding: 20px;
      }
   </style>
   <script>
      function toggle() {
         var myElement = document.getElementById("id1");
         if(myElement.style.backgroundColor == 'red') {
            myElement.style.backgroundColor = 'yellow';
            myElement.style.color = 'black';
         } else {
            myElement.style.backgroundColor = 'red';
            myElement.style.color = 'white';
         }
      }
      window.onload = function() {
         document.getElementById("btn1").onclick = toggle;
      }
   </script>
</head>
```

```
<body>
    <span id="id1">Welcome back to my site.</span>
    <input type="button" id="btn1" value="Toggle" />
</body>
</html>
```

Create the HTML file in your editor and try it out.

You should see that when the page originally loads, the text is in the default black and has no background color. That happens because these style properties are initially not set in the `<style>` instructions in the page head, as an inline style, or via the DOM.

Executing when the button is clicked, the `toggle()` function checks the current background color of the `<span>` element. On finding that its value is not currently red, `toggle()` sets the background color to red and the text color to white.

The next time the button is clicked, the test condition

```
if(myElement.style.backgroundColor == 'red')
```

returns a value of `true`, causing the colors to be set instead to black on a yellow background.

Figure 12.1 shows the program in action.

FIGURE 12.1
Setting style properties in JavaScript

Accessing Classes Using `className`

Earlier in this hour we discussed separating style from content, and the benefits that this can bring.

Using JavaScript to edit the properties of the `style` object, as in the previous exercise, works well—but it does carry with it the danger of reducing this separation of style and content. If your JavaScript code routinely changes elements' style declarations, the responsibility for styling your pages is no longer lodged firmly in CSS. If you later decide to change the styles your JavaScript applies, you'll have to go back and edit all of your JavaScript functions.

Thankfully, we have a mechanism by which JavaScript can restyle pages without overwriting individual style declarations. By using the `className` property of the element, we can switch the value of the `class` attribute and with it the associated style declarations for the element. Take a look at Listing 12.2.

LISTING 12.2 Changing Classes Using `className`

```
<!DOCTYPE html>
<html>
<head>
    <title>Switching classes with JavaScript</title>
    <style>
        .classA {
            width: 180px;
            border: 3px solid black;
            background-color: white;
            color: red;
            font:  normal 24px arial, helvetica, sans-serif;
            padding: 20px;
        }
        .classB {
            width: 180px;
            border: 3px dotted white;
            background-color: black;
            color: yellow;
            font: italic bold 24px "Times New Roman", serif;
            padding: 20px;
        }
    </style>
    <script>
        function toggleClass() {
            var myElement = document.getElementById("id1");
            if(myElement.className == "classA") {
                myElement.className = "classB";
            } else {
                myElement.className = "classA";
            }
```

```
            }
        window.onload = function() {
            document.getElementById("btn1").onclick = toggleClass;
        }
    </script>

</head>
<body>
    <div id="id1" class="classA"> An element with a touch of class.</div>
    <input type="button" id="btn1" value="Toggle" />
</body>
</html>
```

The `<style>` element in the page `<head>` lists style declarations for two classes, `classA` and `classB`. The JavaScript function `toggleClass()` uses similar logic to the earlier function `toggle()` of Listing 12.1, except that `toggleClass()` does not work with the element's `style` object. Instead, `toggleClass()` gets the class name associated with the `<div>` element and switches its value between `classA` and `classB`.

Figure 12.2 shows the script in action.

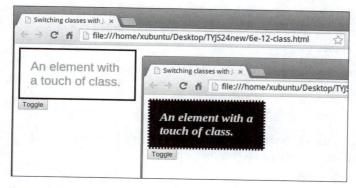

FIGURE 12.2
Switching classes in JavaScript

NOTE

As an alternative to using `className`, you could try setting the class attribute for an element to the value `classA` by using

```
element.setAttribute("class", "classA");
```

Unfortunately, various versions of Internet Explorer have trouble when trying to set the `class` attribute, but work fine with `className`. The statement

```
element.className = "classA";
```

seems to work in all browsers.

The DOM `styleSheets` Object

The `styleSheets` property of the `document` object contains an array of all the stylesheets on the page, whether they are contained in external files and linked into the page head, or declared between `<style>` and `</style>` tags in the page head. The items in the `styleSheets` array are indexed numerically, starting at zero for the stylesheet appearing first.

TIP

You can access the total number of spreadsheets on your page by using

```
document.styleSheets.length
```

Enabling, Disabling, and Switching Stylesheets

Each stylesheet in the array has a property called `disabled`, containing a value of Boolean `true` or `false`. This is a read/write property, so we are able to effectively switch individual stylesheets on and off in JavaScript:

```
document.styleSheets[0].disabled = true;
document.styleSheets[1].disabled = false;
```

The preceding code snippet "switches on" the second stylesheet in the page (index 1) while "switching off" the first stylesheet (index 0).

Listing 12.3 has a working example. The script on this page first declares the variable `which-Sheet`, initializing its value at zero:

```
var whichSheet = 0;
```

This variable keeps track of which of the two stylesheets is currently active. The second line of code initially disables the second of the two stylesheets on the page:

```
document.styleSheets[1].disabled = true;
```

The function `sheet()`, which is attached to the `onClick` event handler to the button on the page when the page loads, carries out three tasks when the button is clicked:

▶ Disable the stylesheet whose index is stored in variable `whichSheet`:

```
document.styleSheets[whichSheet].disabled = true;
```

▶ Toggle variable `whichSheet` between one and zero:

```
whichSheet = (whichSheet == 1) ? 0 : 1;
```

▶ Enable the stylesheet corresponding to the new value of `whichSheet`:

```
document.styleSheets[whichSheet].disabled = false;
```

The combined effect of these activities is to toggle between the two active stylesheets for the page. The script is shown in action in Listing 12.3 and Figure 12.3.

LISTING 12.3   Toggling Between Stylesheets Using the `styleSheets` Property

```html
<!DOCTYPE html>
<html>
<head>
    <title>Switching Stylesheets with JavaScript</title>
    <style>
        body {
            background-color: white;
            color: red;
            font:  normal 24px arial, helvetica, sans-serif;
            padding: 20px;
        }
    </style>
    <style>
        body {
            background-color: black;
            color: yellow;
            font: italic bold 24px "Times New Roman", serif;
            padding: 20px;
        }
    </style>
    <script>
        var whichSheet = 0;
        document.styleSheets[1].disabled = true;
        function sheet() {
            document.styleSheets[whichSheet].disabled = true;
            whichSheet = (whichSheet == 1) ? 0 : 1;
            document.styleSheets[whichSheet].disabled = false;
        }
        window.onload = function() {
            document.getElementById("btn1").onclick = sheet;
        }
    </script>
</head>
<body>
    Switch my stylesheet with the button below!<br />
    <input type="button" id="btn1" value="Toggle" />
</body>
</html>
```

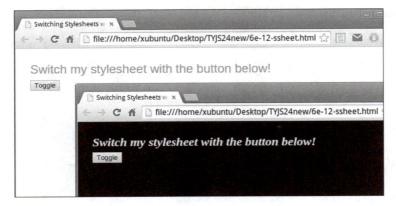

FIGURE 12.3
Switching stylesheets with the `styleSheets` property

▼ TRY IT YOURSELF

Selecting a Particular Stylesheet

Having your stylesheets indexed by number doesn't make it easy to select the stylesheet you need. It would be easier if you had a function to allow you to title your stylesheets and select them by their title attribute.

You need your function to respond in a useful manner if you ask for a stylesheet that doesn't exist; you want it to maintain the previous stylesheet and send the user a message.

First, declare a couple of variables and initialize their values:

```
var change = false;
var oldSheet = 0;
```

The Boolean variable `change` keeps track of whether you've found a stylesheet with the requested name; once you do so, you change its value to `true`, indicating that you intend to change stylesheets.

The integer `oldSheet`, originally set to zero, will eventually be assigned the number of the currently active sheet; in case you don't find a new stylesheet matching the requested title, you set this back to active before returning from the function.

Now you need to cycle through the `styleSheets` array:

```
for (var i = 0; i < document.styleSheets.length; i++) {
    ...
}
```

For each stylesheet:

▶ If you find that this is the currently active stylesheet, store its index in the variable `oldSheet`:

```
if(document.styleSheets[i].disabled == false) {
    oldSheet = i;
}
```

▶ As you cycle through, make sure all sheets are disabled:

```
document.styleSheets[i].disabled = true;
```

▶ If the current sheet has the title of the requested sheet, make it enabled by setting its `disabled` value to `false`, and immediately set your variable `change` to `true`:

```
if(document.styleSheets[i].title == mySheet) {
    document.styleSheets[i].disabled = false;
    change = true;
}
```

When you've cycled through all sheets, you can determine from the state of the variables `change` and `oldSheet` whether you are in a position to change the stylesheet. If not, reset the prior stylesheet to be enabled again:

```
if(!change) document.styleSheets[oldSheet].disabled = false;
```

Finally, the function returns the value of variable `change`—true if the change has been made, or false if not.

The code is listed in Listing 12.4. Save this code in an HTML file and load it into your browser.

LISTING 12.4   **Selecting Stylesheets by Title**

```
<!DOCTYPE html>
<html>
<head>
    <title>Switching stylesheets with JavaScript</title>
    <style title="sheet1">
        body {
            background-color: white;
            color: red;
        }
    </style>
    <style title="sheet2">
        body {
            background-color: black;
            color: yellow;
        }
```

```
        </style>
        <style title="sheet3">
            body {
                background-color: pink;
                color: green;
            }
        </style>
        <script>
            function ssEnable(mySheet) {
                var change = false;
                var oldSheet = 0;
                for (var i = 0; i < document.styleSheets.length; i++) {
                    if(document.styleSheets[i].disabled == false) {
                        oldSheet = i;
                    }
                    document.styleSheets[i].disabled = true;
                    if(document.styleSheets[i].title == mySheet) {
                        document.styleSheets[i].disabled = false;
                        change = true;
                    }
                }
                if(!change) document.styleSheets[oldSheet].disabled = false;
                return change;
            }
            function sheet() {
                var sheetName = prompt("Stylesheet Name?");
                if(!ssEnable(sheetName)) alert("Not found - original stylesheet
                ➥retained.");
            }
            window.onload = function() {
                document.getElementById("btn1").onclick = sheet;
            }
        </script>
    </head>
<body>
    Switch my stylesheet with the button below!<br />
    <input type="button" id="btn1" value="Change Sheet" />
</body>
</html>
```

The small function `sheet()` is added to the button's `onClick` event handler when the page loads. Each time the button is clicked, `sheet()` prompts the user for the name of a stylesheet:

```
var sheetName = prompt("Stylesheet Name?");
```

Then it calls the `ssEnable()` function, passing the requested name as an argument.

If the function returns `false`, indicating that no change of stylesheet has taken place, you alert the user with a message:

```
if(!ssEnable(sheetName)) alert("Not found - original stylesheet retained.");
```

The script is shown operating in Figure 12.4.

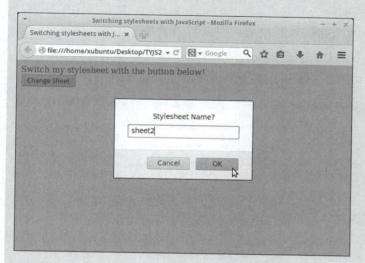

FIGURE 12.4
Selecting a new stylesheet by name

Summary

In this hour you learned a number of ways in which JavaScript can be put to work on the CSS styles of your page. You learned how to use the `style` property of page elements, how to work with CSS classes, and how to manipulate entire stylesheets.

Q&A

Q. Is it possible for JavaScript to work with individual CSS style rules?

A. Yes it is, but at the time of writing this does not work very well cross-browser. Mozilla browsers support the `cssRules` array, while Internet Explorer calls the equivalent array `Rules`. There is also considerable difference among browsers in how the notion of a "rule" is interpreted. It's to be hoped that future browser versions will resolve these differences.

Q. **Is it possible to alter the mouse cursor in JavaScript?**

A. Yes, it is. The `style` object has a property called `cursor` that can take various values. Popular cursors include the following:

  ▶ **Crosshair**—Pointer renders as a pair of crossed lines like a gun sight.

  ▶ **Pointer**—Usually a pointing finger.

  ▶ **Text**—Text entry caret.

  ▶ **Wait**—The program is busy.

Workshop

Try to answer all the questions before reading the subsequent "Answers" section.

Quiz

1. To set the `font-family` property for element `myElement` to Verdana, you would use:

   a. `myElement.style.font-family = "verdana";`

   b. `myElement.style.fontFamily = "verdana";`

   c. `myElement.style.font-family("verdana");`

2. The property `className` can be used:

   a. To access the value of the `class` attribute of an element

   b. To access the value of the `name` attribute of an element

   c. To add the attribute `classname` to an element

3. How can you enable the stylesheet with index `n` in the `styleSheets` array?

   a. `document.styleSheets[n].active = true;`

   b. `document.styleSheets[n].enabled = true;`

   c. `document.styleSheets[n].disabled = false;`

Answers

1. b. `myElement.style.fontFamily = "verdana";`

2. a. To access the value of the `class` attribute of an element.

3. c. `document.styleSheets[n].disabled = false;`

Exercises

▶ Edit the program of Listing 12.1 to change other style properties such as font face and decoration, element borders, padding, and margins.

▶ Change the program of Listing 12.4 so that some of the stylesheets are externally linked, rather than situated between `<style>` and `</style>` tags in the page `<head>`. Does everything work the same?

Introducing CSS3

What You'll Learn in This Hour:

▶ Some of the new abilities CSS3 brings to CSS
▶ Using vendor-specific prefixes and extensions
▶ Cross-browser setting of CSS3 properties
▶ Setting CSS3 properties efficiently in JavaScript

Using CSS3 you can easily achieve plenty of cool new effects without having to use lots of JavaScript code and/or external graphics applications such as Photoshop. You can create rounded borders, add shadows to boxes, use an image as a border, and more. CSS3 contains several new background properties that give you more control over background elements, including multiple background images, while CSS3 gradients let you display smooth transitions between two or more specified colors. New text features include text shadows and word wrap, as well as easy use of web fonts. And CSS3 lets you easily build really cool transitions, transformations, and animations.

In this hour you'll get a flavor of what CSS3 can do for your web pages, and you'll see how to effectively control CSS3's capabilities using JavaScript.

Vendor-Specific Properties and Prefixes

CSS vendor prefixes are a way for the browser companies to add support for new or experimental CSS features before they become part of the formal CSS3 specification, or to implement features of a specification that hasn't yet been finalized. In due course, these prefixes usually become unnecessary as the features become fully supported via their standard CSS3 nomenclature. To make sure that your pages render as you want them to in the maximum number of browsers, though, it pays to use prefixes.

The CSS3 browser prefixes you're likely to need appear in Table 13.1.

TABLE 13.1 Vendor Prefixes for CSS3

Browser/System	Prefix
Android	-webkit-
Chrome	-webkit-
Firefox	-moz-
Internet Explorer	-ms-
iOS	-webkit-
Opera	-o-
Safari	-webkit-

In most cases, where a prefix is necessary you take the CSS3 property as listed in the CSS3 speci-fication and add the relevant prefix from Table 13.1 for the browser in use. For example, later in this hour you'll read about CSS3 transitions. There you'll see that, if you want to add a CSS3 transition to your page, you use the transition property with the prefixes added first:

```
-webkit-transition: background 0.5s ease;
-moz-transition: background 0.5s ease;
-o-transition: background 0.5s ease;
transition: background 0.5s ease;
```

The user's browser will respond to whichever version of the transition feature it understands, ignoring the rest.

Thankfully, browser manufacturers are working hard at fully implementing all of the CSS3 fea-tures, and for most modern browsers the number of properties requiring a prefix is falling quickly.

TIP

At the time of writing there's a really useful roundup of which feature/browser combinations require a prefix at http://shouldiprefix.com/.

For a frequently updated list of which features are supported by a particular browser and version, visit http://www.w3schools.com/cssref/css3_browsersupport.asp.

CAUTION

The prefixed version of a property might not always be exactly the same as the property as described in the CSS3 specification.

Even though vendor-specific extensions usually avoid conflicts (as each vendor has a unique prefix), please remember that such extensions may also be subject to change by the vendor, as they do not form part of the CSS3 specifications, even though they try to behave like the forthcoming CSS3 properties.

Remember, too, that the vendor-specific extensions will almost certainly fail CSS validation.

CSS3 Borders

CSS3 lets you do some really cool things with borders that were only previously possible with lots of ugly, hard-to-maintain code hacks.

In this section we'll look at two examples: box shadows and rounded corners.

Create Box Shadows

The `box-shadow` property lets you add drop shadows to your page's box elements. As Table 13.2 shows, you can separately specify values for color, size, blur, and offset:

TABLE 13.2   Parameters for the `box-shadow` Property

Shadow Parameter	Action
h-shadow (required)	The position of the horizontal shadow. Negative values are allowed.
v-shadow (required)	The position of the vertical shadow. Negative values are allowed.
blur (optional)	The blur distance.
spread (optional)	The size of shadow.
color (optional)	The color of the shadow. The default is black.

Here's an example using a 10px-wide shadow heading down and to the right, blurred across its full width, and colored mid-grey:

```
#div1 {
background-color: #8080ff;
width: 400px;
height: 250px;
box-shadow: 10px 10px 10px #808080;
-webkit-box-shadow: 10px 10px 10px #808080;
-moz-box-shadow: 10px 10px 10px #808080;
}
```

In Figure 13.1 you can see an example of this style applied to a `<div>` element in a web page.

FIGURE 13.1
A CSS3 box shadow

Rounding Corners with the `border-radius` property

The `border-radius` property lets you add rounded corners to your page elements without the need for specially created corner images, and is perhaps one of the most popular features new to CSS3.

The `border-radius` property already has widespread browser support, though Mozilla Firefox required the `-moz-` prefix for a little longer than some of its rivals; therefore, if you need to support Firefox back several versions you should consider including the prefixed version too:

```
#div1 {
-moz-border-radius: 25px;
border-radius: 25px;
}
```

In Figure 13.2 you can see an example of a `<div>` element styled with radiused corners.

FIGURE 13.2
A CSS3 border radius

Rounded corners can be specified independently using the individual properties `border-bottom-left-radius`, `border-top-left-radius`, `border-bottom-right-radius`, and `border-bottom-right-radius`, or for all four corners in one statement by using the `border-radius` property, as we've done here.

CSS3 Backgrounds

CSS3 contains several new background properties that allow more control of the background element.

In this section you'll learn about the `background-size` and `background-origin` properties, as well as how to use multiple background images.

The `background-size` Property

The `background-size` property adds a new feature to CSS that allows you to set the size of your background images using lengths, percentages, or either of two keywords, `contain` or `cover`.

Specifying the background size using lengths and percentages behaves as you might expect. For each background image, two lengths or percentages can be supplied, relating to the width and height, respectively. (When you use percentages, these relate to the space available for the background, not to the width and height of the background image.)

The `auto` keyword can be used in place of either the width or the height value. If you specify only one value for `background-size`, this will be assumed to be the width. The height will then default to `auto`.

```
#div1 {
background-size: 400px;
background-image: url(lake.png);
width: 400px;
height: 250px;
border-radius: 25px;
}
```

Here I've set the background width equal to the size of the `<div>` element (I've also rounded the corners for good measure). The result is shown in Figure 13.3.

FIGURE 13.3
Setting background size in CSS3

The `background-origin` Property

The `background-origin` property is used to set how the position of a background in a box is calculated.

It takes one of three values: `padding-box`, `border-box`, or `content-box`.

When you supply a value of `padding-box`, the position is relative to the upper-left corner of the padding edge. With `border-box` it's relative to the upper-left corner of the border, and `content-box` means the background is positioned relative to the upper-left corner of the content.

Multiple Background Images

CSS3 lets you use multiple background images for box elements, simply by employing a comma-separated list. The order of the list is important, with the first value supplied representing the layer closest to the user, and subsequent entries in the list being rendered as layers successively further behind it. Here's an example:

```
#div1 {
width: 600px;
height: 350px;
background-image: url(boat.png), url(lake.png);
background-position: center bottom, left top;
background-repeat: no-repeat;
}
```

Here, boat.png is a drawing of a yacht upon a transparent background, while lake.png is a photograph. In Figure 13.4 you can see the result when applied to a `<div>` element within a web page.

FIGURE 13.4
Using multiple images in CSS3 backgrounds

Browser support for the multiple backgrounds feature is already quite established, with Mozilla Firefox (3.6+), Safari/Chrome (1.0/1.3+), Opera (10.5+), and Internet Explorer (9.0+) offering support.

CSS3 Gradients

CSS3 gradients allow you to generate smooth transitions between two or more specified colors, where previously you had to employ images to achieve these effects. With CSS3 gradients you can reduce the download time, cache memory, and bandwidth usage that these images would have cost. CSS3 gradients perform better when zoomed, too.

CSS3 offers two types of gradient: *Linear Gradients*, directed down/up/left/right/diagonally, and *Radial Gradients*, directed outwards from a defined center.

Linear Gradients

To create a linear gradient in CSS3, you must define at least two colors to serve as the end points of the gradient. You can also define a starting point and a direction (that is, top to bottom, left to right, or an angle) for the gradient effect.

```
#div1 {
  width: 600px;
  height: 350px;
  background: -webkit-linear-gradient(red, #6699cc);
  background: -o-linear-gradient(red, #6699cc);
```

```
    background: -moz-linear-gradient(red, #6699cc);
    background: linear-gradient(red, #6699cc);
}
```

Here I've mixed the ways the colors are defined, using both color names (here red) and #rrggbb notation. I haven't specified a direction for the gradient, so the default top-to-bottom will be used by the browser, as shown in Figure 13.5.

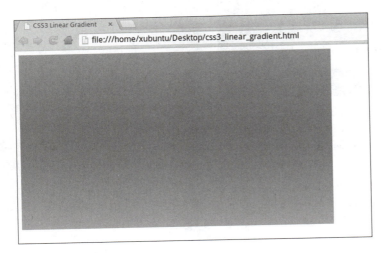

FIGURE 13.5
A CSS3 linear gradient

You can also enter a direction for the gradient; for instance, suppose you want the gradient to be directed left-to-right instead of top-to-bottom, like so:

```
background: linear-gradient(to right, red , #6699cc);
```

The following line defines a diagonal gradient:

```
background: linear-gradient(to bottom right, red , #6699cc);
```

If you want total control over the direction of the gradient, define an angle:

```
background: linear-gradient(135deg, red, #6699cc);
```

Radial Gradients

A radial gradient is defined by its center and (like its linear counterpart) must have at least two colors defined to act as end points for the gradient effect:

```
background: radial-gradient(red, #6699cc);
```

A radial gradient specified this way displays as shown in Figure 13.6.

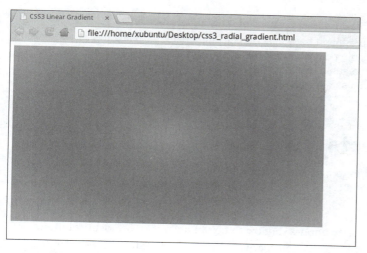

FIGURE 13.6
A CSS3 radial gradient

You can also set a location parameter for the center of the radial gradient, using the `at` keyword:

```
background: radial-gradient(at top left, red, #6699cc);
```

The result is shown in Figure 13.7.

FIGURE 13.7
Moving the center of the radial gradient

TIP

CSS3 gradients can do much more than I have space to describe here, including the use of more than two colors, transparency, and modifications to the shape and size of the gradient. You can even add multiple gradients to the same element. Full details are in the W3C documentation: http://www.w3.org/TR/2011/WD-css3-images-20110217/

CSS3 Text Effects

CSS3 contains some new features to help you manipulate text.

Text Shadow

In CSS3, the `text-shadow` property applies shadow to text in a way almost identical to the `box-shadow` property for block elements. You specify the horizontal and vertical shadow distances and optionally the blur distance and the color of the shadow:

```
h3 {
  text-shadow: 10px 10px 3px #333;
  font-size: 26px;
}
```

You can see an example displayed in Figure 13.8.

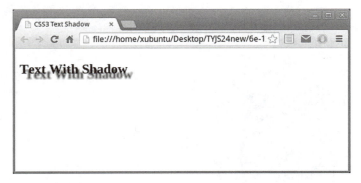

FIGURE 13.8
CSS3 text shadow

Word Wrap

If a word is too long to fit within the block element containing it, it overflows beyond its container. In CSS3, you can use the `word-wrap` property to force the text to wrap, even if has to wrap in the middle of a word:

```
p {
    word-wrap: break-word;
}
```

CSS3 Transitions, Transformations, and Animations

Traditionally, programmers have used custom JavaScript code to create movement in page elements, which can be tricky to implement in a cross-browser way. It would be better if there were easier ways to add simple effects to elements on the page.

These capabilities are currently being introduced in CSS3, in the form of transitions, transformations, and animations. They already have support to varying degrees in most browsers.

In the following simple example, we add a transition effect (in those browsers that support it) to change the background color on link hover. As the background color changes, a transition effect will smooth out the transformation.

Here's the code for our example link:

```
<a href="somepage.html" class="trans" id="link1">Show Me</a>
```

Following are the CSS declarations showing the original and hover background colors, and the declarations used to carry out the transition effect in the various different browsers. Note the range of different prefixes required, as discussed earlier in this hour. The last declaration, without a prefix, will be the one required once the technology moves from an experimental to a finished status.

```
a.trans {
    background: #669999;
    -webkit-transition: background 0.5s ease;
    -moz-transition: background 0.5s ease;
    -o-transition: background 0.5s ease;
    transition: background 0.5s ease;
}
a.trans:hover {
    background: #999966;
}
```

NOTE

You can find comprehensive information about CSS3 transitions, transformations, and animations at http://css3.bradshawenterprises.com/all/.

Referencing CSS3 Properties in JavaScript

The combination of CSS3 and JavaScript promises some great effects with slick performance, high reliability, and minimum code complexity. In this section we look at some ways to get and set CSS3 properties successfully from within your JavaScript code.

Converting CSS Property Names to JavaScript

As I mentioned in Hour 12, "JavaScript and CSS," to make the names of CSS properties compatible with JavaScript naming conventions, CSS property names need a small conversion from the format they have in stylesheets.

Instead of using lowercase names and hyphens as they do in CSS, the JavaScript versions have the hyphens removed and the following characters capitalized. Hence, `border-radius` becomes `borderRadius`. Property names having no hyphens, such as `width`, are unchanged.

You saw in Hour 12 how to access element style properties using this naming convention along with the DOM `style` property:

```
var bRad = document.getElementById("div1").style.borderRadius;
```

As I mentioned at that time, while this can be useful, it is limited to elements with inline styles; for elements with CSS declarations grouped in `<style>` elements in the page head, or in external files, it won't work. Luckily, there's a better way, which I'll discuss now.

The DOM `getComputedStyle()` Method

Nowadays nearly all browsers support the DOM `getComputedStyle()` method, which accesses the final (that is, computed) style of an element. By final style, we mean the style in which the browser finally displays the element after applying (in their appropriate order) all of the styling rules relevant to that element, be they inline, external, or inherited from container elements.

The `getComputedStyle()` method returns an object having various methods, including `getPropertyValue(property)`, which returns the current value for the given CSS property name:

```
var myDiv = document.getElementById("div1");
var bRad = getComputedStyle(myDiv).getPropertyValue("borderRadius");
```

Controlling Lighting Effects

Let's create a small application to use `box-shadow` and `radial-gradient`, both controlled by JavaScript, to control lighting effects in a simple HTML page. The code is shown in Listing 13.1.

LISTING 13.1   Controlling CSS3 Effects

```
<!DOCTYPE html>
<html>
  <title>Controlling CSS3 Effects</title>
<style>
  #div1 {
    width: 600px;
    height: 350px;
    background-color: #6699cc;
  }
  #div2 {
    background-color: #aaaaff;
    width: 80px;
    height: 80px;
    padding: 20px;
    position: relative;
    left: 240px;
    top: 105px;
  }
</style>
<script>
    window.onload = function() {
        document.getElementById("btn1").onclick = function() {
          document.getElementById("div1").style.background =
          ➡"radial-gradient(at top left, white, #6699cc)" ;
          document.getElementById("div2").style.boxShadow =
          ➡"10px 10px 10px #808080" ;
        }
        document.getElementById("btn2").onclick = function() {
          document.getElementById("div1").style.background =
          ➡"radial-gradient(at top right, white, #6699cc)" ;
          document.getElementById("div2").style.boxShadow =
          ➡"-10px 10px 10px #808080" ;
        }
        document.getElementById("btn3").onclick = function() {
          document.getElementById("div1").style.background =
          ➡"radial-gradient(at bottom, white, #6699cc)" ;
          document.getElementById("div2").style.boxShadow =
          ➡"0px -10px 10px #808080" ;
        }
    }
```

```
</script>
</head>
<body>
    <div id="div1">
        <div id="div2">
            LIGHTS:<br/>
            <input type="button" id="btn1" value="Top Left"><br/>
            <input type="button" id="btn2" value="Top Right"><br/>
            <input type="button" id="btn3" value="Bottom">
        </div>
    </div>
</body>
</html>
```

First, take a look at the `<body>` section of the page. It's very simple, containing just two nested `<div>` elements, the inner one containing three buttons, labeled Top Left, Top Right, and Bottom, respectively.

Returning to the `<head>` section of the page, you'll see that the `window.onload` event causes the attachment of an `onclick` event handler to each of these buttons. In each case, the event handler changes the gradient of the outer `<div>` element's background and the direction of the `box-shadow` style of the inner `<div>` element. The combined effect is to simulate a light source emanating from one of three directions.

You can see the page in action in Figure 13.9.

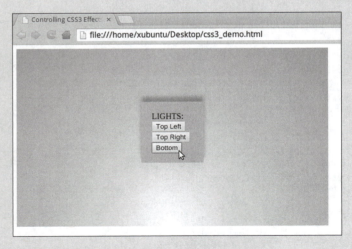

FIGURE 13.9
Controlling CSS3 with JavaScript

> Note how there are no images used to create these effects—something that wouldn't have been possible prior to CSS3.

Setting CSS3 Properties with Vendor Prefixes

So you've seen how to get a CSS property, but how can you *set* a CSS3 property using JavaScript when different browsers support different variations of the property (that is, having different prefixes)?

When a browser supports a particular CSS property, it returns a string value when you request the property from a page element. (This will be an empty string if the property has not yet been set.) If your browser doesn't support the property, the value undefined is returned instead. So you can easily carry out a test before setting a CSS3 property to determine which variant of the property is supported.

Let's write code that accepts an array of potential CSS3 properties and returns the one supported by the browser.

```
function getCss3Property(properties){
    // loop through all possible property names
    for (var i=0; i<properties.length; i++) {
        // if the property exists for this element
        if (properties[i] in document.documentElement.style) {
            // return the associated string
            return properties[i];
        }
    }
}
```

With this we can return the appropriate version of the feature.

Let's see how that might work for the transition used earlier in this hour:

```
//get the correct CSS3 transition property
var myTrans = getCss3Property(['transition', 'MozTransition', 'WebkitTransition',
'msTransition', 'OTransition'])

//set CSS transition for "link1"
document.getElementById("link1").style[myTrans] = "background 0.5s ease" ;
```

Let's suppose that I'm using a version of Firefox that doesn't support the CSS3 transition property, but does support Mozilla's own version, MozTransition (corresponding to -moz-transition).

When called, the `getCss3Property()` function will begin to loop through the list of transition properties corresponding to the various vendor types. Having returned a value of `undefined` for the property transition (as the browser does not support it) it will, on the following trip through the loop, exit the function, returning a string value of `MozTransition`. We now know which version of the property to set in the following line of code.

Summary

In this hour you learned about some of the new capabilities that CSS3 brings to web design. You saw how different browser manufacturers implement new or experimental CSS3 features via custom prefixes, and saw how you can access and set these custom features using JavaScript.

Q&A

Q. What browsers currently support CSS3 transitions, transforms, and animations?

A. At the time of writing, 2D transforms are available in all popular current browsers, while 3D transforms are supported in Safari, Chrome/Chromium, and Firefox. Transitions and 3D transforms were added in IE10. Most of these effects degrade sensibly, so a user having a browser without support will still be OK, but will see the page elements without animation.

Q. Why do several different browser vendors use the `-webkit-` prefix?

A. WebKit is a layout engine used for rendering web pages in web browsers. The webkit engine is the basis of a number of popular browsers, including Safari, Chrome/Chromium, and various other browsers for both desktop and mobile platforms.

Workshop

Try to answer all the questions before reading the subsequent "Answers" section.

Quiz

1. Which of the following will correctly specify a linear gradient from lower left to upper right?

    a. `linear-gradient(upper right, #112244 , #6699cc);`

    b. `linear-gradient(top right, #112244 , #6699cc);`

    c. `linear-gradient(to top right, #112244 , #6699cc);`

2. How would you reference the `text-shadow` property in JavaScript?

    a. `textShadow`

    b. `text-Shadow`

    c. `text-shadow`

3. Which of the following would correctly render multiple background images with image cactus.png visible in front of image desert.jpg?

    a. `background-image: cactus.png, desert.jpg`

    b. `background-image: url(cactus.png), url(desert.jpg);`

    c. `background-image: url(desert.jpg), url(cactus.png);`

Answers

1. c. `linear-gradient(to top right, #112244 , #6699cc);`

2. a. `textShadow`

3. b. `background-image: url(cactus.png), url(desert.jpg);`

Exercises

▶ Using the individual properties `border-bottom-left-radius`, `border-top-left-radius`, `border-bottom-right-radius`, and `border-bottom-right-radius`, use JavaScript to style a `<div>` element to be completely elliptical in shape. (Hint: Set the radius sizes such that all of the element's border is within the radius of exactly one corner.) Use `getComputedStyle()` on your elliptical `<div>` to then report these border radii to the console.

▶ In this hour's "Try It Yourself" section, the box shadow direction was set manually, while you were writing the code, to be appropriate to the simulated lighting direction. Can you write a function in JavaScript to set the shadow properties based on the detected value of the background gradient?

HOUR 14
Using Libraries

What You'll Learn in This Hour:

▶ Why using a library can be a good idea
▶ The sorts of things libraries can help you do
▶ Library extensions from the user community
▶ Introducing some popular libraries
▶ A quick overview of prototype.js

Libraries are reusable collections of JavaScript code that let you do complicated things by adding only a few lines of extra code to your program.

There are many freely available JavaScript libraries that can help you quickly develop capable, cross-browser applications.

Several of the more popular libraries are introduced in this hour.

Why Use a Library?

You'll often see opinions expressed, mainly on the Internet, by JavaScript developers who strongly advocate writing your own code instead of using one of the many available libraries. Popular objections include

▶ You won't ever really know how the code works because you're simply employing someone else's algorithms and functions.

▶ JavaScript libraries contain a lot of code you'll never use but that your users have to download anyway.

Like many aspects of software development, these are matters of opinion. Personally, I believe that there are some very good reasons for using libraries *sometimes*:

▶ Why invent code that somebody else has already written? Popular JavaScript libraries tend to contain the sorts of abstractions that programmers need often—which means you'll likely need those functions too from time to time. The thousands of downloads and pages of online comment generated by the most-used libraries pretty much guarantee that the code they contain will be more thoroughly tested and debugged than your own, home-cooked code would be.

▶ Take inspiration from other coders. There are some *really* clever programmers out there; take their work and use it to improve your own.

▶ Using a well-written library can really take away some of the headaches of writing cross-browser JavaScript. You won't have every browser always at your disposal, but the library writers—and their communities of users—test on every leading browser.

▶ Download size for most libraries is not horrific. For the few occasions where you need the shortest of download times, compressed versions are available for most of the popular libraries that you can use in your "production" websites. There's also the possibility of examining the library code and extracting just the parts you need.

What Sorts of Things Can Libraries Do?

The specifics differ depending on the library concerned and the needs and intentions of its creator. However, there are certain recurring themes that most libraries include:

▶ **Encapsulation of DOM methods**—As you see later in this hour when you look at prototype.js, JavaScript libraries can offer appealing shorthand ways to select and manage page elements and groups of elements.

▶ **Animation**—In Hour 7, "Program Control," you learned about the use of timers. Timers can be used to animate page elements, but writing such code can be tricky and the resulting code complicated to maintain. Many of the popular libraries wrap these sorts of operations into convenient functions to slide, fade, shake, squish, fold, snap, and pulsate parts of your page's interface, all in a cross-browser way and with just a few lines of code.

▶ **Drag and drop**—A truly cross-browser drag and drop has always been one of the trickiest effects to code for all browsers. Libraries can make it easy.

▶ **Ajax**—Easy methods to update page content without needing to worry about the nitty-gritty of instantiating XMLHttpRequest objects and managing callbacks and status codes.

Some Popular Libraries

New libraries are popping up all the time; others have seen continual development over a number of years. This is by no means a complete list; it simply attempts to point out some of the more popular current players.

Prototype Framework

The Prototype Framework (http://www.prototypejs.org) has been around for a few years now and is currently in version 1.7. Prototype's major strengths lie in its DOM extensions and Ajax handling, though it has many more tricks up its sleeve, including JSON support and methods to help with creating and inheriting classes.

Prototype is distributed as a standalone library but also as part of larger projects, such as Ruby on Rails and the script.aculo.us JavaScript library.

NOTE

You look in more detail at the Prototype Framework later in the hour, including some hands-on coding.

Dojo

Dojo (http://www.dojotoolkit.org/) is an open-source toolkit that adds power to JavaScript to simplify building applications and user interfaces. It has features ranging from extra string and math functions to animation and AJAX. The latest versions support not only all major desktop browsers, but also mobile environments, including Apple iOS, Android, and Blackberry with their "Dojo Mobile" HTML5 mobile JavaScript framework.

At the time of writing, Dojo is at version 1.7.

The Yahoo! UI Library

The Yahoo! UI Library (http://developer.yahoo.com/yui/) was developed by Yahoo! and made available to everyone under an open-source license. It includes features for animation, DOM features, event management, and easy-to-use user interface elements such as calendars and sliders.

MooTools

MooTools (http://mootools.net/) is a compact, modular JavaScript framework allowing you to build powerful, flexible, and cross-browser code using a simple-to-understand, well documented API (application programming interface).

jQuery

jQuery (http://jquery.com/) is a fast and compact JavaScript library that simplifies various development tasks, including HTML document traversing, event handling, animation, and Ajax calls for rapid development of interactive websites.

TIP

You find out a lot about the jQuery library and its associated user interface library, jQueryUI, in the following two hours.

Introducing prototype.js

Sam Stephenson's prototype.js is a popular JavaScript library containing an array of functions useful in the development of cross-browser JavaScript applications, and including specific support for Ajax. Shortly you'll see how your JavaScript code can be simplified by using this library's powerful support for DOM manipulation, HTML forms, and the XMLHttpRequest object.

The latest version of the prototype.js library can be downloaded from http://prototypejs.org/.

Including the library in your web application is simple; just include in the <head> section of your HTML document the following line:

```
<script src="prototype.js"></script>
```

The prototype.js library contains a broad range of functions that can make writing JavaScript code quicker and the resulting scripts cleaner and easier to maintain.

The library includes general-purpose functions providing shortcuts to regular programming tasks, a wrapper for HTML forms, an object to encapsulate the XMLHttpRequest object, methods and objects for simplifying DOM tasks, and more.

Let's take a look at some of these tools.

CAUTION

At the time of writing, prototype.js is at version 1.7.2. If you download a different version, check the documentation to see whether there are differences between your version and the one described here.

The $() Function

$() is essentially a shortcut to the `getElementById()` DOM method. Normally, to return the value of a particular element you would use an expression such as

```
var mydata = document.getElementById('someElementID');
```

The $() function simplifies this task by returning the value of the element whose ID is passed to it as an argument:

```
var mydata = $('someElementID');
```

Furthermore, $() (unlike `getElementById()`) can accept multiple element IDs as an argument and return an array of the associated element values. Consider this line of code:

```
mydataArray = $('id1','id2','id3');
```

In this example:

- ▶ `mydataArray[0]` contains value of element with ID `id1`.

- ▶ `mydataArray[1]` contains value of element with ID `id2`.

- ▶ `mydataArray[2]` contains value of element with ID `id3`.

The $F() Function

The $F() function returns the value of a form input field when the input element or its ID is passed to it as an argument. Take a look at the following HTML snippet:

```
<input type="text" id="input1" name="input1">
<select id="input2" name="input2">
    <option value="0">Option A</option>
    <option value="1">Option B</option>
    <option value="2">Option C</option>
</select>
```

Here we could use

```
$F('input1')
```

to return the value in the text box and

```
$F('input2')
```

to return the value of the currently selected option of the select box. The $F() function works equally well on check box and text area input elements, making it easy to return the element values regardless of the input element type.

The `Form` Object

prototype.js defines a `Form` object having several useful methods for simplifying HTML form manipulation.

You can return an array of a form's input fields by calling the `getElements()` method:

```
inputs = Form.getElements('thisform');
```

The `serialize()` method allows input names and values to be formatted into a URL-compatible list:

```
inputlist = Form.serialize('thisform');
```

Using the preceding line of code, the variable `inputlist` would now contain a string of serialized parameter and value pairs:

```
field1=value1&field2=value2&field3=value3...
```

`Form.disable('thisform')` and `Form.enable('thisform')` each do exactly what the name implies.

▼ TRY IT YOURSELF

Using the `getElements()` Method

Let's gather some information about an HTML form using the `getElements()` method. As I mentioned earlier, this method returns an array containing the elements of a particular form.

Here's the code for our simple form:

```
<!DOCTYPE html>
<html>
<head>
    <title>Prototype.js example</title>
</head>
<body>
    <form id="exampleForm" action="#" onsubmit="return false">
        Username: <input type="text" name="username" /><br/>
        Telephone: <input type="text" name="telephone" /><br/>
        Message: <input type="text" name="message" /><br/>
    </form>
    <input type="button" value="Result" onclick="showFormFields();"/>
</body>
</html>
```

For this example, we just have three text fields, as shown in Figure 14.1.

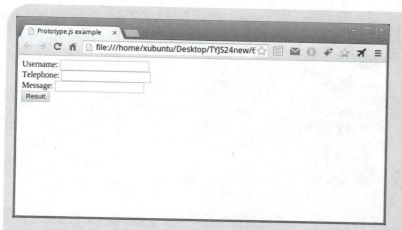

FIGURE 14.1
The simple HTML form

After including prototype.js in the head section of the HTML, we need to write a function to be executed when the form's button is clicked. This function will use the `getElements()` method to build an array of the form's elements. It will then read back the names and the entered values from the form via a JavaScript alert.

The code is shown in Listing 14.1.

LISTING 14.1   Prototype.js Example Form

```
<!DOCTYPE html>
<html>
<head>
<title>Prototype.js example</title>
    <script src="prototype.js"></script>
    <script>

    function showFormFields() {
        var form = $('exampleForm');
        var message = '';
        var fields = form.getElements();
        for(var x=0; x<fields.length;x++)  {
            message += "Field Name : " + fields[x].name + " Value : " +
            ➥fields[x].value + "\n";
        }
        alert(message);
    }

    </script>
```

```
</head>

<body>

  <form id="exampleForm" action="#" onsubmit="return false">
      Username: <input type="text" name="username" /><br/>
      Telephone: <input type="text" name="telephone" /><br/>
      Message: <input type="text" name="message" /><br/>

  </form>

  <input type="button" value="Result" onclick="showFormFields();"/>

</body>
</html>
```

In Figure 14.2 you can see the result of running the example and entering some sample data.

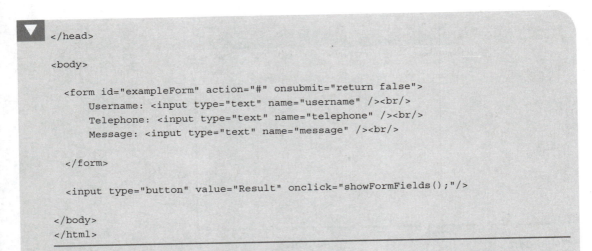

FIGURE 14.2
Form information retrieved using `getElements()`

Summary

In many instances, writing JavaScript can be made a whole lot easier by using libraries. Such libraries wrap many of the commonly used objects and methods into more user-friendly forms; no longer do you have to remember cross-browser methods to, for example, add or remove an event listener or access form elements. In this hour you learned a little about some of the more popular JavaScript libraries.

Q&A

Q. How do I include a third-party JavaScript library into my pages?

A. The process varies slightly from library to library. Usually it's simply a matter of including one or more external .js files into the `<head>` part of your web page. See the documentation supplied with your chosen library for specific details.

Q. Can I use more than one third-party library in the same script?

A. Yes, in theory: If the libraries are well written and designed not to interfere with each other, there should be no problem combining them. In practice, this depends on the libraries you need and how they were written.

Workshop

Try to answer all the questions before reading the subsequent "Answers" section.

Quiz

1. Which of the following objects *is not* a JavaScript library?

    a. MooTools

    b. Prototype

    c. Ajax

2. How can you extend jQuery yourself?

    a. jQuery can't be extended.

    b. By writing server-side scripts.

    c. By writing a plug-in, or using a prewritten one.

3. What other JavaScript third-party library does script.aculo.us employ?

    a. Prototype

    b. Dojo

    c. jQuery

Answers

1. c. Ajax is a programming technique enabling your scripts to use resources hosted on your server. There are many libraries to help you employ Ajax functionality, but Ajax itself is not a library.

2. c. jQuery has a well-documented way to write and use plug-ins.

3. a. Script.aculo.us uses the prototype.js library.

Exercises

▶ Write a simple script using the Prototype library, or use a sample script from the Prototype website at http://www.prototypejs.org.

▶ Visit the Script.aculo.us page at http://script.aculo.us/ and review the complete list of effects made available by this library.

A Closer Look at jQuery

What You'll Learn in This Hour:

▶ Including jQuery in your pages
▶ jQuery's `$(document).ready` handler
▶ Selecting page elements
▶ Working with HTML content
▶ Showing and hiding elements
▶ Animating elements
▶ Command chaining
▶ Handling events
▶ Using jQuery for Ajax applications

Many JavaScript libraries are available, but jQuery is arguably the most popular and also the most extensible. A huge number of developers contribute open source plug-ins for jQuery, and you can find a suitable plug-in for almost any application you might have. The wide range of plug-ins and the simple syntax make jQuery such a great library. In this hour you learn the basics of jQuery and get a taste of how powerful it is.

Including jQuery in Your Pages

Before you can use jQuery, you need to include it in your pages. There are two main options, as detailed in the following sections.

Download jQuery

You can download jQuery from the official website at http://docs.jquery.com/Downloading_jQuery, where you find both Compressed and Uncompressed versions of the code. The Compressed version is for your live pages, as it has been compressed to the smallest possible file size to download as quickly as possible.

For development purposes, choose the Uncompressed version. Thanks to the well-formatted, commented source, you can read the jQuery code to see how it works.

You need to include the jQuery library in the `<head>` section of your pages, using a `<script>` tag. The easiest way is to place the downloaded jquery.js file in the same directory as the page from where you want to use it and then reference it like this:

```
<script src="jquery-1.11.2.js"></script>
```

Of course, if you place jQuery in another directory, you'll have to change the (relative or absolute) path in the value you give to the `src` attribute to reflect the location of the file.

NOTE

The actual filename depends on the version you download. At the time of writing, 1.11.2 is the current release.

Use a Remote Version

Instead of downloading and hosting jQuery yourself, you can include it from a so-called Content Delivery Network, or CDN. In addition to saving you from having to download the jQuery library, using a CDN version has a further advantage: It's quite likely that when users visit your page and their browser requests jQuery, it'll already be in their browser cache. Additionally, CDNs generally ensure that they serve the file from the server geographically closest to them, further cutting the loading time.

The official jQuery site currently lists the following CDNs:

- **Google Ajax API CDN**—http://ajax.googleapis.com/ajax/libs/jquery/1.11.2/jquery.min.js

- **Microsoft CDN**—http://ajax.aspnetcdn.com/ajax/jQuery/jquery-1.11.2.min.js

- **jQuery CDN**—http://code.jquery.com/jquery-1.11.2.min.js (Minified version), http://code.jquery.com/jquery-1.11.2.js (Source version)

You can then modify your `<script>` tag to suit the chosen CDN, for example:

```
<script  src="https://ajax.googleapis.com/ajax/libs/jquery/1.11.2/
jquery.min.js"></script>
```

Unless you have a particular reason for hosting jQuery yourself, this is usually the best way.

TIP

If you want to make sure your code is always using the latest release of jQuery, simply link to http://code.jquery.com/jquery-latest.min.js.

---

jQuery's $(document).ready **Handler**

At various places through this book you used the `window.onload` handler. jQuery has its own equivalent:

```
$(document).ready(function() {
    // jQuery code goes here
});
```

Pretty much all the jQuery code you write will be executed from within a statement like this.

Like `window.onload`, it accomplishes two things:

▶ It ensures that the code does not run until the DOM is available—that is, that any elements your code may be trying to access already exist—so your code doesn't return any errors.

▶ It helps make your code unobtrusive, by separating it from the semantic (HTML) and presentation (CSS) layers.

The jQuery version, though, has an advantage over the `window.onload` event; it doesn't block code execution until the entire page has finished loading, as would be the case with `window.onload`. With jQuery's `(document).ready`, the code begins to execute as soon as the DOM tree has been constructed, before all images and other resources have finished loading, speeding up performance a little.

Selecting Page Elements

jQuery lets you select elements in your HTML by enclosing them in the jQuery wrapper `$("")`.

TIP

You can also use single quotes in the wrapper function, `$('')`.

Here are some examples of sets of page elements wrapped with the $ operator:

```
$("span"); // all HTML span elements
$("#elem"); // the HTML element having id "elem"
$(".classname"); // HTML elements having class "classname"
$("div#elem"); // <div> elements with ID "elem"
$("ul li a.menu"); // anchors with class "menu" that are nested in list items
$("p > span"); // spans that are direct children of paragraphs
$("input[type=password]"); // inputs that have specified type
$("p:first"); // the first paragraph on the page
$("p:even"); // all even numbered paragraphs
```

So much for DOM and CSS selectors. But jQuery also has its own custom selectors, such as the following:

```
$(":header"); // header elements (h1 to h6)
$(":button"); // any button elements (inputs or buttons)
$(":radio"); // radio buttons
$(":checkbox"); // checkboxes
$(":checked"); // selected checkboxes or radio buttons
```

The jQuery statements shown in the preceding examples each return an object containing an array of the DOM elements specified by the expression inside the wrapper function. Note that in none of the preceding lines of code have you specified an action; you are simply getting the required elements from the DOM. In the sections that follow you learn how to work with these selected elements.

Working with HTML Content

One of jQuery's most useful time-saving tricks is to manipulate the content of page elements. The `html()` and `text()` methods allow you to get and set the content of any elements you've selected using the previous statements, while `attr()` lets you get and set the values of individual element attributes. Let's see some examples.

html()

The `html()` method gets the HTML of any element or collection of elements. It works pretty much like JavaScript's `innerHTML`:

```
var htmlContent = $("#elem").html();
/* variable htmlContent now contains all HTML
(including text) inside page element
with id "elem" */
```

Using similar syntax, you can set the HTML content of a specified element or collection of elements:

```
$("#elem").html("<p>Here is some new content.</p>");
/* page element with id "elem"
has had its HTML content replaced*/
```

text()

If you only want the text content of an element or collection of elements, without the HTML, you can use `text()`:

```
var textContent = $("#elem").text();
/* variable textContent contains all the
```

```
text (but not HTML) content from inside a
page element with id "elem" */
```

Once more you can change the text content of the specified element(s):

```
$("#elem").text("Here is some new content.");
/* page element with id "elem"
has had its text content replaced*/
```

If you want to append content to an element, rather than replacing it, you can use the following:

```
$("#elem").append("<p>Here is some new content.</p>");
/* keeps current content intact, but
adds the new content to the end */
```

And likewise:

```
$("div").append("<p>Here is some new content.</p>");
/* add the same content to all
<div> elements on the page. */
```

attr()

When passed a single argument, the `attr()` method gets the value for the specified attribute:

```
var title = $("#elem").attr("title");
```

If applied to a set of elements, it returns the value for only the first element in the matched set.

You can also pass a second argument to `attr()` to set an attribute value:

```
$("#elem").attr("title", "This is the new title");
```

Showing and Hiding Elements

Using plain old JavaScript, showing and hiding page elements usually means manipulating the value of the `display` and `visibility` properties of the element's `style` object. While that works OK, it can lead to pretty long lines of code:

```
document.getElementById("elem").style.visibility = 'visible';
```

You can use jQuery's `show()` and `hide()` methods to carry out these tasks with rather less code. The jQuery methods also offer some useful additional functionality, as you see in the following code examples.

show()

A simple way to make an element or set of elements visible is to call the show() method:

```
$("div").show(); // makes all <div> elements visible
```

However, you can also add some additional parameters to spice up the transition.

In the following example, the first parameter "fast" determines the speed of the transition. As an alternative to "fast" or "slow", jQuery is happy to accept a number of milliseconds for this argument, as the required duration of the transition. If no value is set, the transition will occur instantly, with no animation.

TIP

The value "slow" corresponds to 600ms, while "fast" is equivalent to 200ms.

The second argument is a function that operates as a callback; that is, it executes once the transition is complete:

```
$("#elem").show("fast", function() {
    // do something once the element is shown
});
```

Here we have used an anonymous function, but a named function works just fine too.

hide()

The hide() method is, of course, the exact reverse of show(), allowing you to make page elements invisible with the same optional arguments as you saw for hide():

```
$("#elem").hide("slow", function() {
    // do something once the element is hidden
});
```

toggle()

The toggle() method changes the current state of an element or collection of elements; it makes visible any element in the collection that is currently hidden and hides any currently being shown. The same optional duration and callback function parameters are also available to toggle().

```
$("#elem").toggle(1000, function() {
    // do something once the element is shown/hidden
});
```

TIP
Remember that the `show()`, `hide()`, and `toggle()` methods can be applied to collections of elements, so the elements in that collection will appear or disappear all at once.

Animating Elements

Some of the standard effects that jQuery offers are powerful. Animation of page elements once had to be done by tricky hand-coded routines using JavaScript timers. Those capabilities are neatly wrapped into a few jQuery methods that you can call for your elements or collections of elements.

Fading

You can fade an element in or out, optionally setting the transition duration and adding a callback function.

To fade out to invisibility:

```
$("#elem").fadeOut("slow", function() {
    // do something after fadeOut has finished executing
});
```

Or to fade in:

```
$("#elem").fadeIn(500, function() {
    // do something after fadeIn has finished executing
});
```

You can also fade an element only partially, either in or out:

```
$("#elem").fadeTo(3000, 0.5, function() {
    // do something after fade has finished executing
});
```

The second parameter (here set to 0.5) represents the target opacity. Its value works similarly to the way opacity values are set in CSS. Whatever the value of opacity before the method is called, the element will be animated until it reaches the value specified in the argument.

Sliding

You can slide elements, or collections of elements, upward or downward. The jQuery methods for sliding an element are direct corollaries to the fading methods you've just seen, and their arguments follow exactly the same rules:

```
$("#elem").slideDown(150, function() {
    // do something when slideDown is finished executing
});
```

And to slide up:

```
$("#elem").slideUp("slow", function() {
    // do something when slideUp is finished executing
});
```

In case you need to slide an element up or down depending on its current state, jQuery also provides a handy `slideToggle()` method:

```
$("#elem").slideToggle(1000, function() {
    // do something when slide up/down is finished executing
});
```

Animation

To animate an element, you do so by using jQuery to specify the CSS styles that the item should have applied. jQuery will impose the new styles, but can do so gradually (instead of applying them instantly as in plain CSS/JavaScript), thus creating an animation effect.

You can use `animate()` on a wide range of numerical CSS properties. In this example the width and height of an element are animated to a size of 400 x 500 pixels; once the animation is complete, the callback function is used to fade the element to invisibility:

```
$("#elem").animate(
    {
        width: "400px",
        height: "500px"
        }, 1500, function() {
            $(this).fadeOut("slow");
    }
);
```

Command Chaining

A further handy behavior of jQuery is that most jQuery methods return a jQuery object that can then be used in your call to another method. You could combine two of the previous examples, like this:

```
$("#elem").fadeOut().fadeIn();
```

The preceding code will fade out all the chosen elements, and then fade them back in. The number of items you can chain is arbitrarily large, allowing for several commands to successively work on the same collection of elements:

```
$("#elem").text("Hello from jQuery").fadeOut().fadeIn();
```

A Simple jQuery Animation

Let's use some of what you've learned so far to do a simple animation exercise with jQuery.

Your HTML page will initially display a `<div>` element, styled via CSS, but with no content. Here's the HTML for the page:

```
<!DOCTYPE html>
<html>
<head>
    <style>
        #animateMe {
            position:absolute;
            width: 100px;
            height: 400px;
            top: 100px;
            left: 100px;
            border: 2px solid black;
            background-color: red;
            padding: 20px;
        }
    </style>
</head>
<body>
    <div id="animateMe"></div>
</body>
</html>
```

First you need to add to your page a `<script>` element to link to the jQuery library—in this case, via a CDN:

```
<script src="http://code.jquery.com/jquery-latest.min.js"></script>
```

The first thing to do is add a little text to the `<div>` element using jQuery's `text()` method:

```
$("#animateMe").text("Changing shape...")
```

You can then call `animate()` to change the size (and therefore the shape) of the element:

```
$("#animateMe").animate(
    {
        width: "400px",
        height: "200px"
    }, 5000, function() {
        // callback function
    }
);
```

Of course, since the `text()` and `animate()` methods operate on the same element, you can use command chaining to concatenate the two:

```
$("#animateMe").text("Changing shape...").animate(
    {
        width: "400px",
        height: "200px"
    }, 5000, function() {
        // callback function
    }
);
```

When the animation has completed, let's change the text in the element, and then have the element fade slowly away. We'll chain these two commands, and use the callback function of the previous call to the `animate()` method to execute these additional commands once the animation is complete:

```
$("#animateMe").text("Changing shape...").animate(
    {
        width: "400px",
        height: "200px"
    }, 5000, function() {
        $(this).text("Fading away ...").fadeOut(4000);
    }
);
```

Note the use of `this`. Because you're currently carrying out methods on the `$("#animateMe")` parent element, using `this` inside the code block refers to that parent element.

Finally, you need to carry out all of this activity when the DOM is ready, by wrapping the code inside jQuery's `$(document).ready` handler.

The complete listing is shown in Listing 15.1. Create this page using your text editor, and load it into your browser.

CAUTION
_____

To use a version of jQuery stored on a CDN, you need your computer to be connected to the Internet. If you have no Internet connection, you need to use a local copy of jQuery to try out these examples.

LISTING 15.1   A Simple jQuery Animation

```html
<!DOCTYPE html>
<html>
<head>
    <style>
        #animateMe {
            position:absolute;
            width: 100px;
            height: 400px;
            top: 100px;
            left: 100px;
            border: 2px solid black;
            background-color: red;
            padding: 20px;
        }
    </style>
    <script src="http://code.jquery.com/jquery-latest.min.js"></script>
    <script>
        $(document).ready(function() {
            $("#animateMe").text("Changing shape...").animate(
                {
                    width: "400px",
                    height: "200px"
                }, 5000, function() {
                    $(this).text("Fading away ...").fadeOut(4000);
                }
            );
        });
    </script>
</head>
<body>
    <div id="animateMe"></div>
</body>
</html>
```

When the page has loaded, you should see a red `<div>` element with a black border, and containing the words "Changing shape...." Once animated to its new width and height, the wording changes to "Fading away...," and the element fades out to nothing. Figure 15.1 shows the animation taking place.

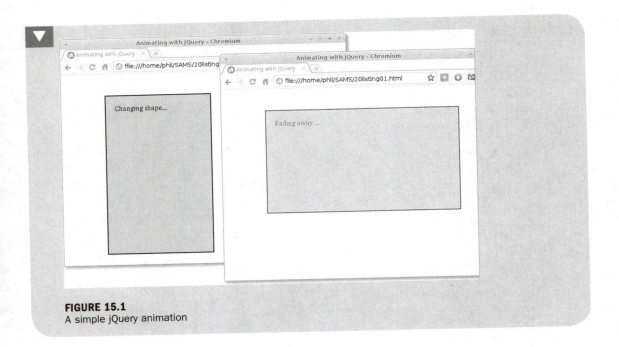

FIGURE 15.1
A simple jQuery animation

Handling Events

You can attach event handlers to elements or collections of elements a number of ways in jQuery. First, you can add event handlers directly, like this:

```
$("a").click(function() {
    // execute this code when any anchor element is clicked
});
```

Alternatively, you can use a named function, like this:

```
function hello() {
    alert("Hello from jQuery");
}
$("a").click(hello);
```

In these two examples the function will be executed when an anchor is clicked. Some other common events you might use in jQuery include blur, focus, hover, keypress, change, mouse-move, resize, scroll, submit, and select.

To help you add multiple event handlers, jQuery wraps the attachEvent and addEventLis-tener JavaScript methods in a cross-browser way:

```
$("a").on('click', hello);
```

The on() method can be used to attach handlers both to elements already present in the original HTML page and to elements that have been dynamically added to the DOM.

NOTE

The on() method was introduced in jQuery 1.7 and is the recommended replacement for several previous event-handling methods, including bind(), delegate(), and live(). See the jQuery documentation for complete details.

Summary

jQuery is a feature-rich and very popular JavaScript library with an easy-to-use API that works across the vast majority of popular browsers. In this hour you took a good look at the basics of jQuery and learned how it can help you to write concise cross-browser JavaScript applications.

Q&A

Q. Where did jQuery come from?

A. jQuery was written by John Resig and launched in 2006. There are currently several jQuery projects, including jQuery Core (used in this hour) and jQuery UI (which you learn about in Hour 16, "The jQuery UI User Interface Library"). These projects are under active development by John and a team of volunteers. You can read about the team and the projects at jquery.org.

Q. Is it possible to use jQuery alongside other libraries? Will there be conflicts?

A. Yes, jQuery can be used with other libraries. jQuery provides a means to prevent conflicts with the jQuery.noConflict() method. You can read about it at http://docs.jquery.com/Using_jQuery_with_Other_Libraries.

Workshop

Try to answer all the questions before reading the subsequent "Answers" section.

Quiz

1. How could you select all page elements having class = "sidebar"?

   a. $(".sidebar")

   b. $("class:sidebar")

   c. $(#sidebar)

2. The expression `$("p:first").show()` does what?

   a. Displays paragraph elements before displaying any other elements

   b. Makes the first paragraph element on the page visible

   c. Makes the first line of all paragraph elements visible

3. When applied to fades, slides, and animations, the value "fast" is equivalent to

   a. 1 second

   b. 600 milliseconds

   c. 200 milliseconds

Answers

1. a. `$(".sidebar")`

2. b. Makes the first paragraph element on the page visible

3. c. 200 milliseconds

Exercises

▶ Review some of the sample programs from earlier in the book. Pick a few to rewrite using jQuery, and try to do so.

▶ Visit the jQuery site at jquery.com and take a look at the documentation and examples, especially for the many jQuery methods that we didn't have space to discuss here.

The jQuery UI User Interface Library

What You'll Learn in This Hour:

▶ What jQuery UI is all about
▶ Using the ThemeRoller
▶ How to include jQuery UI in your pages
▶ Interactions: drag, drop, resize, and sort
▶ Using widgets: accordions, date pickers, and tabs

In the previous hour you learned about the jQuery open source JavaScript library. In this hour you see how to use its companion library jQuery UI.

jQuery UI provides advanced effects and theme-able widgets that help you to build interactive web applications.

What jQuery UI Is All About

The jQuery development team decided to launch an "official" collection of plug-ins for jQuery, bringing together a wide range of popular user interface components and giving them a common interface style. Using these components you can build highly interactive and attractively styled web applications with a minimum of code.

Using jQuery UI in your programs gives you access to

▶ **Interactions**—The jQuery UI library provides support for dragging and dropping, resizing, selecting, and sorting page elements.

▶ **Widgets**—These are feature-rich controls including accordion, autocomplete, button, date picker, dialog, progress bar, slider, and tabs.

▶ **Theme building**—Give your site a coherent look-and-feel across all of the user interface components. A ThemeRoller tool is available at http://jqueryui.com/themeroller/. The ThemeRoller online tool allows you to choose a theme from the gallery of prewritten designs or create a custom theme based on an existing theme as a starting point.

In this hour, you see how to use a selection of the more popular plug-ins. Thanks to the consistent user interface of jQuery UI, it will then be easy to explore the many other available plug-ins by using the jQuery documentation.

How to Include jQuery UI in Your Pages

The first step is to visit the jQuery ThemeRoller online application at http://jqueryui.com/themeroller/.

Using the ThemeRoller

The jQuery UI CSS Framework is a set of classes covering a wide range of user interface requirements. Using the ThemeRoller tool, you can build your own interface styles, either from scratch or based on any of the extensive collection of examples available in the gallery at http://jqueryui.com/themeroller/.

Once you've decided on a style, jQuery UI provides a download builder that packages only the components you need. It also handles any dependencies for your selected items, so you can't download a widget or interaction without all the ancillary files it requires. All you need to do is then download and unpack the zip file.

Once you've unpacked the download, you have the following directories:

```
/css/
/development-bundle/
/js/
```

The `development-bundle` directory holds the jQuery UI source code, demos, and documentation. If you don't intend to change any of the jQuery UI code, you can safely delete it.

Generally, you need to include from the remaining files your theme, jQuery, and jQuery UI on any page that is to use jQuery UI widgets and interactions:

```
<link rel="stylesheet" type="text/css" href="jquery-ui.min.css"/>
<script src="http://code.jquery.com/jquery-latest.min.js"></script>
<script src="http://codeorigin.jquery.com/ui/1.10.3/jquery-ui.min.js"></script>
```

If you use one of the standard gallery themes, you can alternatively link to all of the files you need on a Content Delivery Network:

```
<link rel="stylesheet" type="text/css"
href="http://ajax.googleapis.com/ajax/libs/jqueryui/1.10.3/themes/smoothness/
jquery-ui.css"/>
<script src="http://code.jquery.com/jquery-latest.min.js"></script>
<script src="http://codeorigin.jquery.com/ui/1.10.3/jquery-ui.min.js"></script>
```

Interactions

Let's take a look at some of the things you can do with jQuery UI to improve how page elements interact with the user.

Drag and Drop

Making an element draggable couldn't be simpler with jQuery UI:

```
$("#draggable").draggable();
```

Listing 16.1 shows how you could achieve this in an HTML page.

LISTING 16.1   Making a Page Element Draggable

```
<!DOCTYPE html>
<html>
<head>
    <link rel="stylesheet" type="text/css"
href="http://ajax.googleapis.com/ajax/libs/jqueryui/1.10.3/themes/smoothness/
jquery-ui.css"/>
    <style>
        #dragdiv {
            width: 100px;
            height: 100px;
            background-color: #eeffee;
            border: 1px solid black;
            padding: 5px;
        }
    </style>
    <title>Drag and Drop</title>
    <script src="http://code.jquery.com/jquery-latest.min.js"></script>
    <script src="http://codeorigin.jquery.com/ui/1.10.3/jquery-ui.min.js"></script>
    <script>
        $(function() {
            $("#dragdiv").draggable();
        });
    </script>
</head>
<body>
    <div id="dragdiv"> Drag this element around the page!</div>
</body>
</html>
```

When the page has loaded, the element `<div id="dragdiv">` is made draggable:

```
$(function() {
    $("#dragdiv").draggable();
});
```

You can then drag the item around the page by clicking the mouse on any part of the element, as depicted in Figure 16.1.

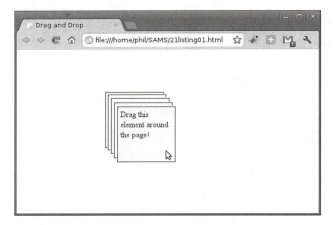

FIGURE 16.1
Dragging a page element

Drag and Drop with jQuery UI

To make an element capable of receiving another element that is dropped on it, you need to use the `droppable()` method. This method can be specified to act on various events, such as draggable items being dropped, being over the droppable area, or leaving the droppable area.

You're going to modify the code from Listing 16.1 to add a further, larger `<div>` element as the drop area:

```
<div id="dropdiv">This is the drop zone ...</div>
```

In addition to making the draggable item draggable, you need to specify that the new `<div>` element is a drop area, like this:

```
$("#dropdiv").droppable();
```

In addition, you're going to make the text on the draggable item change in response to being dropped, or to leaving the droppable area, by adding methods to the handlers of the `drop` and `out` events:

```
$("#dropdiv").droppable({
    drop: function() { $("#dragdiv").text("Dropped!"); },
    out: function() { $("#dragdiv").text("Off and running again ..."); }
});
```

Create an HTML page containing the code of Listing 16.2.

LISTING 16.2   Drag and Drop with jQuery UI

```html
<!DOCTYPE html>
<html>
<head>
    <link rel="stylesheet" type="text/css"
href="http://ajax.googleapis.com/ajax/libs/jqueryui/1.10.3/themes/smoothness/
jquery-ui.css"/>
<style>
        div {
            font: 12px normal arial, helvetica;
        }
        #dragdiv {
            width: 150px;
            height: 50px;
            background-color: #eeffee;
            border: 1px solid black;
            padding: 5px;
        }
        #dropdiv {
            position: absolute;
            top: 80px;
            left: 100px;
            width: 300px;
            height: 200px;
            border: 1px solid black;
            padding: 5px;
            }
    </style>
    <title>Drag and Drop</title>
    <script src="http://code.jquery.com/jquery-latest.min.js"></script>
    <script src="http://codeorigin.jquery.com/ui/1.10.3/jquery-ui.min.js"></script>
    <script>
        $(function() {
            $("#dragdiv").draggable();
            $("#dropdiv").droppable({
```

```
                        drop: function() { $("#dragdiv").text("Dropped!"); },
                        out: function() { $("#dragdiv").text("Off and running again ..."); 
}
                });
            });
    </script>
</head>
<body>
    <div id="dropdiv">This is the drop zone ...</div>
    <div id="dragdiv">Drag this element around the page!</div>
</body>
</html>
```

With the page loaded in your browser, you should now find that the draggable page element can be dropped within the droppable `<div>`, changing its text in response to the drop event.

The text changes once again as you drag the draggable item outside the border of the drop container, as shown in Google Chrome in Figure 16.2.

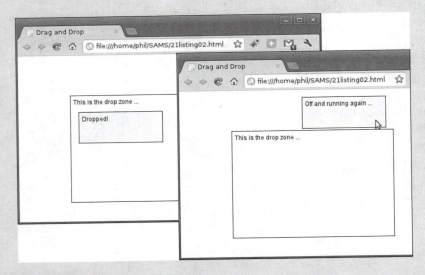

FIGURE 16.2
Drag and drop with jQuery UI

Resize

To add a resizing handle to a block element is equally trivial thanks to jQuery UI (see Figure 16.3):

```
$("#resizable").resizable();
```

To demonstrate, you can chain the `resizable()` method to the droppable container of Listing 16.2:

```
$(function() {
    $("#dragdiv").draggable();
    $("#dropdiv").droppable({
        drop: function() { $("#dragdiv").text("Dropped!"); },
        out: function() { $("#dragdiv").text("Off and running again ..."); }
    }).resizable();
});
```

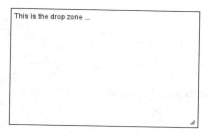

FIGURE 16.3
Adding a resizing handle

Sort

A further wrapper for drag-and-drop functionality is the `sortable()` method, which you can add to items in a list to make the list sortable:

```
$("#sortMe").sortable();
```

Listing 16.3 demonstrates how you might apply this method to an unordered list element.

LISTING 16.3   Making Elements Sortable

```
<!DOCTYPE html>
<html>
<head>
    <link rel="stylesheet" type="text/css"
```

```
href="http://ajax.googleapis.com/ajax/libs/jqueryui/1.10.3/themes/smoothness/
jquery-ui.css"/>
    <title>Sortable</title>
    <script src="http://code.jquery.com/jquery-latest.min.js"></script>
    <script src="http://codeorigin.jquery.com/ui/1.10.3/jquery-ui.min.js"></script>
    <script>
        $(function() {
            $("#sortMe").sortable();
        });
    </script>
</head>
<body>
    <ul id="sortMe">
        <li>One</li>
        <li>Two</li>
        <li>Three</li>
        <li>Four</li>
        <li>Five</li>
    </ul>
</body>
</html>
```

Dragging elements to a new location in the list causes the list to sort, "snapping" the list into a new order when the drop is made, as in Figure 16.4.

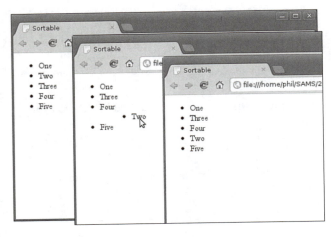

FIGURE 16.4
Sorting a list

Using Widgets

Widgets are interface items you can drop into your application with a minimum of fuss and complication.

Accordion

The accordion widget lets a user expand a list of `<div>` elements by opening just one at a time, leaving the remaining ones reduced to just a title bar.

First you need to add the data in the semantic layer, using pairs of headers and content panels:

```
<div id="accordion">
    <h3><a href="#">First header</a></h3>
    <div>First content</div>
    <h3><a href="#">Second header</a></h3>
    <div>Second content</div>
</div>
```

Next you can activate the accordion by calling the `accordion()` method on the outer container element:

```
$(function() {
        $("#accordion").accordion();
});
```

Listing 16.4 shows a sample application, here dividing the lunch options of a restaurant menu into separate folds of an accordion.

LISTING 16.4   Using the Accordion Widget

```
<!DOCTYPE html>
<html>
<head>
    <link rel="stylesheet" type="text/css"
href="http://ajax.googleapis.com/ajax/libs/jqueryui/1.10.3/themes/smoothness/
jquery-ui.css"/>
    <title>Menu Choices</title>
    <script src="http://code.jquery.com/jquery-latest.min.js"></script>
    <script src="http://codeorigin.jquery.com/ui/1.10.3/jquery-ui.min.js">
    </script>
    <script>
        $(function() {
            $("#accordion").accordion();
```

```
        });
    </script>

</head>
<body>
    <h2>Choose from the following menu options:</h2>

<div id="accordion">
    <h3><a href="#">Starters</a></h3>
    <div>
        <ul>
            <li>Clam Chowder</li>
            <li>Ham and Avocado Salad</li>
            <li>Stuffed Mushrooms</li>
            <li>Chicken Liver Pate</li>
        </ul>
    </div>
    <h3><a href="#">Main Courses</a></h3>
    <div>
        <ul>
            <li>Scottish Salmon</li>
            <li>Vegetable Lasagne</li>
            <li>Beef and Kidney Pie</li>
            <li>Roast Chicken</li>
        </ul>
    </div>
    <h3><a href="#">Desserts</a></h3>
    <div>
        <ul>
            <li>Chocolate Sundae</li>
            <li>Lemon Sorbet</li>
            <li>Fresh Fruit Salad</li>
            <li>Strawberry Cheesecake</li>
        </ul>
    </div>
</div>
</body>
</html>
```

Figure 16.5 shows the accordion widget in action. An accordion doesn't allow multiple content panels to be open at the same time; clicking on the Starters heading will open that section, at the same time closing Main Courses.

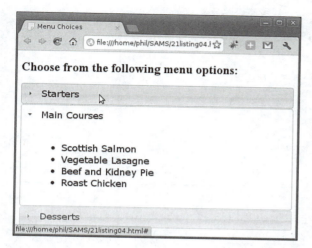

FIGURE 16.5
The accordion widget

Date Picker

Expecting visitors to correctly fill out date fields has always been a tricky business, mainly due to the wide range of possible date formats that may be used.

A date picker is a pop-up calendar widget that allows the user to simply click on the required day, leaving the widget to format the selected date and enter the appropriate data into the correct input field.

Suppose you have a form field to accept a date:

```
<input type="text" id="datepicker">
```

You can implement a date picker widget for that field with a single line of code:

```
$("#datepicker").datepicker();
```

Listing 16.5 has a complete example you can try.

LISTING 16.5   Using a Date Picker Widget

```
<!DOCTYPE html>
<html>
<head>
    <link rel="stylesheet" type="text/css"
href="http://ajax.googleapis.com/ajax/libs/jqueryui/1.10.3/themes/smoothness/
jquery-ui.css"/>
    <title>Date Picker</title>
```

```
<script src="http://code.jquery.com/jquery-latest.min.js"></script>
<script src="http://codeorigin.jquery.com/ui/1.10.3/jquery-ui.min.js"></script>
<script>
    $(function() {
        $( "#datepicker" ).datepicker();
    });
</script>
</head>
<body>
    Date: <input type="text" id="datepicker">
</body>
</html>
```

Figure 16.6 shows the date picker in action.

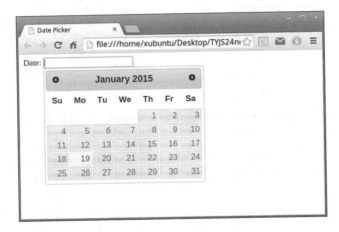

FIGURE 16.6
A date picker widget

Tabs

In the previous section you saw how to use an accordion widget to save some page area by showing just one panel of information from a list of options.

Another common way to achieve such a saving of space is by using a tabbed interface. Once again jQuery makes it a snap. Take a look at the code in Listing 16.6.

LISTING 16.6   A Tabbed Interface

```
<!DOCTYPE html>
<html>
<head>
    <link rel="stylesheet" type="text/css"
href="http://ajax.googleapis.com/ajax/libs/jqueryui/1.10.3/themes/smoothness/
jquery-ui.css"/>
    <title>Tabs</title>
    <script src="http://code.jquery.com/jquery-latest.min.js"></script>
    <script src="http://codeorigin.jquery.com/ui/1.10.3/jquery-ui.min.js"></script>
    <script>
        $(function() {
            $( "#tabs" ).tabs();
        });
    </script>
</head>
<body>
    <div id="tabs">
        <ul>
            <li><a href="#tabs-1">Home</a></li>
            <li><a href="#tabs-2">About Us</a></li>
            <li><a href="#tabs-3">Products</a></li>
        </ul>
        <div id="tabs-1">
            <p>Welcome to our online store....</p>
        </div>
        <div id="tabs-2">
            <p>We've been selling widgets for 5 years ...</p>
        </div>
        <div id="tabs-3">
            <p>We sell all kinds of widgets ...</p>
        </div>
    </div>
</body>
</html>
```

The tabs are contained in an unordered list:

```
<ul>
    <li><a href="#tabs-1">Home</a></li>
    ...
</ul>
```

The title of each tab is wrapped inside an anchor element, the `href` of which points to the ID of the `<div>` containing the content for that panel:

```
<div id="tabs-1">
    <p>Welcome to our online store....</p>
</div>
```

The whole of the preceding is wrapped within a div container with id="tabs", and to acti-vate the tabbed interface all you need to do is call the tabs() method against this container element:

```
$( "#tabs" ).tabs();
```

Once activated, the interface looks like the one shown in Figure 16.7.

FIGURE 16.7
Tabs

Summary

In this hour you learned how to build slick user interfaces using the jQuery UI library in addition to jQuery. You saw how to quickly add interactions and widgets to your pages, and how to set an overall style for your interface items using the ThemeRoller application.

Q&A

Q. **Can I further customize these interface elements?**

A. Yes you can. Due to the limited space in this book, each of the interactions and widgets demonstrated in this hour used the default settings. In reality, each has a host of custom-ization options to make it work just how you want. You'll find extensive documentation and examples at http://docs.jquery.com/UI/.

Q. **How can I make the other elements on my page have the same styles as those generated by jQuery UI?**

A. When jQuery UI generates markup, it applies classes to the newly created markup items. These classes correspond to CSS declarations in the jQuery UI CSS Framework. Full details for each widget are given in the jQuery UI documentation.

Workshop

Try to answer all the questions before reading the subsequent "Answers" section.

Quiz

1. To use the jQuery UI in your pages, each page must contain as a minimum:

    a. The jQuery and jQuery UI JavaScript libraries and a link to a jQuery UI theme CSS file

    b. Just the jQuery and jQuery UI libraries

    c. Just the jQuery UI JavaScript library and a link to a jQuery UI theme CSS file

2. How can you make a `<div>` element with `id = "parking"` capable of accepting items that are dropped on to it?

    a. `$("#parking").drop()`

    b. `$("#parking").dropzone()`

    c. `$("#parking").droppable()`

3. An accordion widget is capable of displaying:

    a. One content section at a time

    b. A definable number of content sections all at once

    c. All content sections at once

Answers

1. a. The jQuery and jQuery UI JavaScript libraries and a link to a jQuery UI theme CSS file

2. c. `$("#parking").droppable()`

3. a. An accordion can display one content section at a time.

Exercises

▶ Use the ThemeRoller to download a jQuery UI theme of your choice. Use it to reproduce some of the sample scripts of this hour, and compare the appearance of your pages with those displayed in the figures.

▶ Visit the jQuery UI documentation at http://docs.jquery.com/UI/ to investigate how some of these widgets can be further customized with options, and try out some examples using the listings in this hour as a starting point.

HOUR 17
Ajax with jQuery

What You'll Learn in This Hour:

▶ What Ajax is and how it helps the user experience
▶ How Ajax is implemented in raw JavaScript
▶ How to implement Ajax smoothly and simply using jQuery

JavaScript is a client-side scripting language, and all of the examples you've used so far have been limited entirely to client-side coding. Ajax allows you to communicate with the server in the background and display the results on your page without having to carry out a page refresh. This lets you create pages that interact more smoothly with the user.

In this hour, you'll learn the basics of the technology that underpins Ajax, and how you can use jQuery to make the whole process slick and simple.

The Anatomy of Ajax

So far we've discussed only the traditional page-based model of a website user interface.

When you interact with such a website, individual pages containing text, images, data entry forms, and so forth are presented to you one at a time. Each page must be dealt with individually before navigating to the next.

For instance, you may complete the data entry fields of a form, editing and re-editing your entries as much as you want, knowing that the data will not be sent to the server until the form is finally submitted.

This interaction is summarized in Figure 17.1.

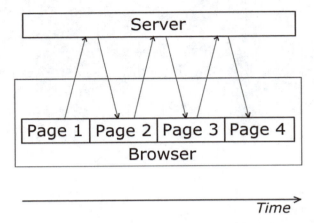

FIGURE 17.1
Traditional client–server interaction

After you submit a form or follow a navigation link, you then must wait while the browser screen refreshes to display the new or revised page that has been delivered by the server.

Unfortunately, interfaces built using this model have quite a few drawbacks. First, there is a significant delay while each new or revised page is loaded. This interrupts what we, as users, perceive as the "flow" of the application.

Furthermore, a *whole* page must be loaded on each occasion, even when most of its content is identical to that of the previous page. Items common to many pages on a website, such as header, footer, and navigation sections, can amount to a significant proportion of the data contained in the page.

This unnecessary download of data wastes bandwidth and further exacerbates the delay in loading each new page.

The combined effect of the issues just described is to offer a much inferior user experience compared to that provided by the vast majority of desktop applications. On the desktop, you expect the display contents of your programs to remain visible, and the interface elements to continue responding to your commands, while the computing processes occur quietly in the background.

Introducing Ajax

Ajax enables you to add to your web application interfaces some of this functionality more commonly seen in desktop applications. To achieve this, Ajax builds an extra "layer" of processing between the web page and the server.

This layer, often referred to as an Ajax Engine or Ajax Framework, intercepts requests from the user and in the background handles server communications quietly, unobtrusively, and *asynchronously*. This means that server requests and responses no longer need to coincide with particular user actions but may happen at any time convenient to the user and to the correct operation of the application. The browser does not freeze and await the completion by the server of the last request, but instead lets you carry on scrolling, clicking, and typing in the current page.

The updating of page elements to reflect the revised information received from the server is also looked after by Ajax, happening dynamically while the page continues to be used.

Figure 17.2 represents how these interactions take place.

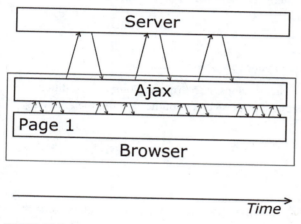

FIGURE 17.2
Ajax client-server interaction

The XMLHttpRequest Object

When you click on a hyperlink or submit an HTML form, you send an HTTP request to the server, which responds by serving to you a new or revised page. For your web application to work asynchronously, however, you must have a means to send HTTP requests to the server *without* an associated request to display a new page.

We can do so by means of the XMLHttpRequest object. This JavaScript object is capable of making a connection to the server and issuing an HTTP request without the necessity of an associated page load.

TIP

As a security measure, the XMLHttpRequest object can generally only make calls to URLs within the same domain as the calling page, and cannot directly call a remote server.

Different Rules for Different Browsers

Since you don't know in advance which browser, version, or operating system your users have, you must have your code adapt its behavior on the fly to ensure that the instance of the object will be created successfully.

For the majority of browsers that support XMLHttpRequest as a native object (Firefox, Opera, and the rest, as well as later versions of Internet Explorer), creating an instance of this object is straightforward. The following line creates an XMLHttpRequest object called request:

```
var request = new XMLHttpRequest();
```

To achieve the equivalent result in some earlier versions of Microsoft Internet Explorer, you need to create an ActiveX object. Here's an example:

```
var request = new ActiveXObject("Microsoft.XMLHTTP");
```

Once again, this assigns the name request to your new object.

To complicate matters a little more, some earlier versions of Internet Explorer have a different version of the Microsoft XML parser installed; in those cases you need to use the following instruction:

```
var request = new ActiveXObject("Msxml2.XMLHTTP");
```

Methods and Properties

Now that you have created an instance of your XMLHttpRequest object, let's look at some of the object's properties and methods, by referring to Table 17.1.

TABLE 17.1   XMLHttpRequest Objects and Methods

Properties	Description
onreadystatechange	Determines which event handler will be called when the object's readyState property changes
readyState	Integer reporting the status of the request:
	0 = uninitialized
	1 = loading
	2 = loaded
	3 = interactive
	4 = completed
responseText	Data returned by the server in text string form
responseXML	Data returned by the server expressed as a document object

Properties	Description
`status`	HTTP status code returned by server
`statusText`	HTTP reason phrase returned by server
Methods	*Description*
`abort()`	Stop the current request
`getAllResponseHeaders()`	Returns all headers as a string
`getResponseHeader(x)`	Returns the value of header x as a string
`open('method','URL','a')`	Specifies the HTTP method (e.g., `GET` or `POST`), the target URL, and whether the request should be handled asynchronously (if yes, `a='true'` [default]; if no, `a='false'`)
`send(content)`	Sends the request, optionally with POST data
`setRequestHeader('x','y')`	Sets a parameter and value pair x=y and assigns it to the header to be sent with the request

Over the next few lessons we examine how these methods and properties are used to create the functions that form the building blocks of your Ajax applications.

Talking with the Server

In the traditional style of web page, when you issue a server request via a hyperlink or a form submission, the server accepts that request, carries out any server-side processing required, and subsequently serves to you a new page with content appropriate to the action you've taken.

While this processing takes place, your user interface is effectively frozen. You are made aware when the server has completed its task by the appearance in the browser of the new or revised page.

With asynchronous server requests, however, such communications occur in the background, and the completion of such a request does not necessarily coincide with a screen refresh or a new page being loaded. You must therefore make other arrangements to find out what progress the server has made in dealing with your request.

The `XMLHttpRequest` object possesses a convenient property to report on the progress of the server request. You can examine this property using JavaScript routines to determine the point at which the server has completed its task, and the results are available for you to use.

Your Ajax armory must therefore include a routine to monitor the status of your request and act accordingly. We look at this in more detail later in the hour.

What Happens at the Server?

So far as the server-side script is concerned, the communication from your `XMLHttpRequest` object is just another HTTP request. Ajax applications care little about what languages or operating environments exist at the server; provided that the client-side Ajax layer receives a timely and correctly formatted HTTP response from the server, everything will work just fine.

Dealing with the Server Response

Once notified that an asynchronous request has been successfully completed, you may then use the information returned by the server.

Ajax allows for this information to be returned to you in a number of formats, including ASCII text and XML data.

Depending on the nature of the application, you may then translate, display, or otherwise process this information within your current page.

But There's an Easier Way, Right?

Luckily, there are plenty of JavaScript libraries out there that make a good job of packaging these rather complicated procedures into easy-to-use functions and methods.

In the remainder of this hour you'll see how the jQuery library can make writing Ajax scripts a piece of cake.

Using jQuery to Implement Ajax

As you probably now realize, Ajax programming from scratch can be a little cumbersome. Fortunately, jQuery solves this for you, letting you write Ajax routines in few lines of code.

There are a number of jQuery methods for performing Ajax calls to the server; the more frequently used ones are described here.

load()

When you simply want to grab a document from the server and display it in a page element, `load()` might be all you require. The following code snippet gets the file newContent.html and adds its content to the element with `id="elem"`:

```
$(function() {
    $("#elem").load("newContent.html");
});
```

A neat trick is that you can pass a selector along with the URL, and only get the part of the page corresponding to that selector:

```
$(function() {
    $("#elem").load("newContent.html #info");
});
```

Here you have added a jQuery selector after the URL, separated by a space. This causes jQuery to pass back only the content of the container specified by the selector; in this case, the element with ID of `info`.

When `load()` gives you too little control, jQuery offers methods to send GET and POST requests too.

get() **and** post()

The two methods are similar, simply invoking different request types. You don't need to select a jQuery object (such as a page element or set of elements); instead, you can call `get()` or `post()` directly using `$.get()` or `$.post()`. In its simplest form, the `get()` or `post()` method takes a single argument, the target URL.

You'll often want to send data to the server using `get()` or `post()`. Such data is sent as a set of parameter and value pairs in an encoded string.

TIP

If you are collecting data from form fields, jQuery offers the handy `serialize()` method that can assemble the form data for you:

```
var formdata = $('#form1').serialize();
```

In most cases, though, you'll want to do something with the returned data. To do that, you pass a callback function as an argument:

```
$.get("serverScript.php",
    {param1: "value1", param2: "value2"},
    function(data) {
        alert("Server responded: " + data);
});
```

The syntax for `post()` is essentially the same:

```
$.post("serverScript.php",
    {param1: "value1", param2: "value2"},
    function(data) {
        alert("Server responded: " + data);
});
```

ajax()

For the ultimate flexibility, the `ajax()` method allows you to set virtually every aspect of the Ajax call and how to handle the response. For full details of using `ajax()` see the documentation at http://api.jquery.com/jQuery.ajax/.

▼ TRY IT YOURSELF

An Ajax Form with jQuery

Let's round off this hour with an example of a simple Ajax form submission powered by jQuery.

We'll work with this simple HTML form:

```
<form id="form1">
    Name<input type="text" name="name" id="name"><br />
    Email<input type="text" name="email" id="email"><br />
    <input type="submit" name="submit" id="submit" value="Submit Form">
</form>
```

You're going to use jQuery to carry out the following tasks:

▶ Check that both input fields contain text.

▶ Submit the form via Ajax using HTTP POST.

▶ Print the data returned from the server into a `<div>` element on the page.

To check that both fields have had data entered, you use a simple function:

```
function checkFields(){
    return ($("#name").val() && $("#email").val());
}
```

For the function to return Boolean true, the value attribute of both form fields must contain some text data; if either field is empty, the blank field will be interpreted as "falsy" and the logical AND (&&) operator will cause false to be returned from the function.

Next, apply jQuery's `submit()` event handler to detect form submission. If your function `check-Fields()` returns false, the default behavior will be canceled and the form won't be submitted; otherwise, jQuery serializes the data and sends a `post()` request to the server script.

The jQuery `serialize()` method is used to collect the form information into a serialized string to send as a data payload with the Ajax call.

For this example, the server script test.php doesn't do anything except format the information it receives and send it back as a little piece of HTML:

```
<?php
echo "Name: " . $_REQUEST['name'] . "<br />Email: " . $_REQUEST['email'];
?>
```

Finally, the callback function displays the returned information on the page:

```
function(data){
    $("#div1").html(data);
}
```

The code is shown in Listing 17.1.

LISTING 17.1   An Ajax Form

```html
<!DOCTYPE html>
<html>
<head>
    <title>Ajax Form Submission</title>
    <script src="http://code.jquery.com/jquery-latest.min.js"></script>
    <script>
        $(document).ready(function(){
            function checkFields(){
                return ($("#name").val() && $("#email").val());
            }

            $("#form1").submit(function(){
                if(checkFields()){
                    $.post(
                        'test.php', $("#form1").serialize(),
                        function(data){
                            $("#div1").html(data);
                        }
                    );
                }
                else alert("Please fill in name and email fields!");
                return false;
            });
        });
    </script>
</head>
<body>
    <form id="form1">
        Name<input type="text" name="name" id="name"><br />
        Email<input type="text" name="email" id="email"><br />
        <input type="submit" name="submit" id="submit" value="Submit Form">
    </form>
    <div id="div1"></div>
</body>
</html>
```

To run this example you need to upload both the file listed in Listing 17.1 and the server file test.php to a web server with PHP support.

Trying to submit the form with one or both of the input fields left blank will cause the script to issue an alert message and prevent the form submission.

A successful form submission should result in the formatted data being presented on the page, as shown in Figure 17.3. The figure also shows Firebug Lite displaying details of the Ajax call and response.

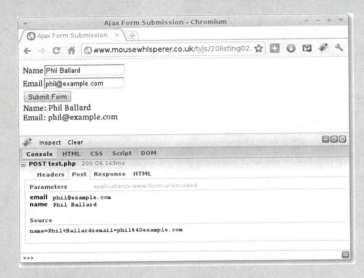

FIGURE 17.3
An Ajax form using jQuery

Summary

In this hour you took a good look at the basics of Ajax programming and learned how you can use the jQuery library to make the whole process much more slick and straightforward.

Q&A

Q. How did Ajax get its name?

A. Ajax is an acronym for Asynchronous JavaScript And XML. In practice, though, Ajax is by no means limited to returning just XML data.

Q. Do other libraries besides jQuery implement Ajax?

A. Certainly. There are many libraries and frameworks that help you implement Ajax, some popular ones being Dojo, MooTools, and Prototype.

Workshop

Try to answer all the questions before reading the subsequent "Answers" section.

Quiz

1. Which of these will grab element with `id=source` from server file examples.html and insert it into a page element with `id=target`?

   a. `$("#target").load("examples.html #source");`

   b. `$("#source").load("examples.html #target");`

   c. `$(#source).load("examples.html #info");`

2. A function used to process the data returned from an Ajax call is called:

   a. An anonymous function

   b. A callback function

   c. An Ajax request

3. The jQuery `serialize()` method:

   a. Encodes a set of form elements as a string for submission.

   b. Encodes a set of form elements as a JSON object for submission.

   c. Encodes a set of form elements as a JavaScript array for submission.

Answers

1. a. `$("#target").load("examples.html #source");`

2. b. A callback function

3. a. The jQuery `serialize()` method encodes a set of form elements as a string for submission.

Exercises

▶ Upload some plain text in a .txt file to your server. Create an HTML page that uses jQuery's `load()` method to return the text and display it in a `<div>` element of your page.

▶ Amend the code of this hour's "Try It Yourself" exercise to disallow form submission if either data entry field is blank *or* contains data less than four characters long.

HOUR 18
Reading and Writing Cookies

Something that the JavaScript techniques that you have seen so far can't do is transfer information from one page to another. Cookies provide a convenient way to give your web pages the means to store and retrieve small pieces of information on a user's own computer, allowing your website to save details such as a user's preferences or dates of his or her prior visits to your site.

In this hour you learn how to create, save, retrieve, and delete cookies using JavaScript.

What Are Cookies?

The HTTP protocol that you use to load web pages into your browser is a so-called *stateless* protocol. This means that once the server has delivered the requested page to your browser, it considers the transaction complete and retains no memory of it. This makes it difficult to maintain certain sorts of continuity during a browsing session (or between one session and the next) such as keeping track of which information the visitor has already read or downloaded, or of his or her login status to a private area of the site.

Cookies are a way to get around this problem; you could, for example, use cookies to remember a user's last visit, save a list of that user's preferences, or keep track of shopping cart items while he or she continues to shop. Correctly used, cookies can help improve the experience perceived by the user while using your site.

The cookies themselves are small strings of information that can be stored on a user's computer by the web pages he or she visits, to be later read by any other web pages from within the correct domain and path. Cookies are set to expire after a specified length of time.

CAUTION

Be aware that many users do not allow websites to leave cookies on their computers, so be sure not to make your websites depend on them.

The usual reason is that some websites use cookies as part of advertising systems, using them to track users' online activities with a view to selecting appropriate advertisements. It may be advisable to show an explanation of why you are going to use the cookie and what you'll use it for.

Limitations of Cookies

Your browser may have a limit to how many cookies it can store—normally a few hundred cookies or more. Usually, 20 cookies per domain name are permitted. A total of 4KB of cookie information can be stored for an individual domain.

In addition to the potential problems created by these size limitations, cookies can also vanish from a hard disk for various reasons, such as the cookie's expiry date being reached or the user clearing cookie information or switching browsers. Cookies should therefore never be used to store critical data, and your code should always be written to cope with situations where an expected cookie cannot be retrieved.

The `document.cookie` Property

Cookies in JavaScript are stored and retrieved by using the `cookie` property of the `document` object.

Each cookie is essentially a text string consisting of a name and a value pair, like this:

```
username=sam
```

When a web page is loaded into your browser, the browser marshals all of the cookies available to that page into a single string-like property, which is available as `document.cookie`. Within `document.cookie`, the individual cookies are separated by semicolons:

```
username=sam;location=USA;status=fullmember;
```

TIP

I refer to `document.cookie` as a *string-like* property, because it isn't really a string—it just behaves like one when you're trying to extract cookie information, as you see during this hour.

Escaping and Unescaping Data

Cookie values may not include certain characters. Those disallowed include semicolons, commas, and whitespace characters such as space and tab. Before storing data to a cookie, you need to encode the data in such a way that it will be stored correctly.

You can use the JavaScript `escape()` function to encode a value before storing it, and the corresponding `unescape()` function to later recover the original cookie value.

The `escape()` function converts any non-ASCII character in the string to its equivalent two- or four-digit hexadecimal format—so a blank space is converted into `%20`, and the ampersand character (&) to `%26`.

For example, the following code snippet writes out the original string saved in variable `str` followed by its value after applying the `escape()` function:

```
var str = 'Here is a (short) piece of text.';
document.write(str + '<br />' + escape(str));
```

The output to the screen would be

```
Here is a (short) piece of text.
Here%20is%20a%20%28short%29%20piece%20of%20text.
```

Notice that the spaces have been replaced by `%20`, the opening parenthesis by `%28`, and the closing parenthesis by `%29`.

All special characters, with the exception of *, @, -, _, +, ., and /, are encoded.

Cookie Ingredients

The cookie information in `document.cookie` may look like a simple string of name and value pairs, each in the form of

```
name=value;
```

but really each cookie has certain other pieces of information associated with it, as outlined in the following sections.

NOTE

The definitive specification for cookies was published in 2011 as RFC6265. You can read it at http://tools.ietf.org/html/rfc6265.

cookieName **and** cookieValue

These are the name and value visible in each `name=value` pair in the cookie string.

domain

The `domain` attribute tells the browser to which domain the cookie belongs. This attribute is optional, and when not specified its value defaults to the domain of the page setting the cookie.

The purpose of the `domain` attribute is to control cookie operation across subdomains. If the domain is set to www.example.com, then pages on a subdomain such as code.example.com cannot read the cookie. If, however, `domain` is set to example.com, then pages in code.example.com will be able to access it.

You cannot set the `domain` attribute to any domain outside the one containing your page.

path

The `path` attribute lets you specify a directory where the cookie is available. If you want the cookie to be only set for pages in directory `documents`, set the path to `/documents`. The `path` attribute is optional, the usual default path being /, in which case the cookie is valid for the whole domain.

secure

The optional and rarely used `secure` flag indicates that the browser should use SSL security when sending the cookie to the server.

expires

Each cookie has an `expires` date after which the cookie is automatically deleted. The `expires` date should be in UTC time (Greenwich Mean Time, or GMT). If no value is set for `expires`, the cookie will only last as long as the current browser session and will be automatically deleted when the browser is closed.

Writing a Cookie

To write a new cookie, you simply assign a value to `document.cookie` containing the attributes required:

```
document.cookie = "username=sam;expires=15/06/2013 00:00:00";
```

To avoid having to set the date format manually, we could do the same thing using JavaScript's Date object:

```
var cookieDate = new Date ( 2013, 05, 15 );
document.cookie = "username=sam;expires=" + cookieDate.toUTCString();
```

This produces a result identical to the previous example.

TIP

Note the use of

```
cookieDate.toUTCString();
```

instead of

```
cookieDate.toString();
```

because cookie dates always need to be set in UTC time.

In practice, you should use `escape()` to ensure that no disallowed characters find their way into the cookie values:

```
var cookieDate = new Date ( 2013, 05, 15 );
var user = "Sam Jones";
document.cookie = "username=" + escape(user) + ";expires=" +
➥cookieDate.toUTCString();
```

A Function to Write a Cookie

It's fairly straightforward to write a function to write your cookie for you, leaving all the escaping and the wrangling of optional attributes to the function. The code for such a function appears in Listing 18.1.

LISTING 18.1 **Function to Write a Cookie**

```
function createCookie(name, value, days, path, domain, secure) {
    if (days) {
        var date = new Date();
        date.setTime(date.getTime() + (days*24*60*60*1000));
        var expires = date.toGMTString();
    }
    else var expires = "";
    cookieString = name + "=" + escape (value);
    if (expires) cookieString += "; expires=" + expires;
    if (path) cookieString += "; path=" + escape (path);
    if (domain) cookieString += "; domain=" + escape (domain);
    if (secure) cookieString += "; secure";
    document.cookie = cookieString;
}
```

The operation of the function is straightforward. The `name` and `value` arguments are assembled into a `name=value` string, after escaping the `value` part to avoid errors with any disallowed characters.

Instead of specifying a date string to the function, we are asked to pass the number of days required before expiry. The function then handles the conversion into a suitable date string.

The remaining attributes are all optional and are appended to the string only if they exist as arguments.

CAUTION

Your browser security may prevent you from trying out the examples in this hour if you try simply loading the files from your local machine into your browser. To see the examples working, you may need to upload the files to a web server on the Internet or elsewhere on your local network.

▼ TRY IT YOURSELF

Writing Cookies

Let's use this function to set the values of some cookies. The code for our simple page is shown in Listing 18.2. Create a new file named testcookie.html and enter the code as listed. Feel free to use different values for the name and value pairs that you store in your cookies.

LISTING 18.2 Writing Cookies

```
<!DOCTYPE html>
<html>
<head>
<title>Using Cookies</title>
<script>
    function createCookie(name, value, days, path, domain, secure) {
    if (days) {
            var date = new Date();
            date.setTime(date.getTime() + (days*24*60*60*1000));
            var expires = date.toGMTString();
        }
        else var expires = "";
        cookieString = name + "=" + escape (value);
        if (expires) cookieString += "; expires=" + expires;
        if (path) cookieString += "; path=" + escape (path);
        if (domain) cookieString += "; domain=" + escape (domain);
        if (secure) cookieString += "; secure";
        document.cookie = cookieString;
    }
    createCookie("username","Sam Jones", 5);
    createCookie("location","USA", 5);
    createCookie("status","fullmember", 5);
</script>
```

```
</head>
<body>
Check the cookies for this domain using your browser tools.
</body>
</html>
```

Upload this HTML file to an Internet host or a web server on your local area network, if you have one. The loaded page displays nothing but a single line of text:

```
Check the cookies for this domain using your browser tools.
```

In the Chromium browser, I can open Developer Tools using Shift+Ctrl+I—if you are using a different browser, check the documentation for how to view cookie information.

My result is shown in Figure 18.1.

TIP

Note that each time the function is called, it sets a new value for `document.cookie`, yet this value does not overwrite the previous one; instead, it appends your new cookie to the cookie values already present. As I said, `document.cookie` sometimes *appears* to act like a string, but it isn't one really.

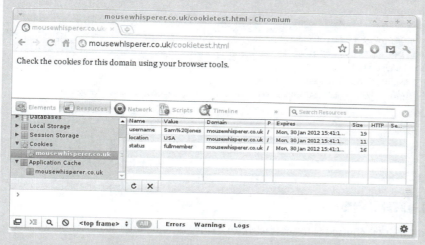

FIGURE 18.1
Displaying our cookies

Reading a Cookie

The function to read the value of a cookie relies heavily on JavaScript's `split()` string method that you learned about in Hour 5, "Numbers and Strings." You may recall that `split()` takes a string and splits it into an array of items, using a specified character to determine where the string should be divided:

```
myString = "John#Paul#George#Ringo";
var myArray = myString.split('#');
```

The preceding statement would divide string `myString` into a series of separate parts, cutting the string at each occurrence of the hash (#) character; `myArray[0]` would contain "John," `myArray[1]` would contain "Paul," and so forth.

Since in `document.cookie` the individual cookies are divided by the semicolon character, this character is initially used to break up the string returned by `document.cookie`:

```
var crumbs = document.cookie.split(';');
```

You want to search for a cookie of a specific name, so the resulting array `crumbs` is next searched for any items having the appropriate `name=` part.

The `indexOf()` and `substring()` methods are combined to return the value part of the cookie, which is then returned by the function after using `unescape()` to remove any encoding:

```
function getCookie(name) {
    var nameEquals = name + "=";
    var crumbs = document.cookie.split(';');
    for (var i = 0; i < crumbs.length; i++) {
        var crumb = crumbs[i];
        if (crumb.indexOf(nameEquals) == 0) {
            return unescape(crumb.substring(nameEquals.length, crumb.length));
        }
    }
    return null;
}
```

Deleting Cookies

To delete a cookie, all that is required is to set it with an expiry date before the current day. The browser infers that the cookie has already expired and deletes it.

```
function deleteCookie(name) {
    createCookie(name,"",-1);
}
```

CAUTION

Some versions of some browsers maintain the cookie until you restart your browser even if you have deleted it in the script. If your program depends on the deletion definitely having happened, do another `getCookie` test on the deleted cookie to make sure it has really gone.

 TRY IT YOURSELF ▼

Using Cookies

Let's put together all you've learned so far about cookies by building some pages to test cookie operation.

First, collect the functions `createCookie()`, `getCookie()`, and `deleteCookie()` into a single JavaScript file and save it as cookie.js, using the code in Listing 18.3.

LISTING 18.3   cookies.js

```javascript
function createCookie(name, value, days, path, domain, secure) {
    if (days) {
        var date = new Date();
        date.setTime( date.getTime() + (days*24*60*60*1000));
        var expires = date.toGMTString();
    }
    else var expires = "";
    cookieString = name + "=" + escape (value);
    if (expires) cookieString +=    "; expires=" + expires;
    if (path) cookieString += "; path=" + escape (path);
    if (domain) cookieString += "; domain=" + escape (domain);
    if (secure) cookieString += "; secure";
    document.cookie = cookieString;
}

function getCookie(name) {
    var nameEquals = name + "=";
    var crumbs = document.cookie.split(';');
    for (var i = 0; i < crumbs.length; i++) {
        var crumb = crumbs[i].trim();
        if (crumb.indexOf(nameEquals) == 0) {
            return unescape(crumb.substring(nameEquals.length, crumb.length));
        }
    }
    return null;
}

function deleteCookie(name) {
    createCookie(name,"",-1);
}
```

This file will be included in the `<head>` of your test pages so that the three functions are available for use by your code.

The code for the first test page, cookietest.html, is listed in Listing 18.4, and that for a second test page, cookietest2.html, in Listing 18.5. Create both of these pages in your text editor.

LISTING 18.4   cookietest.html

```
<!DOCTYPE html>
<html>
<head>
    <title>Cookie Testing</title>
    <script src="cookies.js"></script>
    <script>
        window.onload = function() {
            var cookievalue = prompt("Cookie Value:");
            createCookie("myCookieData", cookievalue);
        }
    </script>
</head>
<body>
    <a href="cookietest2.html">Go to Cookie Test Page 2</a>
</body>
</html>
```

LISTING 18.5   cookietest2.html

```
<!DOCTYPE html>
<html>
<head>
    <title>Cookie Testing</title>
    <script src="cookies.js"></script>
    <script>
        window.onload = function() {
            document.getElementById("output").innerHTML = "Your cookie value: " +
            ➥getCookie("myCookieData");
        }
    </script>
</head>
<body>
    <a href="cookietest.html">Back to Cookie Test Page 1</a><br/>
    <div id="output"></div>
</body>
</html>
```

The only visible page content in cookietest.html is a link to the second page cookietest2.html. However, the `window.onload` event is captured by the code on the page and used to execute a function that launches a `prompt()` dialog as soon as the page has finished loading. The dialog asks you for a value to be saved to your cookie, and then calls `createCookie()` to set a cookie of name `myCookieData` with the value that you just entered.

The page cookietest.html is shown working in Figure 18.2.

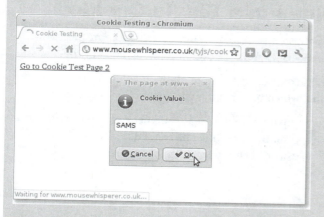

FIGURE 18.2
Enter a value for your cookie.

After setting your cookie, use the link to navigate to cookietest2.html.

When this page loads, the `window.onload` event handler executes a function that retrieves the stored cookie value using `getCookie()` and writes it to the page, as shown in Figure 18.3.

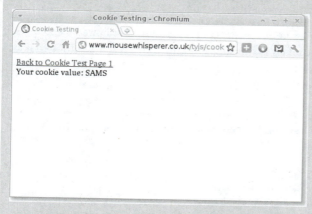

FIGURE 18.3
Retrieving the value of your cookie

To try it out for yourself, you need to upload the files cookietest.html, cookietest2.html, and cookies.js to a web server on the Internet (or one on your local network, if you have one) as browser security will probably prevent you from setting cookies when using the `file://` protocol to view a file on your own computer.

Setting Multiple Values in a Single Cookie

Each cookie contains one `name=value` pair, so if you need to store several separate pieces of data such as a user's name, age, and membership number, you need three different cookies.

However, with a little ingenuity you can make your cookie store all three values by concatenating the required values into a single string, which becomes the value stored by your cookie.

This way, instead of having three separate cookies for name, age, and membership number, you could have just one, perhaps named `user`, containing all three pieces of data. To separate the details later, you place in your value string a special character called a *delimiter* to separate the different pieces of data:

```
var userdata = "Sandy|26|A23679";
createCookie("user", userdata);
```

Here the | (pipe) character acts as the delimiter. When you later retrieve the cookie value, you can split it into its separate variable values by using the | delimiter:

```
var myUser = getCookie("user");
var myUserArray = myUser.split('|');
var name = myUserArray[0];
var age = myUserArray[1];
var memNo = myUserArray[2];
```

Cookies that store multiple values use up fewer of the 20 cookies per domain allowed by some browsers, but remember that your use of cookies is still subject to the 4KB overall limit for cookie information.

NOTE

This is a further example of serialization, which you learned about in Hour 10, "Meet JSON."

Summary

In this hour you learned about cookies, and how to set, retrieve, and delete them using JavaScript. You also learned how to concatenate multiple values into a single cookie.

Q&A

Q. When concatenating multiple values into a single cookie, can you use any character as a delimiter?

A. You can't use any character that might appear in your escaped data (except as the delimiter character), nor can you use equals (=) or the semicolon (;) as these are used to assemble and concatenate the `name=value` pairs in `document.cookie`. Additionally, cookies may not include whitespace or commas, so naturally they cannot be used as delimiters either.

Q. Are cookies safe?

A. Questions are often raised over the security of cookies, but such fears are largely unfounded. Cookies *can* help website owners and advertisers track your browsing habits, and they can (and do) use such information to select advertisements and promotions to show on web pages that you visit. Website owners and advertisers can't, however, find out personal information about you or access other items on your hard disk simply through the use of cookies.

Workshop

Try to answer all the questions before reading the subsequent "Answers" section.

Quiz

1. Cookies are small pieces of text information stored

    a. On a user's hard disk

    b. On the server

    c. At the user's Internet service provider

2. Encoding a string to store it safely in a cookie can be carried out by using

    a. `escape()`

    b. `unescape()`

    c. `split()`

3. A character used to separate multiple values in a single cookie is known as

    a. An escape sequence

    b. A delimiter

    c. A semicolon

Answers

1. a. Cookies are stored on a user's hard disk.

2. a. You can use `escape()` to safely encode string values for storage in a cookie.

3. b. Multiple values are separated by a character called a delimiter.

Exercises

▶ Find out how to view cookie information in your favorite browser. Use the browser tools to examine the cookie set by the code of Listing 18.4.

▶ Rewrite the code for cookietest.html and cookietest2.html to write multiple values to the same cookie and separate them on retrieval, displaying the values on separate lines. Use the hash character (#) as your delimiter.

▶ Add a button to cookietest2.html to delete the cookie set in cookietest.html and check that it works as requested. (Hint: Use the button to call `deleteCookie()`.)

Coming Soon to JavaScript

What You'll Learn in This Hour:

▶ About some of the most important new additions coming soon to JavaScript
▶ How to find out which features are supported by which browsers
▶ How to use some of the new language features right away

ECMAScript 6 (codenamed *Harmony*) is the forthcoming version of the ECMAScript standard that underpins the JavaScript language. This new standard should be ratified sometime in 2015.

ECMAScript 6 is a significant update to the specification, and the first major update to the language since ECMAScript 5 became standardized in 2009. The major browser manufacturers are already working on implementing the new features in their JavaScript engines.

In this hour we'll take a look at a few of the most important new features, some of which you can already use.

TIP

At the time of writing, Google's Chrome browser has support for ECMAScript 6 turned off by default. You can turn it on by visiting the chrome://flags/ page and finding the Enable Experimental JavaScript entry.

NOTE

You can check out the current compatibility status for various browsers and ECMAScript 6 features at http://kangax.github.io/compat-table/es6/.

Classes

In Hour 8, "Object-Oriented Programming," you read about OOP and saw examples of how to create and manipulate objects, including this one:

```
function Car(Color, Year, Make, Miles) {
    this.color = Color;
    this.year = Year;
    this.make = Make;
    this.odometerReading = Miles;
    this.setOdometer = function(newMiles) {
        this.odometerReading = newMiles;
    }
}
```

If you've come to JavaScript from another programming language you may already be familiar with *classes*. A class is a representation of an object.

```
class Car {
    constructor(Color, Year, Make, Miles) {
        this.color = Color;
        this.year = Year;
        this.make = Make;
        this.odometerReading = Miles;
    }

    setOdometer(newMiles) {
        this.odometerReading = newMiles;
    }
}
```

This syntax also allows you to *extend* classes, creating a new class that inherits the properties of the parent. Here's an example:

```
class Sportscar extends Car {
    constructor(Color, Year, Make, Miles) {
        super(Color, Year, Make, Miles);
        this.doors = 2;
    }
}
```

Here I've used the `super` keyword in my constructor, allowing me to call the constructor of a parent class and inherit all of its properties. In truth, this is just syntactic sugar; everything using classes can be rewritten in functions and prototypes, just like you learned in Hour 8. However, it's much more compatible with other popular languages, and somewhat easier to read.

Arrow Functions

The arrow function (=>) is a shorthand syntax for an anonymous function.

```
param => statements or expression
```

Let's explicate this a bit more:

- *param*—The name of an argument or arguments. If the function has zero arguments, this needs to be indicated with (). For only one argument the parentheses are not required.

- *statements or expression*—Multiple statements need to be enclosed in curly braces. A single expression, though, doesn't need braces. The expression is also the return value of that function.

```
var overTen = x => x > 10 ? 10 : x;
overTen(8); // returns 8
overTen(12); // returns 10
```

Note that the `function` keyword isn't required, and that the parentheses can be omitted since there is a single argument. The following example has two arguments:

```
var higher = (x, y) => {
    if (x > y) {
        return x;
    } else {
        return y;
    }
}
higher(7, 9); // returns 9
higher(12, 3); // returns 12
```

As well as being a little simpler to write, arrow functions also have the feature that they inherit the value of `this` from the container. This is really handy when using objects. Previously we needed to assign `this` to a variable to pass it into a function:

```
function myObject() {
  this.height = 13;
  var self = this;

  setTimeout(function fiveSecondsLater() {
    console.log(self.height);
  }, 5000)
}
var o = new myObject();
```

In the preceding example, we couldn't simply use

```
console.log(this.height);
```

because `this` would refer to its immediate container, here the function `fiveSecondsLater()`.
However, by using arrow functions the use of a variable like `self` can be avoided:

```
function myObject() {
  this.height = 13;

  setTimeout(() => {
    console.log(this.height); // 'this' here refers to myObject
  }, 5000)
}
var o = new myObject();
```

Modules

As JavaScript applications grow in complexity, a means needs to be found to make objects
declared in one file available in others. By this means, larger projects can be written in a modular fashion.

By default, anything you declare in one file is not available outside of that file. In ECMAScript 6,
though, you can use the `export` keyword to make it available.

Here's an example of how to export a class:

```
// this code appears in file1.js
export default function Car(Color, Year, Make, Miles) {
 this.color = Color;
 this.year = Year;
 this.make = Make;
 this.odometerReading = Miles;
 this.setOdometer = function(newMiles) {
    this.odometerReading = newMiles;
 }
 // this object can be imported by other files
```

And in the receiving file:

```
//  this code appears in file2.js
import Car from 'file1';
var ferrari = new Car('red', 1986, 'Dino', 75500);
```

Using `let` and `const`

Before ECMAScript 6, JavaScript had only two types of scope—namely, *function scope* and *global
scope*. (The scope of a variable, as you learned in Hour 3, "Using Functions," depends on where-
abouts in the code the variable was declared using the `var` keyword.)

To the frustration of many developers coming to JavaScript from other languages, JavaScript lacked a so-called *block scope*, defining that a variable is only accessible within the block in which it's defined. (A block is everything inside a pair of curly braces.)

The new keyword `let` allows you to declare a variable while limiting its scope to the block, statement, or expression on which it is declared.

The `var` keyword, in contrast, defines a variable either globally or locally to an entire function, taking no account of block scope:

```
function myFunc() {
  {
    let x;
    if(y == 0)
      {
        // this is ok, x has block scope
        let x = "inner";
      }
    // this is an error, x already declared in block
    let x = "outer";
  }
}
```

The `const` declaration creates a constant—that is, a read-only named variable. The value of a constant cannot change through reassignment, nor can a constant be re-declared later.

```
function myFunc() {
  {
    const x = "foo";

    // this is an error, x is constant, can't be re-defined
    x = "bar";
  }
}
```

▼ TRY IT YOURSELF

Checking Out `const`

Let's have a look at how `const` operates. At the time of writing, it works in most browsers, but I'm going to use Google Chrome.

Instead of writing code in a text file, open the JavaScript Console for your browser. In the case of Chrome, I can do that with Ctrl+Shift+J as shown in Figure 19.1.

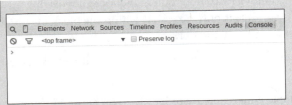

FIGURE 19.1
Chrome's JavaScript Console

First, define a constant using the `const` keyword. You can call it anything you like and choose any value. Mine is called `MYCONST` and I've given it a value of 10 (see Figure 19.2).

FIGURE 19.2
Setting a constant

The console issues undefined because the declaration of a `const` does not return a value.

In Figure 19.3 I try to redefine the value of MYCONST.

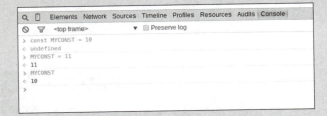

FIGURE 19.3
The constant can't be reassigned

As you can see, the constant `MYCONST` couldn't be reassigned a new value. Let's try to re-declare it instead (see Figure 19.4).

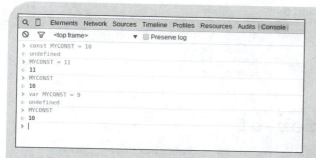

FIGURE 19.4
Redeclaration of a constant doesn't work

Nope, we can't do that either. Finally, let's try to reinitialize it (see Figure 19.5).

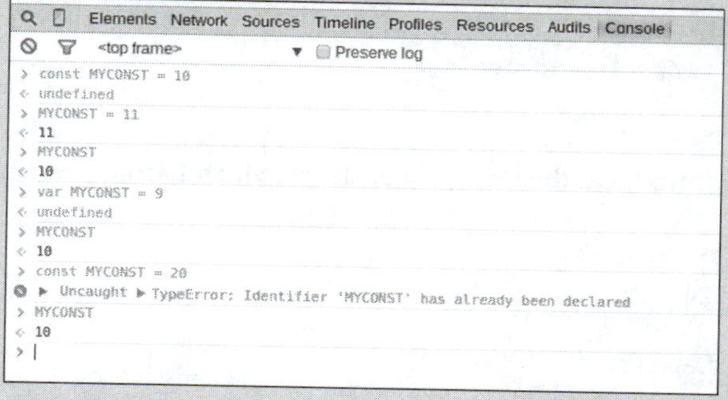

FIGURE 19.5
Trying to reinitialize throws an error

JavaScript throws an error.

Values declared using the `const` keyword, as we can see, cannot be reinitialized, re-declared, or reassigned.

Template Strings

Template strings provide help in constructing strings and are similar to string interpolation features in some other programming languages such as Perl and Python (among others).

```
var name = "John";
var course = "Mathematics III";
var myString = 'Hello ${name}, welcome to ${course}.';
```

You can substitute more complex expressions too:

```
var total = 20;
var tax = 4;
msg = 'Total is ${total} (or ${total + tax}, including tax)';
alert(msg);        // "Total is 20 (or 24, including tax)"
```

Access Arrays with `for-of`

JavaScript has various methods for handling arrays, as you read about in Hour 6, "Arrays." Apart from while and for loops, you can also use for-in. Unfortunately, this loop visits all of an array's *named properties*, not just the actual array *values*:

```
"use strict";
let arr1 = [ 6, 5, 7, 9 ];
arr1.greeting = "hi";

for (var x in arr1) {
    console.log(x); // logs "0", "1", "2", "3", "greeting"
}
```

To get around this problem, ECMAScript 6 introduces the for-of construct, which iterates over just the property values:

```
for (var y of arr1) {
    console.log(y); // logs "6", "5", "7", "9"
}
```

NOTE

Note the use of the directive "use strict" in the preceding code snippet. This directive, introduced in ECMAScript 5, indicates that JavaScript should execute in strict mode, a more rigid set of interpreter rules, and is currently necessary to use certain ECMAScript 6 features.

Transpilation

The examples presented so far in this hour are fine for testing ECMAScript 6 features, but at the time of writing they are not ready for use in your production code. Few visitors to your website will be using a browser with strong ECMAScript 6 support. You *can* start preparing for the future, though.

Traceur is a Google project intended to take ECMAScript 6 code and process it into ECMAScript 5 code that is compatible with most browsers using their default settings. It doesn't support all of the ECMAScript 6 features, but new features are being added all the time.

You can read about the project at https://code.google.com/p/traceur-compiler/wiki/GettingStarted, and also download the code to try for yourself at https://github.com/google/traceur-compiler.

Summary

In this hour, you've read about just some of the important new changes coming to the JavaScript language in the ECMAScript 6 specification.

The new language features bring the JavaScript syntax more into line with other popular languages, as well as making code more concise and readable.

Browser vendors have already begun to implement these and other ECMAScript 6 features into their offerings, and more of the specification will doubtless be supported in upcoming browser versions.

Q&A

Q. How can I follow the progress of the ECMAScript 6 specification?

A. Probably the best online resource is the official ECMAScript wiki (http://wiki.ecmascript.org/).

Q. Who or what is Ecma?

A. Ecma is an international, membership-based, non-profit standards organization, originally called the European Computer Manufacturers Association (ECMA). The organization was founded in 1961 to standardize computer systems throughout Europe.

Workshop

Try to answer all the questions before reading the subsequent "Answers" section.

Quiz

1. A value declared as a `const`:

    a. Can later be reassigned but not re-declared

    b. Can later be re-declared but not reassigned

    c. Can later neither be re-declared nor reassigned

2. You can use the `export` keyword to

    a. Save all your program data into another file

    b. Make something you declare in one file available outside of that file

    c. Make something you declared in another file available inside of the current file

3. Which of the following is a correct arrow function to turn a Centigrade temperature into Fahrenheit?

    a. `var fahr = cent =&gt; cent * 1.8 + 32;`

    b. `var fahr =&gt; cent = cent * 1.8 + 32;`

    c. `function fahr = cent =&gt; cent * 1.8 + 32;`

Answers

1. c. A const can later neither be re-declared nor reassigned.

2. b. Make something you declare in one file available outside of that file

3. a. `var fahr = cent =&gt; cent * 1.8 + 32;`

Exercises

▶ Check out how many ECMAScript6 features are supported in your current browser, by using one of the online resources mentioned earlier. Write some small code examples to check the operation of any supported features described in this hour.

▶ Check out the documentation on the official Ecma wiki for the other ECMAScript 6 features not discussed in this hour.

HOUR 20
Using Frameworks

What You'll Learn in This Hour:

▶ What frameworks are, and why they're useful
▶ About the Model-View-Controller (MVC) architecture
▶ How to get started with Google's AngularJS framework
▶ Details of some other popular frameworks

If you've already written a number of applications, chances are you've had to solve some of the same coding problems over and over again. One of the techniques you can use to cut down on such re-invention of the wheel is to use a *software framework*.

In this hour you'll learn about a popular style of network called an MVC (Model-View-Controller) framework, and see how to implement such a framework for single-page JavaScript applications by using Google's AngularJS.

Software Frameworks

The purpose of a framework is to improve the efficiency with which you can write software applications, at the same time adding consistency, quality, reliability, and robustness to your application.

Choosing a well-written and appropriate framework can leave you more time to focus on the unique requirements of your application rather than spending lots of valuable time on the application's infrastructure.

Why Use a Framework?

Frameworks help you to *reuse code* that has been previously built and tested, improving your application's reliability and reducing the coding and testing work required in its creation.

A framework can also encourage better programming practices, due to the structure it imposes on your application.

Finally, a framework usually provides you with the means to extend its functionality, making it better suited to your application's needs.

Frameworks Are Not the Same as Libraries

Many people confuse the term software framework with a software library, like the ones discussed in Part V of this book.

However, there is a fundamental difference between frameworks and libraries; when you use a library, the objects and methods available within that library already exist, waiting to be invoked by your custom application. You need to know which objects and methods to employ in your code in order to create your application.

When you use a framework, it's you that designs and codes the objects and methods used by your application. The framework provides a consistent structure in which you can do this.

Model-View-Controller (MVC) Architecture

The concept of the Model-View-Controller (MVC) software architecture is fairly simple: to separate our application into units, each of which conforms to one of the following parts.

Models

Models represent the part of the application dealing with business data and business logic. A model might be a single object, or it could be some structure made up from a variety of objects.

Views

A view is a representation of a model used to present information to the user. It usually acts as a presentation filter, showing only certain aspects of the data contained in a model while suppressing others.

A view interrogates its model to obtain the data necessary for presentation. It might also change the data in the model by sending appropriate commands. Such questions and commands all have to be in semantics defined within the model.

Controllers

A controller forms the link between the user and the application, arranging for views to be displayed on the screen, or reading user input by presenting menus, input fields, buttons, or other page elements. The controller interprets user input before passing it to one or more of the views.

The operation of the various parts of the MVC framework is shown in Figure 20.1.

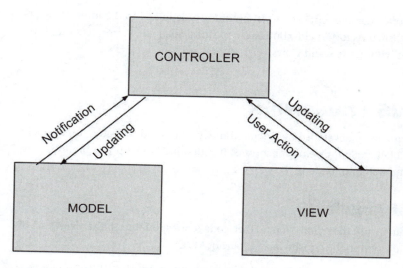

FIGURE 20.1
Model-View-Controller framework interactions

A Real-World Example

Watching TV can be analogous to an MVC framework.

The broadcaster makes available various channels, each containing different data; these channels can be thought of as the *models* of the MVC system.

The *view* is provided by the TV's screen.

You can interact with the TV by using the functions of the remote *control(ler)*.

Using an MVC Framework for Web Apps

The MVC architecture lends itself very well to web applications.

▶ **Model**—The page content is stored in the models that underpin the application. The technical details may vary—the text and images may be stored in a database, as server files, or in some other way—but the content, and the rules of how it all fits together, are encoded into the model part of the framework.

▶ **View**—The HTML and CSS add one or more visual display layers to the content—the veneer we apply to give our web application a particular appearance and style. We can change how the content is displayed without altering the original content, as stored in the model(s), at all.

▶ **Controller**—The controller element consists of program code linked to the interactive elements on the page, such as form fields, buttons, and links. Such code interprets user input and communicates with models and views.

The AngularJS Framework

AngularJS is an MVC framework developed by Google that lets you build well-structured, easily testable, and maintainable JavaScript web applications. It is designed to help you produce powerful, reliable, single-page web applications.

An Overview of AngularJS

AngularJS is an MVC framework that binds your HTML code (corresponding to the *views* part of the MVC paradigm) to JavaScript objects (the *models* part of MVC).

In one direction, any changes to your models update the page automatically. The opposite is also true—a model, for instance associated with a text field, is updated when the content of the field is changed. In the same manner, any changes in the view—such as a user entering information in a field, or clicking on a button—make the required changes to the appropriate model(s).

Behind the scenes, AngularJS handles all the logic, so you don't have to write code to update your page's HTML code, or to listen for and act upon user events.

Including AngularJS in your page

To use AngularJS you have to include it in your page. Perhaps the easiest way to do that is via Google's CDN:

```
<script src="http://ajax.googleapis.com/ajax/libs/angularjs/1.3.14/
angular.min.js"></script>
```

Extending HTML with `ng-` directives

AngularJS employs a number of directives that help you associate your page's HTML elements to models in the MVC architecture. These directives each start with `ng-` and can be added to any element.

The key attribute that you have to include in any page is `ng-app`, which defines an AngularJS application. You need to apply this to an element that contains the rest of the page elements bearing `ng-` directives. You can apply it to the page's `<body>` element (making the whole page part of the application), or a `<div>` element enclosing the application:

```
<body ng-app>
```

AngularJS finds this element when the page loads and processes all ng- directives it sees on its child elements.

Two further important ng- directives are ng-model and ng-bind.

The ng-model directive connects the value of HTML controls such as input fields, select boxes, text areas and so on, to application data stored in models.

The ng-bind directive binds that application data, in the MVC models, to elements in the HTML view.

A trivial example is shown in Listing 20.1.

LISTING 20.1   A Simple AngularJS Example

```
<!DOCTYPE html>
<html>
<head>
<title>AngularJS Example</title>
<style>
 #output {
   font: 28px bold helvetica, arial, sans-serif;
   color: red;
 }
</style>
<script src="http://ajax.googleapis.com/ajax/libs/angularjs/1.3.14/
➥angular.min.js"></script>
</head>
<body ng-app>
  <p>Name: <input type="text" ng-model="name"></p>
  <span id="output" ng-bind="name"></span>
</body>
</html>
```

AngularJS begins work as soon as the web page has loaded. The ng-app directive tells AngularJS that, in this case, it is the <body> element of the page that contains an AngularJS application.

The ng-model directive then binds the value contained by the input field to the variable name.

Similarly, the ng-bind directive binds the HTML content of the <span> element to the variable name. In this way, the <span> element becomes a view in our MVC framework.

Now, any changes in the input field will be immediately reflected in the <span> element, as shown in Figure 20.2.

FIGURE 20.2
A simple AngularJS application

That's it. We already have a dynamic application that would ordinarily have taken much more code to build. We didn't have to worry about writing code for data binding and updating, nor specify any models. In fact, we haven't yet written any JavaScript of our own! The application—simple as it is—already works because of AngularJS's design.

Scopes

A scope is an object that links a DOM element (the *view* part of the MVC architecture) to a controller; in MVC terms, this object becomes the *model*.

The controller and the view both have access to the scope model, so it can be used to communicate between them. This scope object will house the data and the methods to be used in the view.

All AngularJS applications have a `$rootScope`. The `$rootScope` is the top-most scope and belongs to the DOM element that contains the `ng-app` directive.

When explicit scopes are not set in the application, this is the scope used by AngularJS to bind data and functions. This is why the preceding example works.

To get a better idea of how scopes work, let's attach a controller to a particular DOM element, creating a scope for that element, and then interact with it.

Directives

You saw a few directives in the previous example. In AngularJS a *directive* is a function attached to a DOM element that has the capability to run methods, attach controllers and scope objects, and manipulate the DOM.

When an AngularJS application is launched and Angular starts stepping through the DOM (starting from the DOM element having attribute `ng-app`), it will parse the code collecting and running these directives.

Directives handle all of the hard work of making AngularJS applications dynamic. We've seen a few examples of directives previously, including `ng-model` and `ng-bind`:

```
<body ng-app>
    <p>Name: <input type="text" ng-model="name"></p>
    <span id="output" ng-bind="name"></span>
</body>
```

There are many default directives built into AngularJS, some of which we'll look at next.

Expressions

A double set of curly braces is used to encase an expression directive:

```
{{ expression }}
```

AngularJS expressions are rather like JavaScript expressions, in that they can contain literals, operators, and variables. These are all valid AngularJS expressions:

```
{{ 3 + 9 }}
```

```
{{ quantity * cost }}
```

```
{{ firstName + " " + lastName }}
```

AngularJS expressions are interpreted as data in the exact location where the expression is written.

ng-init

The `ng-init` directive runs at startup, before AngularJS has run any application code. With it you can set default variables prior to running any other functions.

ng-click

The `ng-click` directive attaches a listener to a DOM element. When the element is clicked, AngularJS executes the expression defined in the directive.

ng-repeat

The `ng-repeat` directive iterates through a collection and loads a template for each item. The template it copies is the element having the attribute `ng-repeat`.

```
$scope.departments = [
  { name: 'Sales'},
  { name: 'Support'},
  { name: 'Production'},
  { name: 'Shipping'}
];
```

You can iterate through them using `ng-repeat`:

```
<ul>
  <li ng-repeat="dept in departments">{{ dept.name }}</li>
</ul>
```

Here the `<li>` element will be cloned four times to produce the list sent to the view.

Filters

The job of a filter is to select a subset of items from an array and return it as a new array. Here are a few things you might do with an array:

▶ Format a number to a currency format, using `currency`.

▶ Select a subset of items from an array, using `filter`.

▶ Format a string to lowercase, using `lowercase`.

▶ Order an array by an expression, using `orderBy`.

▶ Format a string to uppercase, using `uppercase`.

Here's the general syntax for a filter in AngularJS:

```
{{ filter_expression | filter : expression : comparator }}
```

Let's suppose you want to apply a currency filter to some numeric data:

```
<div ng-app>
Total: <input type="number" ng-model="netTotal">
Tax: <input type="number" ng-model="tax">
<p>Invoice Total = {{ (netTotal + tax) | currency }}</p>
</div>
```

In this example, the expression `{{ netTotal + tax }}` will be evaluated, and the result formatted as currency.

Adding a Filter to a Directive

A filter can also be added to any `ng-` directive by using the pipe character (|) followed by a filter description:

```
<ul>
   <li ng-repeat="dept in departments | filter: uppercase">{{ dept.name }}</li>
</ul>
```

This example will display all list entries in uppercase.

Building an AngularJS Application

You now know enough to put together a basic AngularJS application.

A Basic AngularJS Application

We'll start with a basic HTML page containing a text input field to accept a user's search string and a `<div>` element to contain a list of search results containing the entered string.

Listing 20.2 shows the basic HTML of the page, with the AngularJS framework already included.

LISTING 20.2   HTML code of the AngularJS Application

```
<!DOCTYPE html>
<html>
<head>
    <title>AngularJS Example</title>
    <script src="http://ajax.googleapis.com/ajax/libs/angularjs/1.3.14/
    ➥angular.min.js"></script>
</head>
<body>
    <p>Search Departments: <input type="text"></p>
    <div id="list-container">
        <ul>
            <li></li>
        </ul>
    </div>
</body>
</html>
```

Next, we'll apply the necessary `ng-` directives to the page:

▶ The `ng-app` directive to the `<body>` element, defining this as the container for the AngularJS application.

▶ The `ng-model` directive to the search field, defining it as a model in our MVC framework.

▶ The `ng-repeat` directive to the `<li>` element in our list of search results. The `<li>` element will be repeated once for each search result.

We'll also use the `ng-init` directive to set up some initial data for the application. In a real-world case, this data is more likely to be brought instead from an external source such as a server-side database, but this will serve for our example.

```
ng-init = "departments = [
    { name: 'Sales', contact: 'Marsha Brown'},
    { name: 'Support', contact: 'Dave Price'},
    { name: 'Production', contact: 'Grant Wales'},
    { name: 'Service', contact: 'Sherry Dell'},
    { name: 'Administration', contact: 'Sally Bennett'},
    { name: 'Accounting', contact: 'Kim Sutherland'},
    { name: 'Shipping', contact: 'Sandy Connell'}]"
```

Our initial data comprises an array of fictional departments, each including the department name and the name of the staff contact in charge of it.

Listing 20.3 shows the revised HTML, which also includes a little CSS styling for good measure.

LISTING 20.3   Revised Code of the AngularJS Application

```
<!DOCTYPE html>
<html>
<head>
<title>AngularJS Example</title>
<style>
    body {
        background-color: #ddf;
        font: 16px bold helvetica, arial, sans-serif;
    }
    input {
        padding: 10px;
    }
    #list-container {
        background-color: white;
        color: #448;
        border-radius: 25px;
        border: 1px solid black;
        padding: 25px;
    }
</style>
<script src="http://ajax.googleapis.com/ajax/libs/angularjs/1.3.14/
➥angular.min.js"></script>
</head>
<body ng-app ng-init = "departments = [
    { name: 'Sales', contact: 'Marsha Brown'},
    { name: 'Support', contact: 'Dave Price'},
    { name: 'Production', contact: 'Grant Wales'},
```

```
    { name: 'Service', contact: 'Sherry Dell'},
    { name: 'Administration', contact: 'Sally Bennett'},
    { name: 'Accounting', contact: 'Kim Sutherland'},
    { name: 'Shipping', contact: 'Sandy Connell'}]">
  <p>Search Departments: <input type="text" placeholder="Enter search
string" ng-model="searchString"></p>
  <div id="list-container">
    <ul>
        <li ng-repeat="dept in departments">{{ dept.name }}</li>
    </ul>
  </div>
</body>
</html>
```

Save this code to an .html file and open it in your browser. You should see the departments and contacts listed in a page looking something like the one in Figure 20.3.

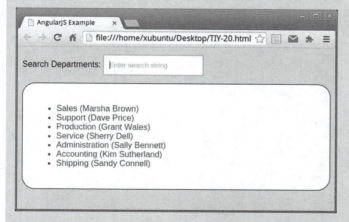

FIGURE 20.3
Our AngularJS app ready for use

All well and good, but the search field doesn't currently do anything. We'll fix that by adding a filter to the `ng-repeat` directive, based on the data entered in the search field, as shown in Listing 20.4.

LISTING 20.4   The Finalized AngularJS Application

```
<!DOCTYPE html>
<html>
<head>
```

```
<title>AngularJS Example</title>
<style>
    body {
        background-color: #ddf;
        font: 16px bold helvetica, arial, sans-serif;
    }
    input {
        padding: 10px;
    }
    #list-container {
        background-color: white;
        color: #448;
        border-radius: 25px;
        border: 1px solid black;
        padding: 25px;
    }
</style>
<script src="http://ajax.googleapis.com/ajax/libs/angularjs/1.3.14/
➥angular.min.js"></script>
</head>
<body ng-app>
  <p>Search Departments: <input type="text" placeholder="Enter search string"
ng-model="searchString"></p>
  <div ng-init = "departments = [
  { name: 'Sales', contact: 'Marsha Brown'},
  { name: 'Support', contact: 'Dave Price'},
  { name: 'Production', contact: 'Grant Wales'},
  { name: 'Service', contact: 'Sherry Dell'},
  { name: 'Administration', contact: 'Sally Bennett'},
  { name: 'Accounting', contact: 'Kim Sutherland'},
  { name: 'Shipping', contact: 'Sandy Connell'}]"></div>
  <div id="list-container">
      <ul>
          <li ng-repeat="dept in departments | filter: searchString">{{ dept.name +
          ➥" (" + dept.contact + ")" }}</li>
      </ul>
  </div>
</body>
</html>
```

And that's all we need to do! AngularJS handles the data binding so the filter acts in real time as
a user types (see Figure 20.4).

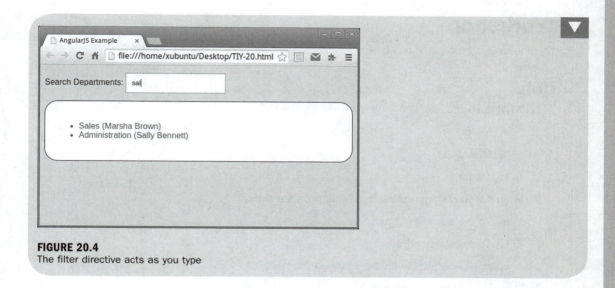

FIGURE 20.4
The filter directive acts as you type

Summary

In this hour, you learned the basics about the Model-View-Controller framework architecture, and how that can be usefully applied to web applications.

You were introduced to Google's AngularJS framework, and used it to build a simple web application with little or no additional code.

In truth, we've barely touched the surface of what AngularJS can do. Take a look at the official website at https://angularjs.org/ to learn more.

Q&A

Q. What is the background of AngularJS?

A. AngularJS was developed in 2009 by a company called Brat Tech LLC as part of a commercial JSON storage service. It was later released as an open-source library, which Google employees continue to maintain and support.

Q. Where can I get AngularJS documentation and help?

A. The official website at https://angularjs.org/ has links to extensive documentation, tutorials, developer guides, and much more.

Workshop

Try to answer all the questions before reading the subsequent "Answers" section.

Quiz

1. What does the M stand for in an MVC framework?

    a. Mirror

    b. Managed

    c. Model

2. In an AngularJS application, `ng-` directives are added:

    a. To the document head

    b. To page elements

    c. In a separate file linked into the document

3. The `ng-init` directive runs:

    a. On application startup, before the AngularJS application code

    b. When called by the user

    c. After the application terminates

Answers

1. c. Model

2. b. To page elements

3. a. On application startup, before the AngularJS application code

Exercises

▸ Modify the code of the "Try It Yourself" example to search only within the department name, but still to report both department name and contact name in the displayed list.

▸ Check out the AngularJS API docs at https://docs.angularjs.org/api and discover just how much more you can do with AngularJS.

JavaScript Beyond the Web Page

What You'll Learn in This Hour:

▶ Some examples of applications for JavaScript outside straightforward web pages
▶ How to write a browser extension for Google Chrome

Up to now you've learned a wide range of uses for JavaScript in the writing of web pages. However, JavaScript can also be used for extending browsers by building add-ons and extensions. Also, JavaScript interpreters are embedded in a number of tools apart from web browsers. Such applications often provide their own object model representing the host environment, although the core JavaScript language may remain essentially the same in each instance.

In this hour, you learn about uses for JavaScript above and beyond writing simple web content. You also write your own extension for Google's Chrome browser.

JavaScript Outside the Browser

There are a number of applications for JavaScript to control the actions of other applications in addition to web pages:

▶ Browser extensions for Google's Chrome, Opera, and Apple's Safari 5 browsers, and widget/gadget collections for Apple's Dashboard, Microsoft, Yahoo!, and Google Desktop can all be written using JavaScript.

▶ JavaScript is supported in PDF files used by Adobe's Acrobat and Adobe Reader, as well as many third-party applications.

▶ Adobe tools such as Photoshop, Illustrator, Dreamweaver, and others allow scripting via JavaScript.

▶ The OpenOffice.org office application suite (and its sibling LibreOffice) have JavaScript as one of the included macro scripting languages. These suites are written largely in Java and provide a JavaScript implementation based on Mozilla Rhino. JavaScript macros can access the application's variables and objects, much like web browsers host scripts that access the browser's Document Object Model (DOM) for a web page.

▶ Sphere, an open source and cross-platform program for writing role-playing games, and the Unity game engine support JavaScript for scripting.

▶ Google Apps Script allows users access and control over Google Spreadsheets and other products using JavaScript.

▶ ActionScript, the programming language used in Adobe Flash, is another implementation of the ECMAScript standard.

▶ The Mozilla platform, which is the basis of Firefox, Thunderbird, and other projects, uses JavaScript for the graphical user interface of these applications.

In this hour of the book, you're going to try your hand at one of these—writing an extension for Google's Chrome web browser.

Writing Google Chrome Extensions

Extensions are small applications that run inside a web browser and provide additional services, integrate with third-party websites or data sources, and customize the user's experience of the browser application. A Google Chrome extension is nothing more or less than a collection of files (HTML, CSS, JavaScript, images, and so on) bundled into a .zip file (although it's renamed as a .crx file).

The extension basically creates a web page that can use all the interface elements that the browser provides to regular web pages, including JavaScript libraries, CSS style sheets, XMLHttpRequest objects, and so on.

Extensions can interact with web pages or servers, and can also interact via program code with browser features such as bookmarks and tabs.

Building a Simple Extension

The first step is to create a folder on your computer to contain the code for your extension.

Each extension has a manifest file, named manifest.json, that is formatted in JSON and provides important information.

The manifest file can contain a wide range of parameters and options, but here we'll begin with a basic example. In your new folder create a text file called manifest.json and edit it like this:

```
{
    "name": "My First Extension",
    "version": "1.0",
```

```
    "manifest_version": 2,
    "description": "Hello World extension.",
    "browser_action": {
        "default_icon": "icon.png",
        "default_popup": "popup.html"
    },
    "web_accessible_resources": [
        "icon.png",
        "popup.js"
    ]
}
```

Put an icon called icon.png in the same folder—I used a small graphic image of a star, but you can use whatever you want. Create the file popup.html listed in Listing 21.1 and put that in the folder too.

LISTING 21.1   popup.html Google Chrome Extension

```html
<!DOCTYPE html>
<html>
<head>
    <style>
        body {
            width: 350px;
        }
        div {
            border: 1px solid black;
            padding: 20px;
            font: 20px normal helvetica, verdana, sans-serif;
        }
    </style>
    <script src="popup.js"></script>
</head>
<body>
</body>
</html>
```

Here is the JavaScript code contained in popup.js:

```javascript
function sayHello() {
    var message = document.createTextNode("Hello World!");
    var out = document.createElement("div");
    out.appendChild(message);
    document.body.appendChild(out);
}
window.onload = sayHello;
```

All this does is, on page load, create a `<div>` element containing the message "Hello World!" and append it to the DOM's `<body>` element.

Now display Chrome's Extensions page by clicking the settings icon and selecting **More Tools > Extensions**.

Click the box next to Developer Mode to show a little more information.

Then click the Load Unpacked Extensions button. Navigate to the folder containing your extension and select it. You should see something like Figure 21.1.

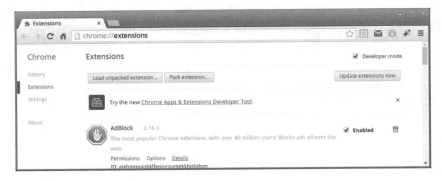

FIGURE 21.1
Your new extension visible on the Extensions page

Make sure the extension is enabled by checking the box next to it. You can now run your extension by clicking on the toolbar icon, as shown in Figure 21.2.

FIGURE 21.2
Hello World as a Google Chrome extension

Debugging the Extension

Right-click on the icon that launches your extension, and you see a content menu containing options to enable and disable the extension, plus an option called *Inspect popup*. Click on that and Chrome's Developer Tools pop open to let you examine the pop-up window, as shown in Figure 21.3.

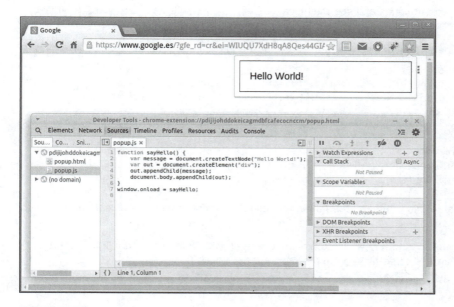

FIGURE 21.3
Inspecting the pop-up window

A Chrome Extension to Get Airport Information

This time you're going to make a Chrome extension that's a little more useful. With the help of the jQuery library, your pop-up is going to retrieve current information about U.S. airports.

TIP

Refer to Hour 15, "A Closer Look at jQuery," if you need a refresher on the jQuery library.

To do that, you're going to have your code make an Ajax call to an information feed at http://services.faa.gov/. To demonstrate how this service works, open your browser and navigate to http://services.faa.gov/airport/status/SFO?format=application/json.

"SFO" is the three-letter code for San Francisco International airport; you can replace it in the preceding URL with the code for another U.S. airport; for example, you could use LAX for Los Angeles International or SEA for Seattle-Tacoma International.

TIP
You can read the airport codes and see their locations at http://www.fly.faa.gov/flyfaa/usmap.jsp.

The format parameter tells the service that you want the information returned as a JSON string:

```
{"name":"San Francisco
International","ICAO":"KSFO","state":"California","status":{"avgDelay":"",
"closureEnd":"", "closureBegin":"","type":"","minDelay":"","trend":"",
"reason":"No known delays for this airport.","maxDelay":"","endTime":""},
"delay":"false","IATA":"SFO","city":"San Francisco","weather":{"weather":"Partly
Cloudy",
"meta":{"credit":"NOAA's National Weather Service","url":"http://weather.gov/",
"updated":"1:56 AM Local"},"wind":"Southwest at 9.2mph","temp":"44.0 F (6.7 C)",
"visibility":"10.00"}}
```

Your code will parse this returned information and use it to construct a more user-friendly display.

To begin the project, create a new directory somewhere on your computer and call it "airport." In this directory, you need three files, as in the previous example.

An Icon File

Choose an icon to display on your Chrome toolbar and from which to launch the extension. I used a 20 × 20 pixel airplane icon in a file called plane.png, but you can use any icon you have on hand.

The `manifest.json` File

The manifest file will be pretty familiar from the previous example, but with one notable addition: a new parameter, `permissions`. You are going to make an Ajax call to services.faa.gov to retrieve the information you want, and Ajax calls can only be made to pages on the same domain as the caller; adding a `permissions` entry allows Chrome to fulfil this requirement by sending a suitable header to the server. The manifest.json file is shown in Listing 21.2.

LISTING 21.2   The manifest.json File

```json
{
    "name": "Airport Information",
    "version": "1.0",
    "manifest_version": 2,
    "description": "Information on US airports",
    "browser_action": {
        "default_icon": "plane.png",
        "default_popup": "popup.html"
    },
    "web_accessible_resources": [
    "plane.png",
    "popup.js"
  ],
    "permissions": [
    "http://services.faa.gov/"
  ]
}
```

The HTML File

Once again the main HTML file will be called popup.html. You can call it something else if you want to, so long as you edit manifest.json and suitably set the value of the "popup" parameter.

The simple HTML page is shown listed in Listing 21.3.

LISTING 21.3   The Basic HTML File popup.html

```html
<!DOCTYPE html>
<html>
<head>
    <title>Airport Information</title>
    <style>
        body {
            width:350px;
            font: 12px normal arial, verdana, sans-serif;
        }
        #info {
            border: 1px solid black;
            padding: 10px;
        }
    </style>
</head>
<body>
    <h2>Airport Information</h2>
```

```
     <input type=Text id="airportCode" value="SFO" size="6" />
     <input id="btn" type="button" value="Get Information" />
     <div id="info"></div>
</body>
</html>
```

Apart from a little CSS styling, the page only contains a few items: an input field to accept the airport code, with default value set to SFO, a button to request that data is fetched, and a `<div>` to hold the returned results.

Now you need to start adding JavaScript to the page.

You're going to use jQuery to simplify things, so first you need to include that. The Google Chrome security policy doesn't allow the use of a content delivery network, so we need to download and include a copy of the jQuery library:

```
<script src="jquery-1.11.2.min.js" /></script>
```

When the page has fully loaded, you need to attach code to the Get Information button. The button needs to assemble the required URL based on the airport code value entered in the input field and instigate the Ajax call. Since the remote service may take some moments to respond, it would also be good if the user received a little message to indicate that the program was working.

Here's the code to carry out these tasks:

```
$(document).ready(function(){
   $("#btn").click(function(){
      $("#info").html("Getting information ...");
      var code = $("#airportCode").val();
      $.get("http://services.faa.gov/airport/status/" + code +
      ➡"?format=application/json",
         '',
         function(data){
            displayData(data);
         }
      );
   });
});
```

Once the page has loaded, jQuery adds code to the `onclick` event handler of the button.

First it uses jQuery's `html()` method to add a user message to the output `<div>` element. This message will later be overwritten when the "real" information is received.

```
$("#info").html("Getting information ...");
```

Next, the desired airport code is retrieved from the input field:

```
var code = $("#airportCode").val();
```

Then the Ajax call is assembled, here using GET:

```
$.get("http://services.faa.gov/airport/status/" + code + "?format=application/
json",
    '',
    function(data){
        displayData(data);
    }
);
```

The callback function specified for the Ajax call is displayData(), which will format the
returned data and display it to the user. Here's the complete contents of popup.js. including the
callback function:

```
function displayData(data) {
    var message = "Airport: " + data.name + "<br />";
    message += "<h3>STATUS:</h3>";
    for (i in data.status) {
        if(data.status[i] != "") message += i + ": " + data.status[i] + "<br />";
    }
    message += "<h3>WEATHER:</h3>";
    for (i in data.weather) {
        if(i != "meta") message += i + ": " + data.weather[i] + "<br />";
    }
    $("#info").html(message);
}
$(document).ready(function(){
    $("#btn").click(function(){
        $("#info").html("Getting information ...");
        var code = $("#airportCode").val();
        $.get("http://services.faa.gov/airport/status/" + code +
        ➡"?format=application/json",
            '',
            function(data){
                displayData(data);
            }
        );
    });
});
```

Recall from Hour 10, "Meet JSON," that JSON data can be interpreted directly as a hierarchy of
JavaScript objects. The displayData(data) function takes the returned JSON object data and
picks out data.name (a string), data.status, and data.weather (themselves objects) from
which to construct the message.

TIP

Look back a few pages to the JSON data returned from the remote server to see how these values were encoded.

The complete HTML page with code included is in Listing 21.4.

LISTING 21.4 The Complete popup.html for the Extension

```
<!DOCTYPE html>
<html>
<head>
    <title>Airport Information</title>
    <style>
        body {
            width:350px;
            font: 12px normal arial, verdana, sans-serif;
        }
        #info {
            border: 1px solid black;
            padding: 10px;
        }
    </style>
    <script src="jquery-1.11.2.min.js" /></script>
    <script src="popup.js"></script>
</head>
<body>
    <h2>Airport Information</h2>
    <input type=Text id="airportCode" value="SFO" size="6" />
    <input id="btn" type="button" value="Get Information" />
    <div id="info"></div>
</body>
</html>
```

Having assembled the required files in their allocated directory, you can add the extension to Google Chrome exactly as in the previous example.

Clicking on the associated icon brings up a small form where you can enter the airport code of your choice. Clicking the Get Information button will cause the program to consult the remote service, assemble the returned information into a readable form, and present it in the pop-up window.

Figure 21.4 shows the extension in operation.

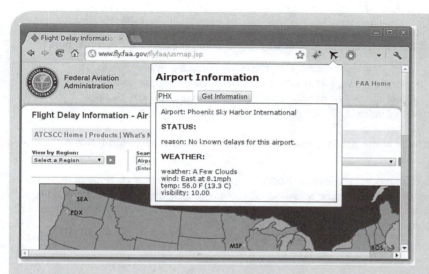

FIGURE 21.4
The Airport Information extension

Packaging the Extension

When you've finished developing your extension, click on the Pack Extension button in the Extensions page. Your extension will be packed into a .crx file for you. You can serve the .crx file from your web pages, and your visitors will be able to install it on their own copy of Google Chrome.

Going Further

The exercises of this hour barely scratched the surface of what can be done with Chrome extensions. Because Chrome has good support for HTML5 and CSS3, you can use the latest web technologies such as `canvas`, `localStorage`, and CSS animations in your extensions, as well as access to external APIs and data sources. Your extensions can even add buttons to the Chrome browser's user interface, or create pop-up notifications that exist outside the browser window.

Summary

In this hour, you learned about some applications of JavaScript beyond its use in HTML web pages. As an example, you wrote a small extension for Google's Chrome browser using JavaScript.

Q&A

Q. Can I write a Firefox extension in a similar way to the Chrome extension described here?

A. The Mozilla way of creating extensions is a little more complex; in addition to JavaScript, you'll have to mess a little with XML too. You'll find some good information to help you get started at https://developer.mozilla.org/en/XUL_School/ Getting_Started_with_Firefox_Extensions.

Q. Is it possible to write whole applications in JavaScript that don't have to run inside a browser?

A. Yes it is. As an example, take a look at Node.js (http://www.nodejs.org). Node.js is a platform built on top of Google Chrome's JavaScript runtime engine and designed for building server-side network applications such as web servers, chat applications, network monitoring tools, and much more.

Workshop

Try to answer all the questions before reading the subsequent "Answers" section.

Quiz

1. Information about a Google Chrome extension is contained in a file called:

    a. manifest.json

    b. manifest.js

    c. manifest.txt

2. A Google Chrome extension is distributed as which type of file?

    a. .js

    b. .xml

    c. .crx

Answers

1. a. manifest.json

2. c. Google Chrome extensions can be distributed as a .crx file.

Exercises

▶ Browse the available JSON APIs listed at http://www.programmableweb.com/apitag/ weather?format=JSON and try writing your own simple Chrome extension to display the data.

▶ Take a look at the documentation for Node js (http://www.nodejs.org) to see how JavaScript can be used to write server-side scripts.

Good Coding Practice

What You'll Learn in This Hour:

▶ How to avoid overuse of JavaScript
▶ Writing readable and maintainable code
▶ About graceful degradation
▶ About progressive enhancement
▶ How to separate style, content, and code
▶ Writing unobtrusive JavaScript
▶ Using feature detection
▶ Avoiding inline code such as event handlers
▶ How to handle errors well

JavaScript has gained an unfortunate reputation in certain circles. Since its main goal as a scripting language was to add functionality to web page designs, accessibility for first-time programmers has always been an important aspect of the language. Unfortunately, that has often led to poorly written code being allowed into web pages, leading to frustration for more software-savvy users.

Throughout the book so far I've made reference to aspects of coding that are good and bad. In this hour we pull all that together to form some general guidelines for good coding practice.

Don't Overuse JavaScript

How much JavaScript do you need? There's often a temptation to include JavaScript code and enhanced interaction where it's not strictly necessary or advisable.

▶ It's important to remember that your users are likely to spend most of their Internet time on sites other than yours. Experienced Internet users become accustomed to popular interface components such as menus, breadcrumb trails, and tabbed browsing. These elements are popular, in general, because they work well, can be made to look good, and don't require the user to read a manual first. Is familiarity with a site's operation likely to increase a user's productivity more than the potential benefits of your all-new whizz-bang design?

▶ Many of the visual effects that once needed to be coded in JavaScript can now be achieved perfectly well using CSS. Where both approaches are possible (image rollovers and some types of menus come immediately to mind), CSS is usually preferable. It's well supported across browsers (despite a few variations) and isn't as commonly turned off by the user. In the rare case that CSS isn't supported, the page is rendered as standard HTML, usually leaving a page that's at least perfectly functional, even if it's not so pretty.

▶ Users in many areas of the world are still using outdated, underpowered, hand-me-down computers and may also have slow and/or unreliable Internet access. The CPU cycles taken up by your unnecessary code may be precious to them.

▶ In some cases you may cost yourself a degree of search engine page rank, since their spiders don't always correctly index content that's been generated by JavaScript, or designs that require it for navigation.

Used carefully and with forethought, JavaScript can be a great tool, but sometimes you can have too much of a good thing.

Writing Readable and Maintainable Code

There is no way of knowing who will one day need to read and understand your code. Even if that person is you, several years and many projects may have intervened; the code that is so familiar to you at the time of writing can seem mystifying further down the line. If somebody else has to interpret your code, they may not share your coding style, naming conventions, or areas of expertise, and you may not be available to help them out.

Use Comments Sensibly

Well-chosen comments at critical places in your code can make all the difference in such situations. Comments are your notes and pointers for those who come later. The trick is in deciding what comments are likely to be helpful. The subject has often raised debate, and opinions vary widely, so what follows is largely my own opinion.

It's perhaps reasonable to assume that the person who ends up reading your code has an understanding of JavaScript, so a commentary on the way the language itself works is going too far; JavaScript developers may vary widely in their styles and abilities, but the one thing we do all share is the language syntax!

Harder to interpret when reading code are the thought processes and algorithms that lie behind the code's operation. Personally, when reading code written by others I find it helpful to see

- A prologue to any object or function containing more than a few lines of simple code.

```
function calculateGroundAngle(x1, y1, z1, x2, y2, z2) {
    /**
     * Calculates the angle in radians at which
     * a line between two points intersects the
     * ground plane.
     * @author Phil Ballard phil@www.example.com
     */
    if(x1 > 0) {
        .... more statements
```

- Inline comments wherever the code would otherwise be confusing or prone to misinterpretation.

```
// need to use our custom sort method for performance reasons
var finalArray = rapidSort(allNodes, byAngle) {
    .... more statements
```

- A comment wherever the original author can pass on specialist knowledge that the reader is unlikely to know.

```
// workaround for image onload bug in browser X version Y
if(!loaded(image1)) {
    .... more statements
```

- Instructions for commonly used code modifications.

```
// You can change the following dimensions to your preference:
var height = 400px;
var width = 600px;
```

TIP

Various schemes use code comments to help you generate documentation for your software. See, for example, http://code.google.com/p/jsdoc-toolkit/.

Choose Helpful File, Property, and Method Names

The amount of comments required in your source code can be greatly reduced by making the code as self-commenting as possible. You can go some way toward this by choosing meaningful human-readable names for methods and properties.

JavaScript has rules about the characters allowed in the names of methods (or functions) and properties (or variables), but there's still plenty of scope to be creative and concise.

A popular convention is to put the names of constants into all uppercase:

```
MONTHS_PER_YEAR = 12;
```

For regular function, method, and variable names, so-called CamelCase is a popular option; names constructed from multiple words are concatenated with each word except the first initialized. The first letter can be upper- or lowercase:

```
var memberSurname = "Smith";
var lastGroupProcessed = 16;
```

It's recommended that constructor functions for instantiating objects have the first character capitalized:

```
function Car(make, model, color) {
    .... statements
}
```

The capitalization provides a reminder that the new keyword needs to be used:

```
var herbie = new Car('VW', 'Beetle', 'white');
```

Reuse Code Where You Can

Generally, the more you can modularize your code, the better. Take a look at this function:

```
function getElementArea() {
    var high = document.getElementById("id1").style.height;
    var wide = document.getElementById("id1").style.width;
    return high * wide;
}
```

The function attempts to return the area of screen covered by a particular HTML element. Unfortunately it can only ever work with an element having id = "id1", which is really not very helpful at all.

Collecting your code into modules such as functions and objects that you can use and reuse throughout your code is a process known as *abstraction*. We can give the function *a higher level of abstraction* to make its use more general by passing as an argument the ID of the element to which the operation should be applied:

```
function getElementArea(elementId) {
    var elem = document.getElementById(elementId);
    var high = elem.style.height;
    var wide = elem.style.width;
```

```
    return parseInt(high) * parseInt(wide);
}
```

You could now call your function into action for any element having an ID:

```
var area1 = getElementArea("id1");
var area2 = getElementArea("id2");
```

Don't Assume

What happens in the previous function when we pass a value for `elementId` that doesn't correspond to any element on the page? The function causes an error, and code execution halts.

The error is to assume that an allowable value for `elementId` will be passed. Let's edit the function `getElementArea()` to carry out a check that the page element does indeed exist, and also that it has a numeric area:

```
function getElementArea(elementId) {
    if(document.getElementById(elementId)) {
        var elem = document.getElementById(elementId);
        var high = elem.style.height;
        var wide = elem.style.width;
        var area = parseInt(high) * parseInt(wide);
        if(!isNaN(area)) {
            return area;
        } else {
            return false;
        }
    } else {
        return false;
    }
}
```

That's an improvement. Now the function will return `false` if it cannot return a numeric area, either because the relevant page element couldn't be found, or because the ID corresponded to a page element without accessible `width` and `height` properties.

Graceful Degradation

Among the earliest web browsers were some that didn't even support the inclusion of images in HTML. When the `<img>` element was introduced, a way was needed to allow those text-only browsers to present something helpful to the user whenever such a nonsupported tag was encountered.

In the case of the `<img>` tag, that facility was provided by the `alt` (alternative text) attribute. Web designers could assign a string of text to `alt`, and text-only browsers would display this text to the user instead of showing the image. At the whim of the page designer, the `alt` text might be simply a title for the image, a description of what the picture would have displayed, or a suggestion for an alternative source of the information that would have been carried in the graphic.

This was an early example of *graceful degradation*, the process by which a user whose browser lacks the required technical features to make full use of a web page's design—or has those features disabled—can still benefit as fully as possible from the site's content.

Let's take JavaScript itself as another example. Virtually every browser supports JavaScript, and few users turn it off. So do you really need to worry about visitors who don't have JavaScript enabled? The answer is probably yes. One type of frequent visitor to your site will no doubt be the spider program from one of the search engines, busy indexing the pages of the Web. The spider will attempt to follow all the navigation links on your pages to build a full index of your site's content; if such navigation requires the services of JavaScript, you may find some parts of your site not being indexed. Your search ranking will probably suffer as a result.

Another important example lies in the realm of accessibility. No matter how capable a browser program is, there are some users who suffer with other limitations, such as perhaps the inability to use a mouse, or the necessity to use screen-reading software. If your site does not cater to these users, they're unlikely to return.

Progressive Enhancement

When we talk about graceful degradation, it's easy to imagine a fully functional web page with all the bells and whistles providing charitable assistance to users whose browsers have lesser capabilities.

Supporters of *progressive enhancement* tend to look at the problem from the opposite direction. They favor the building of a stable, accessible, and fully functional website, the content of which can be accessed by just about any imaginable user and browser, to which they can later add extra layers of additional usability for those who can take advantage of them.

This ensures that the site will work for even the most basic browser setup, with more advanced browsers simply gaining some additional enhancements.

Separate Style, Content, and Code

The key resource of a web page employing progressive enhancement techniques is the content. HTML provides markup facilities to allow you to describe your content semantically; the markup tags themselves identify page elements as being headings, tables, paragraphs, and so on. We might refer to this as the *semantic layer*.

What this semantic layer should ideally *not* contain is any information about how the page should appear. You can add this additional information afterwards, using CSS techniques to form the *presentation layer*. By linking external CSS stylesheets into the document, you avoid any appearance-related information from appearing in the HTML markup itself. Even a browser having no understanding of CSS, however, can still access and display all of the page's information, even though it might not look so pretty.

When you now come to add JavaScript into the mix, you do so as yet another notional layer—you might think of it as the *behavior layer*. Users without JavaScript still have access to the page content via the semantic markup; if their browser understands CSS, they'll also benefit from the enhanced appearance of the presentation layer. If the JavaScript of the behavior layer is applied correctly, it will offer more functionality to those who can use it, without prejudicing the abilities of the preceding layers.

To achieve that, you need to write JavaScript that is *unobtrusive*.

Unobtrusive JavaScript

There is no formal definition of unobtrusive JavaScript, but the concepts upon which it's built all involve maintaining the separation between the behavior layer and the content and presentation layers.

Leave That HTML Alone

The first and perhaps most important consideration is the removal of JavaScript code from the page markup. Early applications of JavaScript clutter the HTML with inline event handlers such as the onClick event handler in this example:

```
<input type="button" style="border: 1px solid blue;color: white"
onclick="doSomething()" />
```

Inline style attributes, such as the one in the preceding example, can make the situation even worse.

Thankfully you can effectively remove the style information to the style layer, for example, by adding a class attribute to the HTML tag referring to an associated style declaration in an external CSS file:

```
<input type="button" class="blueButtons" onclick="doSomething()" />
```

And in the associated CSS definitions:

```
.blueButtons {
    border: 1px solid blue;
    color: white;
}
```

You could, of course, define your style rule for the button via any one of a number of different selectors, including the `input` element or via an `id` instead of a `class` attribute.

To make your JavaScript unobtrusive you can employ a similar technique to the one we just used for CSS. By adding an `id` attribute to a page element within the HTML markup, you can attach the required `onClick` event listener from within your external JavaScript code, keeping it out of the HTML markup altogether. Here's the revised HTML element:

```
<input type="button" class="blueButtons" id="btn1" />
```

The `onClick` event handler is attached from within your JavaScript code:

```
function doSomething() {
    .... statements ....
}
document.getElementById("btn1").onclick = doSomething;
```

Remember that you can't use DOM methods until the DOM is available, so any such code must be attached via a method such as `window.onload` to guarantee DOM availability. There are plenty of examples throughout this book.

Use JavaScript Only as an Enhancement

In the spirit of progressive enhancement, you want your page to work even if JavaScript is turned off. Any improvements in the usability of the page that JavaScript may add should be seen as a bonus for those users whose browser setup permits them.

Let's imagine you want to write some form validation code—a popular use for JavaScript. Here's a little HTML search form:

```
<form action="process.php">
<input id="searchTerm" name="term" type="text" /><br />
<input type="button" id="btn1" value="Search" />
</form>
```

You want to write a routine to prevent the form from being submitted if the search field is blank. You might write this function `checkform()`, which will be attached to the `onClick` handler of the search button:

```
function checkform() {
    if(document.forms[0].term.value == "") {
        alert("Please enter a search term.");
```

```
            return false;
        } else {
            document.forms[0].submit();
        }
    }
}
window.onload = function() {
    document.getElementById("btn1").onclick = checkform;
}
```

That should work just fine. But what happens when JavaScript is switched off? The button now does nothing at all, and the form can't be submitted by the user. Your users would surely prefer that the form could be used, albeit without the *enhancement* of input checking.

Let's change the form slightly to use an input button of `type="submit"` rather than `type="button"`, and edit the `checkform()` function:

```
<form action="process.php">
    <input id="searchTerm" name="term" type="text" /><br />
    <input type="submit" id="btn1" value="Search" />
</form>
```

Here's the modified `checkform()` function:

```
function checkform() {
    if(document.forms[0].term.value == "") {
        alert("Please enter a search term.");
        return false;
    } else {
        return true;
    }
}
window.onload = function() {
    document.getElementById("btn1").onclick = checkform;
}
```

If JavaScript is active, returning a value of `false` to the submit button will prevent the default operation of the button, preventing form submission. Without JavaScript, however, the form will still submit when the button is clicked.

Feature Detection

Where possible, try to directly detect the presence or absence of browser features, and have your code use those features only where available.

As an example, let's look at the `clipboardData` object, which at the time of writing is only supported in Internet Explorer. Before using this object in your code, it's a good idea to perform a couple of tests:

▶ Does JavaScript recognize the object's existence?

▶ If so, does the object support the method you want to use?

The following function `setClipboard()` attempts to write a particular piece of text directly to the clipboard using the `clipboardData` object:

```
function setClipboard(myText){
    if((typeof clipboardData != 'undefined') && (clipboardData.setData)){
        clipboardData.setData("text", myText);
    } else {
        document.getElementById("copytext").innerHTML = myText;
        alert("Please copy the text from the 'Copy Text' field to your clipboard");
    }
}
```

First it tests for the object's existence using `typeof`:

```
if((typeof clipboardData != 'undefined') ....
```

NOTE

The `typeof` operator returns one of the following, depending on the type of the operand:

`"undefined"`, `"object"`, `"function"`, `"boolean"`, `"string"`, or `"number"`

Additionally, the function insists that the `setData()` method must be available:

```
... && (clipboardData.setData)){
```

If either test fails, the user is offered an alternative, if less elegant, method of getting the text to the clipboard; it is written to a page element and the user is invited to copy it:

```
document.getElementById("copytext").innerHTML = myText;
alert("Please copy the text from the 'copytext' field to your clipboard");
```

At no point does the code try to explicitly detect that the user's browser is Internet Explorer (or any other browser); should some other browser one day implement this functionality, the code should detect it correctly.

Handling Errors Well

When your JavaScript program encounters an error of some sort, a warning or error will be created inside the JavaScript interpreter. Whether and how this is displayed to the user depends on the browser in use and the user's settings; the user may see some form of error message, or the failed program may simply remain silent but inactive.

Neither situation is good for the user; he or she is likely to have no idea what has gone wrong, or what to do about it.

As you try to write your code to handle a wide range of browsers and circumstances, it's possible to foresee some areas in which errors might be generated. Examples include

▶ The uncertainty over whether a browser fully supports a certain object, and whether that support is standards compliant

▶ Whether an independent procedure has yet completed its execution, such as an external file being loaded

Using `try` and `catch`

A useful way to try to intercept potential errors and deal with them cleanly is by using the `try` and `catch` statements.

The `try` statement allows you to attempt to run a piece of code. If the code runs without errors, all is well; however, should an error occur you can use the `catch` statement to intervene before an error message is sent to the user, and determine what the program should then do about the error.

```
try {
    doSomething();
}
catch(err) {
    doSomethingElse();
}
```

Note the syntax:

```
catch(identifier)
```

Here `identifier` is an object created when an error is caught. It contains information about the error; for instance, if you wanted to alert the user to the nature of a JavaScript runtime error, you could use a code construct like

```
catch(err) {
    alert(err.description);
}
```

to open a dialog containing details of the error.

▼ TRY IT YOURSELF

Converting Code into Unobtrusive Code

From time to time you may find yourself in the position of having to modernize code to make it less obtrusive. Let's do that with some code we wrote way back in Hour 4, "DOM Objects and Built-in Objects," presented once again here in Listing 22.1.

LISTING 22.1   An Obtrusive Script

```
<!DOCTYPE html>
<html>
<head>
    <title>Current Date and Time</title>
    <style>
        p {font: 14px normal arial, verdana, helvetica;}
    </style>
    <script>
        function telltime() {
            var out = "";
            var now = new Date();
            out += "<br />Date: " + now.getDate();
            out += "<br />Month: " + now.getMonth();
            out += "<br />Year: " + now.getFullYear();
            out += "<br />Hours: " + now.getHours();
            out += "<br />Minutes: " + now.getMinutes();
            out += "<br />Seconds: " + now.getSeconds();
            document.getElementById("div1").innerHTML = out;
        }
    </script>
</head>
<body>
    The current date and time are:<br/>
    <div id="div1"></div>
    <script>
        telltime();
    </script>
    <input type="button" onclick="location.reload()" value="Refresh" />
</body>
</html>
```

As it stands, this script has a number of areas of potential improvement:

▶ The JavaScript statements are placed between `<script>` and `</script>` tags on the page; they would be better in a separate file.

▶ The button has an inline event handler.

▶ A user without JavaScript would simply see a page with a nonfunctioning button.

First, let's move all the JavaScript to a separate file and remove the inline event handler. We also give the button an id value, so we can identify it in JavaScript to add the required event handler via our code.

Next, we need to address the issue of users without JavaScript enabled. We use the `<noscript>` page element so that users without JavaScript enabled will see, instead of the button, a short message with a link to an alternative source of time information:

```
<noscript>
    Your browser does not support JavaScript<br />
    Please consult your computer's operating system for local date and
time information or click <a href="clock.php" target="_blank">HERE</a>
to read the server time.
</noscript>
```

TIP

The `<noscript>` element provides additional page content for users with disabled scripts or with a browser that can't support client-side scripting. Any of the elements that you can put in the `<body>` element of an HTML page can go inside the `<noscript>` element, and will automatically be displayed if scripts cannot be run in the user's browser.

The HTML file after modification is listed in Listing 22.2.

LISTING 22.2 The Modified HTML Page

```
<!DOCTYPE html>
<html>
<head>
    <title>Current Date and Time</title>
    <style>
        p {font: 14px normal arial, verdana, helvetica;}
    </style>
    <script src="datetime.js"></script>
</head>
<body>
    The current date and time are:<br/>
    <div id="div1"></div>
    <input id="btn1" type="button" value="Refresh" />
    <noscript>
        <p>Your browser does not support JavaScript.</p>
        <p>Please consult your computer's operating system for local date and time
information or click <a href="clock.php" target="_blank">HERE</a> to read the server
```

```
time.</p>
    </noscript>
</body>
</html>
```

Within our JavaScript source file telltime.js, we use `window.onload` to add the event listener for the button. Finally we call `telltime()` to generate the date and time information to display on the page. The JavaScript code is shown in Listing 22.3.

LISTING 22.3   datetime.js

```
function telltime() {
    var out = "";
    var now = new Date();
    out += "<br />Date: " + now.getDate();
    out += "<br />Month: " + now.getMonth();
    out += "<br />Year: " + now.getFullYear();
    out += "<br />Hours: " + now.getHours();
    out += "<br />Minutes: " + now.getMinutes();
    out += "<br />Seconds: " + now.getSeconds();
    document..getElementById("div1").innerHTML = out;
}

window.onload = function() {
    document.getElementById("btn1").onclick= function() {location.reload();}
    telltime();
}
```

With JavaScript enabled, the script works just as it did in Hour 4. However, with JavaScript disabled, the user now sees the page as shown in Figure 22.1.

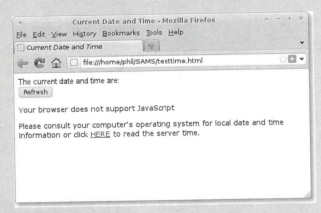

FIGURE 22.1
Extra information for users without JavaScript

Summary

In this hour we rounded up and presented various examples of good practice in writing JavaScript. Used together they should help you deliver your code projects more quickly, with higher quality and much easier maintenance.

Q&A

Q. **Why would a user turn off JavaScript?**

A. Remember that the browser might have been set up by the service provider or employer with JavaScript turned off by default, in an effort to improve security. This is particularly likely in an environment such as a school or an Internet cafe.

Additionally, some corporate firewalls, ad-blocking, and personal antivirus software prevent JavaScript from running, and some mobile devices have web browsers without complete JavaScript support.

Q. **Are there any other options besides `<noscript>` for dealing with users who don't have JavaScript enabled?**

A. An alternative that avoids `<noscript>` is to send users who *do* have JavaScript support to an alternative page containing JavaScript-powered enhancements:

```
<script>window.location="enhancedPage.html";</script>
```

If JavaScript is available and activated, the script redirects the user to the enhanced page. If the browser doesn't have JavaScript support, the script won't be executed, and the user is left viewing the more basic version.

Workshop

Try to answer all the questions before reading the subsequent "Answers" section.

Quiz

1. The modularization of code into reusable blocks for more general use is called:

    a. Abstraction

    b. Inheritance

    c. Unobtrusive JavaScript

2. The CSS for your page should be confined as much as possible to the:

   a. Semantic layer

   b. Presentation layer

   c. Behavior layer

3. Unobtrusive JavaScript code should, wherever possible, be placed

   a. In an external file

   b. Between `<script>` and `</script>` tags in the page `<head>`

   c. Inline

Answers

1. a. Abstraction

2. b. Where possible, all CSS goes in the presentation layer.

3. a. Use external JavaScript files where it's feasible to do so.

Exercises

▶ Pick some Try It Yourself sections from earlier in the book and see what you can do to make the code more unobtrusive, without adversely affecting the script's operation.

▶ Can you work out how to further modify the code of Listing 22.2 and Listing 22.3 to ensure that users without JavaScript enabled see just the content of the `<noscript>` tag, without the additional text and button being present? (Hint: Write these items to the page with innerHTML or via DOM methods.)

Debugging Your Code

What You'll Learn in This Hour:

▶ The types of errors common in JavaScript code
▶ How to carry out simple debugging with `alert()`
▶ Using the browser console and `console.log()`
▶ Grouping messages in the console
▶ Using breakpoints

As you delve into more advanced scripting, you're going to now and then create JavaScript programs that contain errors.

JavaScript errors can be caused by a variety of minor blunders, such as mismatched opening and closing parentheses, mistyping of variable names or keywords, making calls to nonexistent methods, and so on. This hour aims to offer some straightforward tips and suggestions for diagnosing errors and correcting your code, making your programming hours more pleasurable and productive.

An Introduction to Debugging

The process of locating and correcting bugs is known as *debugging*, and it can be one of the most tricky and frustrating parts of the development process.

Types of Errors

The errors that can crop up in your code usually conform to one of three types:

▶ **Syntax errors**—These can include typographical and spelling errors, missing or mismatched quote marks, missing or mismatched parentheses/braces, and case-sensitivity errors.

▶ **Runtime errors**—Errors that occur when the JavaScript interpreter tries to do something it can't make sense of. Examples include trying to treat a string as if it were a numerical value and trying to divide a number by zero.

▶ **Faulty program logic**—These mistakes don't always generate error messages—the code may be perfectly valid—but your script doesn't do what you want it to. These are usually problems associated with algorithms or logical flow within the script.

Choosing a Programmer's Editor

Whatever platform you work on, and whatever your browser of choice, it makes sense to have a good code editor. While it's certainly possible to write code in simple programs like the Windows Notepad text editor, a dedicated editor makes life a lot easier.

Many such programs are available, often free of charge under open source and similar licenses. Here I list a small selection of no-cost editors, but look around for one that suits your platform, your working style, and your pocket.

▶ Notepad++ (Windows)

▶ JEdit (should work on any platform that has Java installed)

▶ PSPad (Windows)

▶ JuffEd (Windows, Linux)

▶ Geany (Windows, Linux)

Editors offer a range of features and capabilities, but as a minimum I would suggest looking for an editor with the following:

▶ **Line numbering**—This is especially useful if you store your JavaScript in external files (and is yet another reason you should do so, wherever feasible). That way the line numbers of any error messages generated by your browser's debugger will usually match those in the source file open in the editor.

▶ **Syntax highlighting**—When you become familiar with your editor's scheme of syntax highlighting, you can on many occasions spot coding errors simply because the code in the editor "looks wrong." It's surprising how quickly you get used to the colors of keywords, variables, string literals, objects, and so on in your favorite editing program. Many editors let you alter the syntax highlighting color scheme to your own taste.

▶ **Parentheses matching**—As an error-seeking missile, parentheses matching is invaluable. Good editors will show matching pairs of open/close occurrences and for all types of brackets, braces, and parentheses. When your code has several levels of nested parentheses it's easy to lose count.

▶ **Code completion or tooltip-style syntax help**—Some editors offer pop-up tooltip-style help for command functions and expressions. This can save you having to take your eyes from the editor window to look up an external reference.

Simple Debugging with `alert()`

Sometimes you want a really simple and quick way to read a variable's value, or to track the order in which your code executes.

Perhaps the easiest way of all is to insert JavaScript `alert()` statements at appropriate points in the code. Let's suppose you want to know whether an apparently unresponsive function is actually being called, and if so, with what parameters:

```
function myFunc(a, b) {
   alert("myFunc() called.\na: " + a + "\nb: " + b);
   // .. rest of function code here ...
...}
```

When the function is called at runtime, the `alert()` method executes, producing a dialog like the one in Figure 23.1.

FIGURE 23.1
Using a JavaScript `alert()`

Remember to put a little more information in the displayed message than just a variable value or one-word comment; in the heat of battle, you'll likely forget to what variable or property the value in the `alert()` refers.

More Advanced Debugging

Placing `alert()` calls in your code is perhaps OK for a quick-and-dirty debug of a short piece of code. The technique does, however, have some serious drawbacks:

▶ You have to click OK on each dialog to allow processing to continue. This can be demoralizing, especially when dealing with long loops!

▶ The messages received are not stored anywhere, and disappear when the dialog is cleared; you can't go back later and review what was reported.

▶ You need to go back into the editor and erase all the `alert()` calls before your code can "go live."

In this section, we'll look at some more advanced debugging techniques.

The Console

Thankfully, most modern browsers provide a JavaScript Console that you can use to better effect for logging debugging messages. How to open the console varies from browser to browser:

▶ In Internet Explorer, to open the Developer Tools: F12

▶ For Chrome's Developer Tools and Opera's Dragonfly Debugger: Ctrl+Shift+I

▶ Using Firefox with the Firebug extension: F12

The examples in this section assume that you're using one of the previous debuggers. If not, you may have to consult your debugger's documentation to see how to carry out some of the tasks I describe. How your browser presents such errors to you differs from browser to browser.

▼ TRY IT YOURSELF

Using Your Browser's Debugging Tools

Have a look at the code in Listing 23.1.

LISTING 23.1   A Program with Errors

```
<!DOCTYPE html>
<html>
<head>
    <title>Strings and Arrays</title>
</head>
<body>
    <script>
        function sayHi() {
            alert("Hello!");
        }
    </script>
    <input type="button" value="good" onclick="sayHi()" />
    <input type="button" value="bad" onclick="sayhi()" />
</body>
</html>
```

This code listing has two different types of errors. First, in the call to the `alert()` method, our argument is missing its closing quotation mark.

Second, the `onclick` handler of the second button calls the function `sayhi()`—remember that function names are case sensitive, so in fact there is no function defined with the name `sayhi()`.

Loading the page into Firefox, we can see the expected two buttons, one labeled "good" and the other "bad." Neither seems to do anything. I can open Firefox's Error Console by pressing Ctrl+Shft+J, and the result is shown in Figure 23.2.

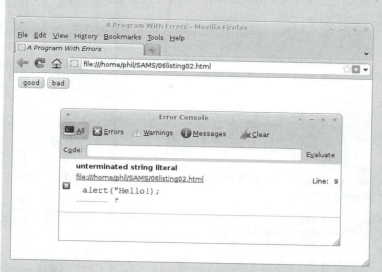

FIGURE 23.2
The Firefox Error Console

That's a helpful start. Firefox tells me it found an *unterminated string literal*, gives me the line number, and even shows me the line of code with an arrow pointed at the section where it has a problem.

With the error corrected and the file saved again, I'm ready to try again. First I click Clear on the toolbar of the Error Console to remove the old error message; then I reload my test page.

That looks better. My page comes up again, and the Error Console stays blank. Clicking on the button labeled "good" opens the expected `alert()` dialog—so far, so good.

But clicking on the button labeled "bad" doesn't seem to do anything—so I refer again to the Error Console, as shown in Figure 23.3.

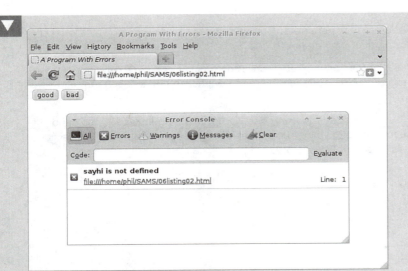

FIGURE 23.3
The second error

Firefox again identifies the problem: "sayhi is not defined." Now we're well on the way to having our code fully debugged and working correctly.

Every browser has its own way of dealing with errors. Figure 23.4 shows how the Chromium browser reports the initial error of the unterminated string literal.

NOTE
Google Chrome and Chromium are almost identical browsers, differing mainly in how they are packaged and distributed. Essentially, Google Chrome is the Chromium open source browser packaged and distributed by Google.

Chromium's message is a slightly more cryptic "Uncaught syntax error: Unexpected token ILLEGAL," but it also gives the line number in a clickable link that shows me the faulty line of code.

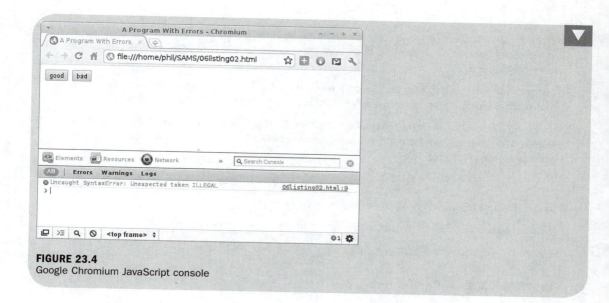

FIGURE 23.4
Google Chromium JavaScript console

To open Internet Explorer's developer tools, press F12 or select Developer Tools from the IE9 Tools menu. Select the Console tab to view error messages returned by JavaScript.

TIP
_____

It's worth getting to know the debugging tools in your favorite browser, and even think about switching browsers if you particularly prefer the tools on offer in another. If you plan to regularly write JavaScript code, it makes sense to do so in a development environment in which you feel comfortable, where you'll be more productive and less frustrated.

TRY IT YOURSELF ▼

A Banner-Cycling Script

Let's put to use some of what you learned in this hour by writing a script to cycle images on the page. I'm sure you have seen this sort of program before, either as an image slideshow, or perhaps to rotate advertisement banners.

First, I want to introduce you to two new items. The first is an event handler that you haven't met before—the `onLoad` method of the `window` object. Its operation is simple: We can attach it to the `<body>` element like this:

```
<body onload="somefunction()" >
```

When the page has finished loading completely, the `onLoad` event fires, and the code specified in the event handler runs. We use this event handler to run our banner rotator as soon as the page has loaded.

Second, we are going to use JavaScript's `setInterval()` function. This function allows us to run a JavaScript function repeatedly, with a preset delay between successive executions.

The `setInterval()` function takes two arguments. The first is the name of the function we want to run, the second the delay (in milliseconds) between successive executions of the function. As an example, the line

```
setInterval(myFunc, 5000);
```

would execute the function `myFunc()` every five seconds.

We use `setInterval()` to rotate the banner image at a regular interval.

Create a new file named banner.html and enter the code from Listing 23.2.

LISTING 23.2   A Banner Rotator

```
<!DOCTYPE html>
<html>
<head>
    <title>Banner Cycler</title>
    <script>
        var banners = ["banner1.jpg", "banner2.jpg", "banner3.jpg"];
        var counter = 0;
        function run() {
            setInterval(cycle, 2000);
        }
        function cycle() {
            counter++;
            if(counter == banners.length) counter = 0;
            document.getElementById("banner").src = banners[counter];
        }
    </script>
</head>
<body onload = "run();">
    <img id="banner" alt="banner" src="banner1.jpg" />
</body>
</html>
```

The HTML part of the page could hardly be simpler—the body of the page just contains an image element. This image will form the banner, which will be "rotated" by changing its `src` property.

Now let's take a look at the code.

The function `run()` contains only one statement, the `setInterval()` function. This function executes another function, `cycle()`, every two seconds (2000 milliseconds).

Every time the function `cycle()` executes, we carry out three operations:

1. Increment a counter.

```
counter++;
```

2. Use a conditional statement to check whether the counter has reached the number of elements in the array of image names; if so, reset the counter to zero.

```
if(counter == banners.length) counter = 0;
```

3. Set the `src` property of the displayed image to the appropriate file name selected from the array of images file names.

```
document.getElementById("banner").src = banners[counter];
```

The operation of the script is shown in Figure 23.5.

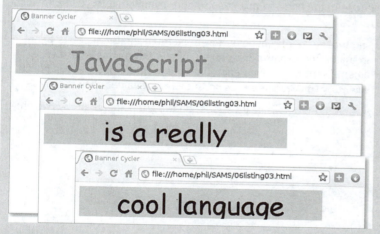

FIGURE 23.5
Our banner cycler

Now let's examine the script operation using browser-based debug tools. I'm using Chromium, so I open the Developer Tools console again like I did in Figure 23.4. In Chromium that's **Settings > More Tools > Developer Tools** or the shortcut Ctrl+Shift+I.

This time I select the Scripts tab in the lower pane. To the left of the lower pane, the code is listed; I'm going to click on the line number of line 15 to set a breakpoint, as shown in Figure 23.6.

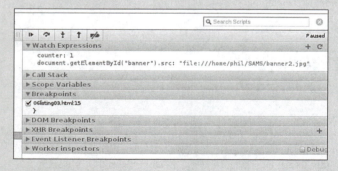

FIGURE 23.6
Setting a breakpoint

While this breakpoint remains set, code execution will halt every time this line of code is reached, before executing the code in the line—in this case, before completing the current execution of the function `cycle()`.

On the right-hand side of the same pane, our breakpoint now appears in the Breakpoints panel. In the same pane, I can click in the Watch Expressions panel and add the names of any variables or expressions whose values I want to examine each time the program pauses; I'm going to enter `counter` and `getElementById("Banner").src` to see what values they contain.

Figure 23.7 shows the display when the program next pauses, showing the values of my two chosen expressions.

FIGURE 23.7
Showing variable values at a breakpoint

Pressing the Play icon above the panel allows the script to restart.

Try using your own browser's debugging tools to explore the program's operation.

TIP

I have only scratched the surface here of the capabilities of the debugger in Google Chrome/Chromium. To learn more, there is a good tutorial at https://developer.chrome.com/devtools/docs/javascript-debugging to get you started.

If Firefox is your browser of choice for development work, you would do well to install the popular Firebug extension, which you can read about at http://getfirebug.com/javascript and which has broadly similar capabilities.

Those using Microsoft Internet Explorer will find good information on debugging with the F12 Developer Tools at https://msdn.microsoft.com/en-us/library/ie/gg589512(v=vs.85).aspx.

Opera contains the Dragonfly debugging tool, which you can read about at http://www.opera.com/dragonfly/documentation/.

The console provides a number of methods you can use in your code in place of the cumbersome and limited `alert()` call, perhaps the most well-known being `console.log()`:

```
function myFunc(a, b) {
    console.log("myFunc() called.\na: " + a + "\nb: " + b);
    // .. rest of function code here ...
...}
```

Rather than interrupt program operation, `console.log()` operates invisibly to the user unless he or she happens to be looking at the console. Figure 23.8 shows the result of running the preceding code with the console open in Firefox with the Firebug extension installed.

FIGURE 23.8
A message logged in the console

In addition to `console.log()`, you can also take advantage of `console.warn()`, `console.info()`, and `console.error()`. These all record messages at the console in slightly different styles, allowing you to build up a picture of how your script is running.

Figure 23.9 shows how Firebug's console displays each one; the display will be slightly different in other browsers.

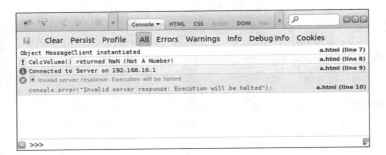

FIGURE 23.9
Different types of console messages

Grouping Messages

Sorting console debugging messages into groups makes them even more readable. You can name the individual message groups any way you like:

```
function myFunc(a, b) {
    console.group("myFunc execution");
    console.log("Executing myFunc()");
    if(isNaN(a) || isNaN(b)) {
        console.warn("One or more arguments non-numeric");
    }
    console.groupEnd();
    myOtherFunc(a+b);
}

function myOtherFunc(c) {
    console.group("myOtherFunc execution");
    console.log("Executing myOtherFunc()");
    if(isNaN(c)) {
        console.info("Argument is not numeric");
    }
```

```
    console.groupEnd();
    // .. rest of function code here ...
}
```

In this code snippet I've defined two `console.group()` sections, and named them to associate them with the functions in which they execute. Each group ends with a `console.groupEnd()` statement. When the code runs, any console messages display in groups, as shown in Figure 23.10.

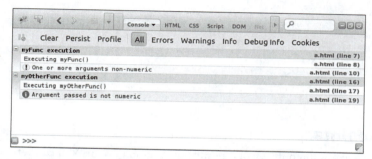

FIGURE 23.10
Grouped messages

Using Breakpoints to Halt Code Execution

As your scripts grow in complexity, you're likely to find that even console logging isn't enough to let you debug effectively.

To perform more detailed debugging, you can set so-called breakpoints in the code at places of interest. When code execution arrives at a breakpoint, it pauses; while time remains frozen you can examine how your code is operating, check variable values, read logged messages, and so on.

To set a breakpoint in most popular debuggers you need to go to the Scripts panel, where you'll see your code listed. Click on a line number (or just to the left of it) to set a breakpoint at that line. In Figure 23.11, a breakpoint has been set on line 8 of the code. The execution has stopped at this point, and you can see the current values of the individual variables in the right panel. You can remove breakpoints by clicking again on the breakpoint icon in the left margin.

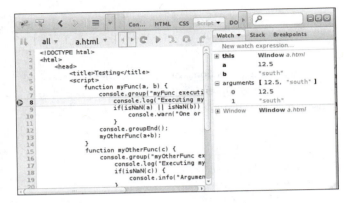

FIGURE 23.11
Execution stopped at a breakpoint

Conditional Breakpoints

Sometimes it helps to break code execution only when a particular situation occurs. You can set a conditional breakpoint by right-clicking the breakpoint icon in the left column and entering a conditional statement.

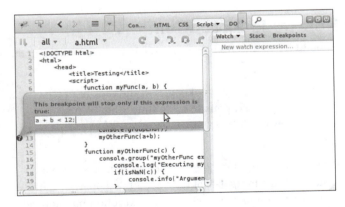

FIGURE 23.12
A conditional breakpoint

Your code will execute without interruption until the condition is fulfilled, at which point execution will halt. For instance, in Figure 23.12, the code will halt if the sum of a and b is less than 12. You can edit the expression at any time just by right-clicking once more on the breakpoint icon.

When code execution halts at a breakpoint you can choose to continue code execution, or step through your code one statement at a time, by using one of the code execution buttons; these usually look something like VCR controls, and appear at the top of one of the panels in the debugger. In most debuggers, the options are:

- ▶ **Continue**—Resume execution and only pause again if/when another breakpoint is reached.

- ▶ **Step Over**—Execute the current line, including any functions that are called, then move to the next line.

- ▶ **Step Into**—Move to the next line, as with Step Over, unless the line calls a function; in that case jump to the first line of the function.

- ▶ **Step Out**—Leave the current function and return to the place from which it was called.

Launching the Debugger from Your Code

It's also possible, and often useful, to set breakpoints from within the JavaScript code. We can do this by using the keyword `debugger`:

```
function myFunc(a, b) {
    if(isNaN(a) || isNaN(b)) {
    debugger;
    }
// .. rest of function code here ...
}
```

In this example, code execution will be halted and the debugger opened only if the conditional expression evaluates to true.

The debugging tools allow you to halt code execution in other circumstances too, such as when the DOM has been altered, or when an uncaught exception has been detected, but these are more advanced cases outside the scope of this discussion.

Watch Expressions

A watch expression is a valid JavaScript expression that the debugger continuously evaluates, making the value available for you to inspect. Any valid expression can be used, ranging from a simple variable name to a formula containing logical and arithmetic expressions or calls to other functions.

You can enter a new watch expression via the right-hand panel of the Script tab, as shown in Figure 23.13 (Firefox/Firebug).

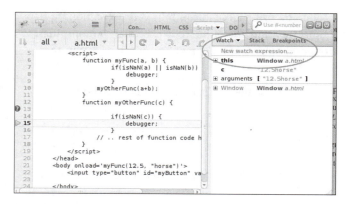

FIGURE 23.13
A watch expression

Validating JavaScript

A different and complementary approach to checking your JavaScript code for problems is to use a validation program. This will check that it conforms to the correct syntax rules of the language. These programs are sometimes bundled with commercial JavaScript editors, or you can simply use Douglas Crockford's JavaScript Lint, which is available free online at http://www.jslint.com/.

Here you can simply paste your code into the displayed window and click the button.

Don't be too dismayed if the program reports a lot of errors—just work through them one at a time. JSLint is very thorough and will even report various issues of coding style that wouldn't affect your code's running at all, but do help to improve how you program!

Summary

In this hour you learned a lot about debugging your JavaScript code, including using the browser console, as well as setting breakpoints and stepping through code in the debugger.

Q&A

Q. How should I choose a programmer's editor?

A. It's completely up to personal choice. Many are free or have a free version, so there's nothing to stop you from trying several before deciding.

Q. Where can I find out more about JavaScript debugging?

A. Many tutorials exist online. Start with the one published by W3Schools, at http://www.w3schools.com/js/js_debugging.asp.

Workshop

Try to answer all the questions before reading the subsequent "Answers" section.

Quiz

1. Which of these error types are you not likely to find in your JavaScript programs?

   a. Syntax errors

   b. Compilation errors

   c. Runtime errors

2. What does a breakpoint do?

   a. Pauses code execution at a given place

   b. Causes JavaScript to step out of a loop

   c. Produces a JavaScript error

3. What line in your code will launch the debugger?

   a. `debug;`

   b. `debugger;`

   c. `pause;`

Answers

1. b. JavaScript is an interpreted, rather than a compiled, language, so you won't encounter compilation errors.

2. a. Pauses code execution at a given place.

3. b. To launch the debugger, type

   ```
   debugger;
   ```

Exercises

▶ How would you modify the banner-cycling script to add links to the banners, such that each image displayed linked to a different external page?

▶ Using your knowledge of random number generation using the Math object, can you rewrite the banner-cycling script to show a random banner at each change, instead of cycling through them in order? Use your browser's built-in debugging tools to help you.

JavaScript Unit Testing

What You'll Learn in This Hour:

▸ What unit testing is and why it's used

▸ How to make your JavaScript code more easily testable

▸ Some examples of JavaScript test suites

▸ About the QUnit test suite and the CommonJS unit testing specification

Often, a little JavaScript hack that started out as just a few lines of code subsequently grows to ten, then twenty, then fifty. Meanwhile, functions are tweaked to do a little more, conditional statements gain a few extra conditions, or a couple extra variables are created.

When such an application (inevitably) breaks, it can be a nightmare to unravel the code and find the problem.

As you already read in Hour 22, "Good Coding Practice," good coding practice can help to make your code easier to understand and to maintain, but there's something else you can do, too. As your JavaScript applications grow in size, complexity, and sophistication, it becomes even more important to write code that can be easily tested.

In this hour you'll learn some ways to write your code to make it suitable for unit testing, and how to write and perform such tests.

What Is Unit Testing?

If you're unfamiliar with the concept of unit testing, don't worry, as it's not too complicated to understand.

Usually when somebody thinks about testing a JavaScript application, they imagine testing the completed system to see if it works as expected. This is essentially a test to see if the various pieces of the application work correctly together, and is often known as *integration testing*.

Unit testing is a software verification and validation method in which an application is broken down into its smallest testable parts, called *units*, then these units are individually examined and tested for proper operation. A unit is the smallest testable part of an application, such as an individual function or method.

Unit testing can be done manually, but such testing is usually automated.

Essentially, you write a series of tests for each fundamental element of your code, to test that unit's performance under all conceivable types of input. If all of these tests are passed, you can be confident that each tested element is fit for purpose.

▼ TRY IT YOURSELF

A Home-Cooked Unit Test

Let's jump right in and perform a unit test from scratch.

In this example we'll write some tests, perform them on a sample unit, and send a summary of the results to the browser console.

Let's look at a function we wrote way back in Hour 3, "Using Functions," to add tax at a given percentage to a net figure and return the gross amount:

```
function addTax(subtotal, taxRate) {
    var total = subtotal * (1 + (taxRate/100));
    return total;
}
```

This function forms the unit that we'll subject to some tests.

We'll save this function in a file tax.js, and include it in the HTML page that will serve as a test suite. In the real world, it's more likely that tax.js would contain a number of different functions, perhaps as part of a financial application, but for this example it'll do just fine. The HTML code is shown in Listing 24.1.

LISTING 24.1   HTML Code for the Test Suite

```
<!DOCTYPE html>
<html>
<head>
  <title>Manual Unit Testing Examples</title>
  <script src="tax.js"></script>
  <script>
  function test(amount, rate, expected) {
    results.total++;
    var result = addTax(amount, rate);
    if (result !== expected) {
      results.failed++;
```

```
      console.log("Expected " + expected + ", but instead got " + result);
    }
  }
  var results = {
    total: 0,
    failed: 0
  };

  // Our unit tests
  test(1, 10, 1.1);
  test(5, 12, 5.6);
  test(100, 17.5, 117.5);

  // Output results to the console
  console.log(results.total + " tests carried out, " + results.failed + " failed, "
➥+(results.total - results.failed) + " passed.");
  </script>
</head>
<body>
</body>
</html>
```

In a script element on this page I've defined a function called `test()`, which takes three arguments. The parameters `amount` and `rate` are the values to be passed to the function under test (in this case `addTax()`) while the third parameter, `expected`, is the result we expect to have returned if the `addTax()` function is working the way we want it to.

If the function under test returns the expected result, the `test()` function increments a counter of successful tests; if not, it increments a counter of failed tests and also logs a message to the console indicating which test failed, and the incorrect value that was returned.

To run the test I can simply save the code as an .html file and load this page into my browser. The result is shown in Figure 24.1.

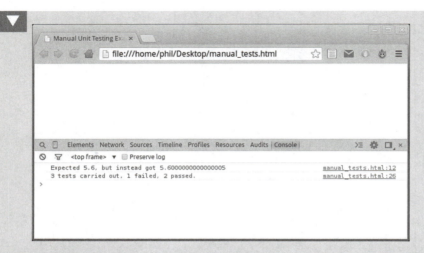

FIGURE 24.1
The results of our unit tests

As you can see, one of our tests failed; JavaScript added a small rounding error. This result is a starting point from which I can reexamine the code of the function `addTax()` to remove this anomaly—perhaps by using rounding on the output value before returning it.

Of course, you don't have to log the results to the console; they could just as easily be printed to the page, saved to a database, and so on. Later we'll look at QUnit, an open source unit testing application that displays a nicely formatted test result directly in the HTML of the test page.

Writing JavaScript for Unit Testing

Looking again at the preceding example, some things immediately become clear:

▶ The function `addTax()` was, of course, a *named* function. Had it been an anonymous function, it would have been much harder—perhaps impossible—to test this way.

▶ The function having been contained in an external JavaScript file (here tax.js) also aided in its inclusion in our test suite.

These are just a couple of examples of how coding style can affect the testability of your JavaScript code.

Applications written in the old-fashioned procedural manner of coding can be hard to unit test. However, if you write your code with unit testing in mind, you'll not only make it easier to write those tests, but also write code that's so much easier to read, maintain, and extend.

In the next section I'll round up a few coding techniques that will make your code easier to test.

Refactoring Code

The process of reorganizing your JavaScript code into a different form, but without modifying its operation, is known as *refactoring*. Refactoring is a great method of improving the design of a program, as it generally involves separating the program logic from the user interaction and display elements.

Where your code is based around a library such as jQuery and/or a framework such as AngularJS, some of that discipline might already have been imposed on your code. Where JavaScript has been written from scratch, however, there's more likelihood that a lot of refactoring will be needed. This is especially true where code has been initially written with little or no concern for separating HTML and program logic—for instance, where inline event handlers have been used.

Here are a few of the things you can do to make your code easier to test.

Externalize Scripts

JavaScript code collected into external files and later linked into your application is generally easier to test. In an ideal case, the same JavaScript file to be included in your production application can simply be linked into your test harness instead in order to have the tests performed.

Keep Functions and Methods Simple

The more you try to do with a single procedure, the more complex and numerous your tests will have to be, and the more difficult it may be to untangle that function from the code around it in order to test it.

The QUnit Test Suite

The previous example shows that you can run practical unit tests without a huge amount of code. However, for more than just a few tests it's much more productive to use a purpose-designed unit testing framework providing more advanced tools for writing and running your tests. In this section we'll look at one such framework, *QUnit*.

QUnit is a powerful, open source JavaScript unit testing framework. It's written by members of the jQuery team, and is used in the jQuery, jQuery UI, and jQuery Mobile projects. However, QUnit is capable of testing any regular JavaScript code.

Installing QUnit

QUnit is a self-contained library, needing only one JavaScript file (`qunit.js`) and one CSS file (`qunit.css`), both of which you can download from the QUnit website. Alternatively, you can use versions that are hosted on a CDN, as in the following examples.

A Minimal QUnit Setup

Once again, our test setup will be a simple HTML page, as shown in Listing 24.2. This time, QUnit is included from a CDN.

LISTING 24.2   Code for QUnit Test Suite

```
<!DOCTYPE html>
<html>
<head>
<title>Hello QUnit Example</title>
<link rel="stylesheet" href="http://code.jquery.com/qunit/qunit-1.16.0.css">
</head>
<body>
<div id="qunit"></div>
<div id="qunit-fixture"></div>
<script src="http://code.jquery.com/qunit/qunit-1.16.0.js"></script>
<script src="tests.js"></script>
</body>
</html>
```

Note the layout of this file, and how similar it is to our manual test suite used in the previous section. There are a few differences, however:

▶ Instead of logging information to the console, QUnit outputs nicely formatted results into the `<div>` having ID #qunit.

▶ The #qunit-fixture element is required in instances where you need to set up a so-called *mock DOM* of elements that are used during testing, usually things like form elements. The mock DOM is reset after every unit test. QUnit expects the mock DOM to be in the #qunit-fixture element.

We include the CSS file in the head, while the body includes the QUnit JavaScript file, followed by a further file called tests.js that contains just the following code:

```
QUnit.test( "Hello QUnit test", function( assert ) {
assert.ok( 1 == "1", "Passed!" );
});
```

Let's see what's happening here. The test method is called, giving a name to the test as the first argument, and passing a function as the second argument. It's this function that will run our test.

```
assert.ok( 1 == "1", "Passed!" );
```

In this trivial example the test will *always* be passed. The `ok` method is one of several *assertions* that QUnit provides, and returns a value of true if the first parameter passed to it returns something that itself evaluates to true.

QUnit Assertions

An *assertion* evaluates expressions to true or false. QUnit's `assert` has a number of additional methods you can use to build your tests. Examples include `equal()`, which unsurprisingly, tests equality; `notEqual()`, which tests for inequality; and `strictEqual()`, which once again tests equality, but this time with a strict type and value comparison.

Check out all of the assertions in QUnit's documentation at http://api.qunitjs.com/category/assert/.

The result is shown in Figure 24.2.

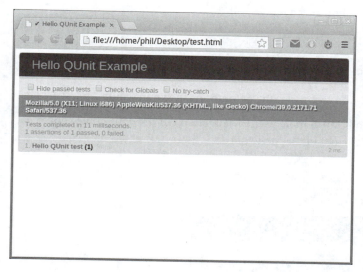

FIGURE 24.2
The result of our sample unit test

Retesting Our `addTax()` Function

Now let's modify the preceding example to retest our function `addTax()`, this time using QUnit. The test harness is similar to before, except it now includes the file tax.js:

```
<!DOCTYPE html>
<html>
<head>
<title>Test of addTax Function with QUnit</title>
```

```
<link rel="stylesheet" href="http://code.jquery.com/qunit/qunit-1.16.0.css">
<script src="tax.js"></script>
</head>
<body>
<div id="qunit"></div>
<div id="qunit-fixture"></div>
<script src="http://code.jquery.com/qunit/qunit-1.16.0.js"></script>
<script src="tests.js"></script>
</body>
</html>
```

Now we need to modify the file tests.js to include the tests we want to run. Here, I've used a different assertion, assert.equal, which is passed if the two parameters offered to it are equal. The first parameter in each test is the value returned from the addTax() function being tested, while the second parameter is our expected result:

```
QUnit.test( "addTax test", function( assert ) {
    assert.equal(addTax(1, 10), 1.1);
    assert.equal(addTax(5, 12), 5.6);
    assert.equal(addTax(100, 17.5), 117.5);
}};
```

When the test harness is loaded into a browser, the output is as shown in Figure 24.3.

You'll notice that the formatting is much more user-friendly than our previous home-cooked version, but the result is identical; one test of the three failed.

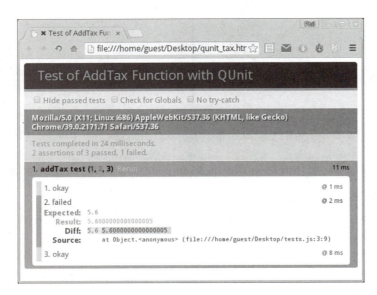

FIGURE 24.3
Testing our addTax function with QUnit

Summary

In this hour, you learned some methods for unit testing your JavaScript code.

Testing JavaScript often requires some important changes in the structure of your code, and you read about some of the coding techniques you might employ to make code testing easier.

You saw how to run some tests with a home-cooked testing framework, then replaced that with the purpose-designed QUnit framework to carry out further testing.

Q&A

Q. Is there a common standard for unit testing?

A. Although there is no universal standard, the CommonJS project (http://en.wikipedia.org/wiki/CommonJS) has a unit testing specification (http://wiki.commonjs.org/wiki/Unit_Testing), which is the one utilized by the QUnit test suite described in this hour.

Q. Where did QUnit come from?

A. Originally, QUnit was developed by John Resig as part of the jQuery library. In 2008 it became a self-contained project, allowing non-jQuery users to use it for their own unit testing. A rewrite in 2009 removed its dependence on jQuery, and now QUnit runs standalone.

Workshop

Try to answer all the questions before reading the subsequent "Answers" section.

Quiz

1. In unit testing, the term *unit* refers to:

    a. The smallest testable part of an application, such as an individual function or method

    b. All of the JavaScript code active on a single web page

    c. All of the JavaScript code in a .js file included in your web page

2. An assertion:

    a. Always declares a test experssion to be true

    b. Evaluates a test expression as being true or false

    c. Sets the value of a JavaScript variable

3. Reworking your JavaScript code to make it more testable is usually referred to as:

    a. Restructuring your code

    b. Refactoring your code

    c. Recompiling your code

Answers

1. a. The smallest testable part of an application, such as an individual function or method

2. b. Evaluates an expression as being true or false

3. b. Refactoring your code

Exercises

▶ Modify the "home cooked" unit testing code to display a neatly formatted report into the HTML page instead of logging it to the console (as QUnit does).

▶ Pick some other functions from throughout the book and subject them to unit tests using QUnit. Do they all work as you expected?

Tools for JavaScript Development

JavaScript development doesn't require any special tools or software other than a text editor and a browser.

Most operating systems come bundled with at least one of each, and in many cases these tools will be more than sufficient for you to write your code.

However, many alternative and additional tools are available, some of which are described here.

TIP

Be sure to check the license terms on the individual websites and/or included in the download package.

Editors

The choice of an editor program is a personal thing, and most programmers have their favorite. Listed in the following sections are some popular, free editors that you can try.

Notepad++

If you develop on the Windows platform, you're probably already aware of the Notepad editor usually bundled with Windows. Notepad++ (http://notepad-plus-plus.org/) is a free application that aims to be a more powerful replacement, while still being light and fast.

Notepad++ offers line numbering, syntax and brace highlighting, macros, search and replace, and a whole lot more.

jEdit

jEdit is a free editor written in Java. It can therefore be installed on any platform having a Java virtual machine available, such as Windows, Mac OS X, OS/2, Linux, and so on.

A fully featured editor in its own right, jEdit can also be extended via 200+ available plug-ins to become, for example, a complete development environment or an advanced XML/HTML editor.

Download jEdit from www.jedit.org.

SciTE

Initially developed as a demonstrator for the Scintilla editing component, SciTE has developed into a complete and useful editor in its own right.

A free version of SciTE is available for Windows and Linux users via download from www.scintilla.org/SciTE.html, while a commercial version is available via the Mac Apps Store for Mac OS X users.

Geany

Geany (www.geany.org/) is a capable editor that can also be used as a basic integrated development environment (IDE). It was developed to provide a small and fast IDE, and can be installed on pretty much any platform supported by the GTK toolkit, including Windows, Linux, Mac OS X, and FreeBSD.

Geany is free to download and use under the terms of the GNU General Public License.

Validators

To make sure your pages work as intended regardless of the user's browser and operating system, it's always advisable to check your HTML code for correctness and conformance to standards.

A number of online tools and facilities are available to help you, as discussed next.

The W3C Validation Services

The W3C offers an online validator at http://validator.w3.org/ that will check the markup validity of web documents in HTML, XHTML, SMIL, MathML, and other markup languages. You can enter the URL of the page to be checked, or cut-and-paste your code directly into the validator.

CSS can be validated in a similar way at http://jigsaw.w3.org/css-validator/validator.html.en.

Web Design Group (WDG)

WDG also offers an online validation service at www.htmlhelp.com/tools/validator/.

This is similar to the W3C validator, but in some circumstances gives slightly more helpful information, such as warnings about valid but dangerous code, or highlighting undefined references rather than simply listing them as errors.

Debugging and Verifying Tools

Debugging tools can save you hours when trying to track down elusive problems in your JavaScript code and help you speed up your scripts by analyzing execution timing.

Verifying tools help you to write tidy, concise, readable, and problem-free code.

Numerous debugging and verifying tools are available, including the following.

Firebug

Firebug integrates with the Mozilla Firefox browser to offer excellent debugging, editing, and profiling tools. Go to http://getfirebug.com/javascript.

JSLint

JSLint (http://www.jslint.com/), written by Douglas Crockford, analyzes your JavaScript source code and reports potential problems, including both style conventions and coding errors.

JavaScript Quick Reference

Table B.1, Table B.2, Table B.3, and Table B.4 in this appendix contain a quick look-up for some of the more commonly used elements of JavaScript syntax, along with properties and methods for a selection of the built-in objects.

TABLE B.1 The JavaScript Operators

Operator	Description
Arithmetic Operators	
*	Multiplies two numbers.
/	Divides two numbers.
% (Modulus)	Returns the remainder left after dividing two numbers using integer division.
String Operators	
+	(String addition) Joins two strings.
+=	Joins two strings and assigns the joined string to the first operand.
Logical Operators	
&&	(Logical AND) Returns a value of true if both operands are true; otherwise, returns false.
||	(Logical OR) Returns a value of true if either operand is true. However, if both operands are false, returns false.
!	(Logical NOT) Returns a value of false if its operand is true; true if its operand is false.
Bitwise Operators	
&	(Bitwise AND) Returns a one in each bit position if both operands' bits are one.
^	(Bitwise XOR) Returns a one in a bit position if the bits of one operand, but not both operands, are one.
|	(Bitwise OR) Returns a one in a bit if either operand has a one in that position.

Operator	Description
~	(Bitwise NOT) Changes ones to zeros and zeros to ones in all bit positions—that is, flips each bit.
<<	(Left shift) Shifts the bits of its first operand to the left by the number of places given in the second operand.
>>	(Sign-propagating right shift) Shifts the bits of the first operand to the right by the number of places given in the second operand.
>>>	(Zero-fill right shift) Shifts the bits of the first operand to the right by the number of places given in the second operand, and then shifts in zeros from the left.

Assignment Operators

=	Assigns the value of the second operand to the first operand, if the first operand is a variable.
+=	Adds two operands and assigns the result to the first operand, if it is a variable.
-=	Subtracts two operands and assigns the result to the first operand, if it is a variable.
*=	Multiplies two operands and assigns the result to the first operand, if it is a variable.
/=	Divides two operands and assigns the result to the first operand, if it is a variable.
%=	Calculates the modulus of two operands and assigns the result to the first operand, if it is a variable.
&=	Executes a bitwise AND operation on two operands and assigns the result to the first operand, if it is a variable.
^=	Executes a bitwise exclusive OR operation on two operands and assigns the result to the first operand, if it is a variable.
|=	Executes a bitwise OR operation on two operands and assigns the result to the first operand, if it is a variable.
<<=	Executes a left shift operation on two operands and assigns the result to the first operand, if it is a variable.
>>=	Executes a sign-propagating right shift operation on two operands and assigns the result to the first operand, if it is a variable.
>>>=	Executes a zero-fill right shift operation on two operands and assigns the result to the first operand, if it is a variable.

Comparison Operators

==	(Equality operator) Returns true if the two operands are equal to each other.
!=	(Not-equal-to) Returns true if the two operands are not equal to each other.

Operator	Description
===	(Strict equality) Returns true if the two operands are both equal and of the same type.
!==	(Strict not-equal-to) Returns true if the two operands are either not equal and/or not of the same type.
>	(Greater-than) Returns true if the first operand's value is greater than the second operand's value.
>=	(Greater-than-or-equal-to) Returns true if the first operand's value is greater than or equal to the second operand's value.
<	(Less-than) Returns true if the first operand's value is less than the second operand's value.
<=	(Less-than-or-equal-to) Returns true if the first operand's value is less than or equal to the second operand's value.

Special Operators

? :	(Conditional operator) Executes an "if...else" test.
,	(Comma operator) Evaluates two expressions and returns the result of evaluating the second expression.
delete	(Deletion) Deletes an object and removes it from memory, or deletes an object's property, or deletes an element in an array.
function	Creates an anonymous function.
in	Returns true if the property you're testing is supported by a specific object.
instanceof	Returns true if the given object is an instance of the specified type.
new	Creates a new object from the specified object type.
typeof	Returns the name of the type of the operand.
void	Allows evaluation of an expression without returning a value.

TABLE B.2 String Methods

Method	Description
substring	Returns a portion of the string.
toUpperCase	Converts all characters in the string to uppercase.
toLowerCase	Converts all characters in the string to lowercase.
indexOf	Finds an occurrence of a string within the string.
lastIndexOf	Finds an occurrence of a string within the string, starting at the end of the string.

Method	Description
replace	Searches for a match between a substring and a string, and replaces the substring with a new substring.
split	Splits a string into an array of substrings, and returns the new array.
link	Creates an HTML link using the string's text.
anchor	Creates an HTML anchor within the current page.

TABLE B.3   The Math Object

Property	Description
Constants	
E	Base of natural logarithms (approximately 2.718).
LN2	Natural logarithm of 2 (approximately 0.693).
LN10	Natural logarithm of 10 (approximately 2.302).
LOG2E	Base 2 logarithm of *e* (approximately 1.442).
LOG10E	Base 10 logarithm of *e* (approximately 0.434).
PI	Ratio of a circle's circumference to its diameter (approximately 3.14159).
SQRT1_2	Square root of one half (approximately 0.707).
SQRT2	Square root of two (approximately 1.4142).

Method	Description
Algebraic	
acos	Arc cosine of a number in radians.
asin	Arc sine of a number.
atan	Arc tangent of a number.
cos	Cosine of a number.
sin	Sine of a number.
tan	Tangent of a number.
Statistical and Logarithmic	
exp	Returns *e* (the base of natural logarithms) raised to a power.
log	Returns the natural logarithm of a number.
max	Accepts two numbers and returns whichever is greater.
min	Accepts two numbers and returns the smaller of the two.

Property	Description
Basic and Rounding	
abs	Absolute value of a number.
ceil	Rounds a number up to the nearest integer.
floor	Rounds a number down to the nearest integer.
pow	One number to the power of another.
round	Rounds a number to the nearest integer.
sqrt	Square root of a number.
Random Numbers	
random	Random number between 0 and 1.

TABLE B.4   The Date Object

Method	Description
getDate()	Returns day of the month (1-31).
getDay()	Returns day of the week (0-6).
getFullYear()	Returns year (four digits).
getHours()	Returns hour (0-23).
getMilliseconds()	Returns milliseconds (0-999).
getMinutes()	Returns minutes (0-59).
getMonth()	Returns month (0-11).
getSeconds()	Returns seconds (0-59).
getTime()	Returns number of milliseconds since midnight Jan 1, 1970.
getTimezoneOffset()	Returns time difference between GMT and local time, in minutes.
getUTCDate()	Returns day of the month, according to Universal Time (1-31).
getUTCDay()	Returns day of the week, according to Universal Time (0-6).
getUTCFullYear()	Returns year, according to Universal Time (4 digit).
getUTCHours()	Returns hour, according to Universal Time (0-23).
getUTCMilliseconds()	Returns milliseconds, according to Universal Time (0-999).
getUTCMinutes()	Returns minutes, according to Universal Time (0-59).
getUTCMonth()	Returns month, according to Universal Time (0-11).
getUTCSeconds()	Returns seconds, according to Universal Time (0-59).

Method	Description
`parse()`	Parses a date string and Returns number of milliseconds since midnight of January 1, 1970.
`setDate()`	Sets the day of the month (1-31).
`setFullYear()`	Sets the year (four digits).
`setHours()`	Sets the hour (0-23).
`setMilliseconds()`	Sets the milliseconds (0-999).
`setMinutes()`	Set the minutes (0-59).
`setMonth()`	Sets the month (0-11).
`setSeconds()`	Sets the seconds (0-59).
`setTime()`	Sets a date and time by adding or subtracting a specified number of milliseconds to or from midnight January 1, 1970.
`setUTCDate()`	Sets the day of the month, according to Universal Time (1-31).
`setUTCFullYear()`	Sets the year, according to Universal Time (four digits).
`setUTCHours()`	Sets the hour, according to Universal Time (0-23).
`setUTCMilliseconds()`	Sets the milliseconds, according to Universal Time (0-999).
`setUTCMinutes()`	Set the minutes, according to Universal Time (0-59).
`setUTCMonth()`	Sets the month, according to Universal Time (0-11).
`setUTCSeconds()`	Set the seconds, according to Universal Time (0-59).
`toDateString()`	Converts the date part of a `Date` object into a readable string.
`toLocaleDateString()`	Returns the date part of a `Date` object as a string, using locale conventions.
`toLocaleTimeString()`	Returns the time part of a `Date` object as a string, using locale conventions.
`toLocaleString()`	Converts a `Date` object to a string, using locale conventions.
`toString()`	Converts a `Date` object to a string.
`toTimeString()`	Converts the time part of a `Date` object to a string.
`toUTCString()`	Converts a `Date` object to a string, according to Universal Time.
`UTC()`	Returns the number of milliseconds in a date string since midnight of January 1, 1970, according to Universal Time.
`valueOf()`	Returns the primitive value of a `Date` object.

Index

How can we make this index more useful? Email us at indexes@samspublishing.com

H

I

How can we make this index more useful? Email us at indexes@samspublishing.com

comparison operators, 90

logical operators, 96

negation operator, 79

precedence, 28

P

packaging Google Chrome extension, 321

parameters

for box-shadow property (CSS), 205

JSON, 152

passing to functions, 40-43

parentNode property, 129

parseFloat() function, 71

parseInt() function, 71

parsing JSON strings, 155-157

passing arguments to functions, 40-43

multiple arguments, 41

pause() command, 170

play() command, 170

playing

sound, <audio> tag (HTML5), 171-172

videos

pause() and play() commands, 170

<video> tag (HTML5), 168-170

post() method, 267

precedence rules for operators, 28

prefixes, CSS3, 203-205

procedural programming, 105

progressive enhancement, 330-331

prompt() method, 52-53

properties

of arrays, length, 82

background-origin property (CSS3), 208

background-size property (CSS3), 207

border-radius property (CSS3), 206-207

box-shadow property (CSS3), 205

childNodes property, 126-129

CSS3

setting with vendor prefixes, 215-218

CSS3, converting to JavaScript, 214

document.cookie property, 274

innerHTML, 54-55

of Math object, 376

nodeName property, 130

of objects, reading, 16-17

parentNode property, 129

prefixed versions, 205

text-shadow (CSS3), 212

word-wrap (CSS3), 213

of XMLHttpRequest object, 264-265

properties (HTML5). *See* attributes (HTML5)

Prototype Framework library, 223

prototype keyword

extending objects, 114-115

inheritance, 115-117

prototype.js, 224-228

$() function, 225

$F() function, 225

Form object, 226

getElements() method, 226-228

purpose of libraries, 222

How can we make this index more useful? Email us at indexes@samspublishing.com

X-Y-Z

Learning Labs!
Learn online with videos, live code editing, and quizzes

SPECIAL 50% OFF – Introductory Offer
Discount Code: STYLL50

FOR A LIMITED TIME, we are offering readers of **Sams Teach Yourself** books a **50% OFF** discount to **ANY online Learning Lab** through Dec 31, 2016.

Visit informit.com/learninglabs to see available labs, try out full samples, and order today.

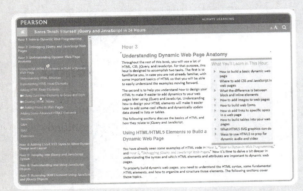

■ **Read** the complete text of the book online in your web browser

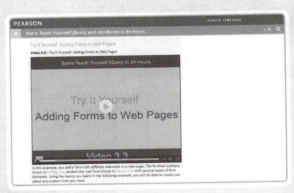

■ **Watch** an expert instructor show you how to perform tasks in easy-to-follow videos

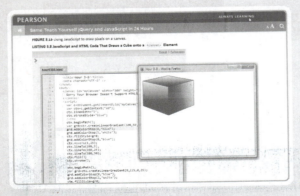

■ **Try** your hand at coding in an interactive code-editing sandbox in select products

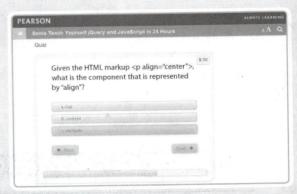

■ **Test** yourself with interactive quizzes